5-08

OPEN ROAD'S BEST OF

Italy

by Douglas E. Morris

Open Road Travel Guides – designed for the
amount of time you *really* have for your trip!

Open Road Publishing

Open Road's new travel guides.
Designed to cut to the chase.
You don't need a huge travel encyclopedia – you need a *selective guide* to steer you right. If you're going on vacation for a few weeks or less, get a guide that brings you the *best* of any destination for the amount of time you *really* have for your trip!

Open Road – the guide you need for the trip you want.

The New Open Road *Best Of* Travel Guides.
Right to the point.
Uncluttered.
Easy.

Open Road Publishing
P.O. Box 284, Cold Spring Harbor, NY 11724
www.openroadguides.com

Text Copyright © 2007 by Douglas E. Morris
- All Rights Reserved -
ISBN 1-59360-092-5
Library of Congress Control No. 2006940248

The author has made every effort to be as accurate as possible, but neither he nor the publisher assumes responsibility for the services provided by any business listed in this guide; for any errors or omissions; or any loss, damage, or disruptions in your travels for any reason.

About the Author

Douglas E. Morris is also the author of Open Road's *Italy Guide*, *Venice Made Easy*, *Rome Made Easy*, and *Florence Made Easy*.

CONTENTS

Your Passport to the **Perfect Trip!**

Maps

1. INTRODUCTION

Italy is filled with so many great cities to visit, amazing sights to see, wonderful restaurants to sample, that it can be difficult to decide where to go and what to do. That's where *Open Road's Best of Italy* comes in. The author has lived in Italy for almost 10 years, knows the country like a native, understands what travelers need, and has collected the best of everything in an easy-to-use format.

So if you're looking for stunning architecture, unparalleled artwork, dazzling museums, ancient ruins, stunning hill towns, world-class accommodations, relaxing cafes, seaside resorts, incredible eateries, vibrant community life, and all manner of outdoor activities, *Open Road's Best of Italy* is the guide for you!

With this book, your days and nights in Italy will be filled with all the exciting possibilities the land of *La Dolce Vita* has to offer, serving up the best parks, piazzas, shopping areas, local neighborhoods, and more, to help take the guess work out of creating the perfect vacation for your particular needs.

It's easy to see why so many Americans choose to visit the boot-shaped peninsula that juts into the Mediterranean. From the big tourist cities of Rome, Florence, and Venice to historic hill towns such as Perugia, Ravello and Lucca, small mountain villages like Gubbio or Todi, as well as breathtaking coastal towns, Italy is romantic, beautiful, fun and exciting.

2. OVERVIEW

Italy is one of the world's most magical destinations. Some experts estimate that between sixty and eighty percent of the world's artistic patrimony reside in this boot shaped country. Italy is also **home to more UNESCO World Heritage sites** than any other country. The *centro storico*, old historic centers, of Rome and Florence, as well as the entire city of Venice have been so designated. Not just a single building, or a row of structures as might be the case in the United States, but entire cities have been deemed significant enough to preserve.

Rome's major influences were the ancient Roman Empire and the Catholic Church, and as a result you will be able to see an incredible display of ancient ruins including the Colosseum, the Roman Forum, Palatine Hill, Baths of Diocletian, along with the Vatican, St.Peter's, and Sistine Chapel. And that is just scratching the surface. Rome is also home to the ancient Pantheon, Trevi Fountain, Spanish Steps, as well as an abundance of churches and museums.

Then there is **Florence**, the cradle of the Renaissance and the jewel in Italy's crown. Michelangelo, Da Vinci, Raphael, and more all made their home and plied their trade here. Master-

pieces of painting, sculpture and architecture are everywhere. Brunelleschi's dome dominates the cityscape along with the spire of the Palazzo Vecchio, framing the city's terracotta rooftops.

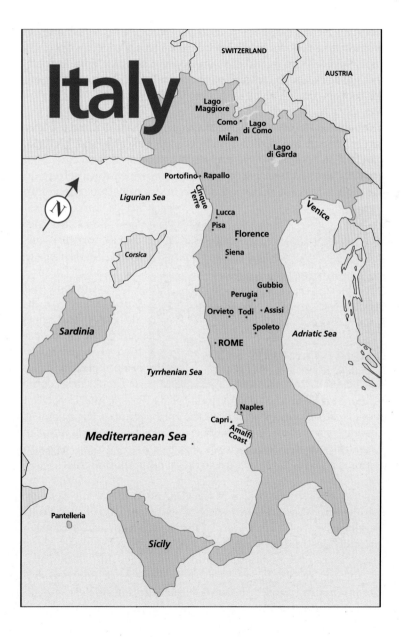

Venice, the most unique and romantic city in the world, set in the middle of a lagoon, is a wonderland of canals and bridges. Venice's riches came from its trade with the Far East and its architecture reflects those exotic influences. Peaceful, calm, serene, Venice is an island city, immensely popular with tourists, this guide helps you find those places off the beaten path where the local heart of Venice still beats strongly.

Though these cities stand out, there is more to Italy than the "big three." Much more! The hill towns of **Tuscany** and **Umbria**, perched in their verdant backdrop, seem as if God and man actively worked together to create the most beautiful setting on the planet. In these regions, **Lucca** is one of only two cities left in  all of Europe that have their entire Medieval fortifications intact, **Pisa** is home to the famous Leaning Tower, **Cortona** and **Gubbio** seem to radiate peace and tranquility, **Orvieto's** cathedral is second to none, **Perugia** is like an Escher print come to life, **San Gimignano** is famous for its towers, and in each of these locations, and throughout the entire country, the cuisine is absolutely amazing. Salamis, cheeses, pastas, sauces and more all vary dramatically from region to region, and town to town within regions, offering a tantalizing array of culinary delights.

Try to see the rustic charm of the **Cinque Terre**, or the majestic setting of the **Amalfi Coast** with its towns perched on steep hills overlooking the azure waters of the Mediterranean. Or **Capri**, a vacation destination since ancient Rome, filled with stunning vistas, incredible restaurants, and vibrant nightlife. In this area are the city of **Naples** and the ancient towns of **Pompeii** and **Herculaneum** trapped in time by the eruption of Vesuvius almost 2,000 years ago.

If you can, visit the **Lake Country** up north, with natural settings carved out of the landscape by retreating glaciers. The city of **Milan** is your gateway to this region, and while I would not spend too much time in Milan, there are enough sights here to make it worth your time for a day or two. But the real prize in this region are the lakes and their lovely towns: **Como**, **Bellagio**, and the pretty lakeside destinations along the shore of **Lago Maggiore**.

3. ROME

Rome is a magical city filled with ancient ruins, medieval streets, Renaissance palazzi, superb restaurants, lively nightlife, relaxing cafés, savory wine bars, and unique shopping. Each step you take in Rome is a walk through history. See ancient ruins such as the **Colosseum** and the **Forum**, set against the glory of **Renaissance churches**, all complemented by **peerless museums** overflowing with stunning relics and art. All of which are surrounded by a community life that is vibrant and congenial.

Along with the architectural and artistic splendor, Rome is also a city made up of neighborhoods, places where communities fill the piazzas and spill out of cafes, offering visitors a delightful introduction to Roman life. I will steer

you to the best of Rome, both the well-known sights as well as those off the beaten path, for in the narrow streets of old Rome behind the **Piazza Navona** or near the **Pantheon**, perhaps more than in the impressive ruins of antiquity, the true heart of ancient Rome is revealed.

ONE GREAT DAY IN ROME

If a day's all you've got, all you are going to get is a glimpse. On this tour we will show you the Spanish Steps and the shopping and ambiance of surrounding it. From here we will move onto the Trevi Fountain and throw a coin in the fountain. Amble over to the Pantheon and admire the architectural wonder of this 2000-year old structure. From here, we'll wander over to Piazza Navona, admire the Fountain of the Four Rivers by Bernini; then cross the Tevere to Castel Sant'Angelo, finally ending up our visit at St. Peter's.

Morning

There is no better way to start the day than at the top of the **Spanish Steps** with a quality view over the rooftops of Rome. At the base of the steps to the right is the world famous **Babington's Tea Room**. Not the most Italian place to break our fast, but a slice of Roman history nonetheless. This ancient café, with its heavy furniture, 18th century decor, and creaky floors has been

serving customers for several centuries, and is where Shelley, Lord Byron, Keats and other literary luminaries would start their days when in Rome. *Info:* 23 Piazza di Spagna, Tel. 06/678-6027. Credit cards accepted. Closed Thursdays.

Across the Piazza di Spagna is the world renowned **Via Condotti** with extremely high-end boutiques such as Gucci, Fendi and others. All around this area, known as **Il Tridente**, are wonderful streets filled with all manner of stores, cafes, and restaurants. A great place to wander around, shopping, people watching, sipping a glass of wine or enjoying a meal. You can either spend time

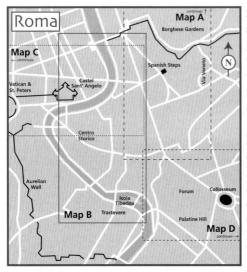

now perusing the possibilities, or as is suggested at the end of this section, do so after dinner, as a relaxing way to end your day in Rome.

From this area, head over to the **Trevi Fountain**, the largest and most impressive of Rome's fountains. Commissioned by Pope Clement XII and built by Nicola Salvi in 1762 from a design he borrowed from Bernini, the fountain takes up an entire exterior wall of the Palazzo Poli that was built in 1730.

There is an ancient custom that guarantees that all who throw a coin into the fountain are destined to return to Rome. So turn your back to the fountain and toss a coin over your left shoulder, with your right hand, into the fountain and fate will carry you back to the Eternal City. However, please don't try and recreate Anita Ekberg's scene in the film *La Dolce Vita* when she waded through the fountain to taunt Marcello Mastroiani. It is completely illegal to walk in the Trevi fountain, and the authorities enforce this regulation stringently.

Rome's Best Cafes

- **Babington's Tea Room** is an expensive, refined way to grab a cuppa. *Info:* 23 Piazza di Spagna, Map A.
- **Caffé Greco** is a refined and elegant place for a brief repast. *Info:* Via Condotti 86, Map A.
- **La Cafetteria** is an upscale local place. *Info:* Piazza di Pietra 65, Map A.
- **Teichner** is located in my favorite piazza in Rome. *Info:* Piazza San Lorenzo in Lucina 17, Map A, B & C.

From here wander over to the oldest structure in Rome's *centro storico* (historic district), the **Pantheon**. Constructed by Agrippa in 27 BCE as a pagan temple, in 609 CE, it was dedicated as a Christian Church and called Santa Maria Rotunda. In the Middle Ages it served as a fortress. In 1620 the building's bronze ceiling was removed and melted into

the cannons for Castel Sant'Angelo and Bernini's Baldacchino (Grand Canopy) in Saint Peter's. The building is made up of red and gray Egyptian granite, and each of the sixteen columns is 12.5 meters high and is composed of a single block of stone.

You enter the building by way of the original bronze doors. The marvelous dome (diameter 43 meters) is inspiring, even with the hole in the middle that allows rain in during moments of inclement weather. There are three niches in the building that contain the following tombs: **Victor Emmanuel II** (died 1878), **Umberto I** (died 1900) **Queen Margherita** (died 1926), and the renowned artist whose last name of **Sanzio** is not nearly as well known as his first, **Raphael** (died 1520). *Info:* Piazza della Rotonda. Tel. 06/6830-0230. www.roma2000.it/zpanthe.html. Open Monday-Saturday 9am-6:30pm, Sundays 9am-1pm. At 10am on Sundays is a mass. Tel. 06/6830-0230.

From the Pantheon, head over to the **Piazza Navona**. Though a tourist haven, and prices at some of the restaurants and cafes may be a little steep, for first time visitors to Rome, this is an ideal location to find a place to eat. If all you want is a snack or some

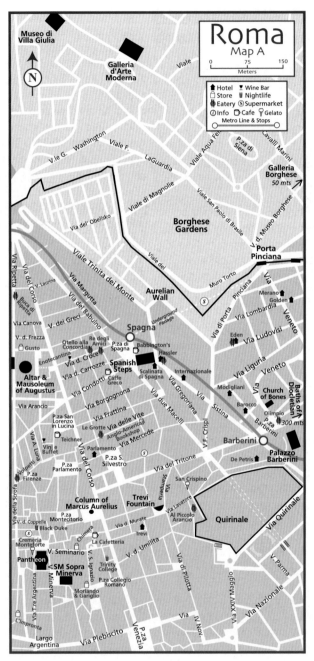

Roma
Map A

0   75   150
Meters

🏨 Hotel   🍷 Wine Bar
🏪 Store   🍸 Nightlife
🍴 Eatery   Ⓢ Supermarket
ⓘ Info   ☕ Cafe 🍦 Gelato
⊙━━━━⊙ Metro Line & Stops

Museo di Villa Giulia

Galleria d'Arte Moderna

N

Viale

V.le G. Washington

Viale F.

LaGuardia

Viale Aqua Fel.

P.za di Siena

Cavalli Marini

Galleria Borghese 50 mts

Viale di Magnolie

Viale San Paolo di Brasile

V. d. Museo Borghese

Via del' Obelisko

Borghese Gardens

Porta Pinciana

Via del Corso

Via Ripetta

Buca di Ripetta

Via del Corso

Viale Trinita dei Monte

Via Margutta

Via del Babuino

Viale del

Aurelian Wall

Muro Torto

Via di Porta Pinciana

Via Pinciana

Via Lombardia

Via Veneto

V. Laurina

Via Canova

V. dei Greci

V. d. Frezza

🏪 Gusto

Otello alla Concordia

Re degli Amici

Spagna

P.za di Spagna

Babbington's

Hassler

Underground Passage

Merano 🏨 Golden 🏨

Eden 🍴

Via Ludovisi

Enotecantina

Via d. Croce

Via d. Carrozze

Spanish Steps

Caffe Greco

Scalinata di Spagna

Internazionale

Via Gregoriana

Via due Macelli

Via Liguria

Veneto

Altar & Mausoleum of Augustus

Via Condotti

Via Borgognona

Via Frattina

Modigliani 🍴

Barocco

Sistina

Church of Bones

Baths of Diocletian

Via Arancio

Via A. Luna

P.za San Lorenzo in Lucina

Le Grotte

Via delle Vite

Anglo-American Bookshop

Via Mercede

V.F. Crispi

Olimpio

P.za Barberini 300 mts

Teichner

Vini e Buffet

Via del Corso

Parlamento

P.za S. Silvestro

Barberini

Palazzo Barberini

De Petris 🍴

Via Volpe

Via della Strofa

P.za Parlamento

P.za Firenze

Via del Tritone

San Crispino

Via Stamperia

Column of Marcus Aurelius

Trevi Fountain

Via Lavatore

Al Piccolo Arancio

Quirinale

Via Quirinale

V. d. Coppelle

P.za Montecitorio

Black Duke

Chimera

Via d. Murate

Trevi

La Cafetteria

V. d. Umilta

Cremeria Monteforte

V. Seminario

V. S. Ignazio

Trinity College

Via di Pilotta

V. Parma

Pantheon

SM Sopra Minerva

P.za Collegio Romano

Via Minerva

Via Tre Argentina

Morlando & Gariglio

C'impronta

Largo Argentina

Via Plebiscito

P.za Venezia

Via IV Nov.

Via XXIV Maggio

Via Nazionale

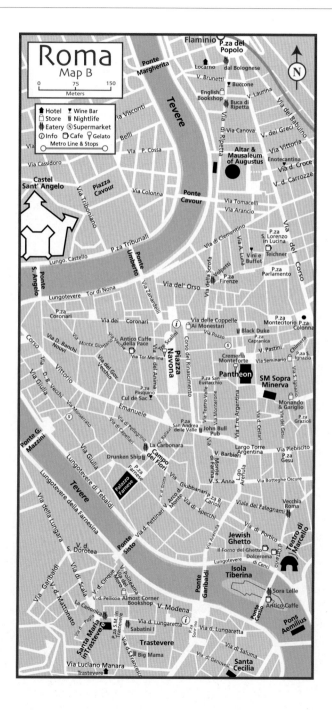

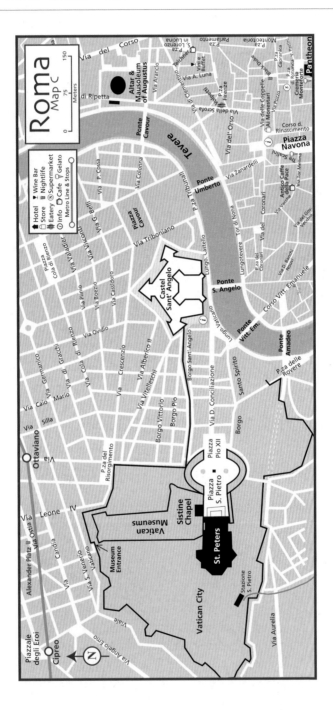

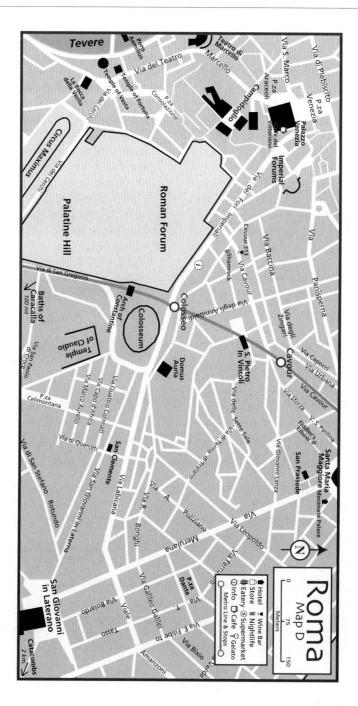

Italian ice cream, sample the offerings at the world-famous **Tre Scalini** (Piazza Navona 28).

Culinary pursuits aside, Piazza Navona is located on the site of a stadium built by Domitian in 86 CE that was used for mock naval battles, gladiatorial contests, and horse races. The stadium's old north entrance has been excavated allowing us to see some original stone arches located 20 feet below the current street level, indicating how much silt, dirt and detritus has accumulated since the days of the Roman Empire.

Rome's Best Gelato

• **Cremeria Monteforte** serves all natural and great tasting gelato. *Info:* Via della Rotonda 22, Map B & C.
• **San Crispino** is the best *gelateria* in Rome. *Info:* Via della Panetteria 42, Map A.
• **Tre Scalini** is world-famous, in a great location, and serves expensive but yummy gelato. *Info:* Piazza Navona 28, Map B & C.

After the Roman era the piazza was lined with small squatters' homes that followed the tiers of the stadium. However, because of its wide open space it soon became a prime spot for upscale buildings. Today the style of the piazza is richly Baroque, featuring works by two great masters, **Bernini** and **Borromini**.

Located in the middle of the square is Bernini's fantastic **Fontana Dei Quattro Fiumi** (Fountain of Four Rivers), sculpted from 1647-51. The four figures supporting the large obelisk (a Bernini trademark) represent the four major rivers known at the time: the Danube, the Ganges, the Nile, and the Plata Rivers.

Within this statue Bernini has hidden a window back in time. Notice the figure representing the Nile shielding its eyes from the facade of the church it is facing, **Santa Agnese in Agone**. This church was designed by Bernini's rival at the time, Borromini; and Bernini is playfully showed his disdain for his rival's creation through the sculpted disgust in his statue.

Afternoon

Before we snake our way through the heart of the *centro storico*, over the Ponte Sant'Angelo to St. Peter's, let's stop for a bite at one of Rome's most popular wine bars, **Cul de Sac** (*see Best Eats*). This intimate wine bar has over 1,400 Italian and foreign vintages for you to sample as well as light and fast hot and cold meals.

Now head over to the most famous church in Christendom, **Saint Peters**. *Info:* Piazza San Pietro. Hours 8am-6pm, but only until 5pm in the winter. Tel. 06/6988-4466. Metro-Ottaviano.

Saint Peter's is the largest church in the world. Around the piazza fronting the church, above the oval structure are 140 statues of saints. In the center is an obelisk with four bronze lions at its base, brought from Heliopolis during the reign of Caligula (circa 40 CE).

On the floor of the central nave you'll find lines drawn identifying where other churches in the world would fit if placed inside Saint Peter's. Also on the floor, near the front entrance, is a red disk indicating the spot where **Charlemagne** was crowned Holy Roman Emperor by Leo III on Christmas Day in 800 CE. To the right of this, in the first chapel, is the world famous **Pieta** carved by Michelangelo in the year 1498 when he was only 24.

Proper Attire Alert!

In most museums, monuments and churches in Italy, women should wear either long pants or a long skirt or dress, and a top with sleeves. Men should wear long pants and no tank tops. **Both men and women will be denied entry to St. Peter's,** and to many other sights as well, if wearing shorts or short skirts and/or a revealing top!

Throughout the Basilica you'll find a variety of superb statues and monuments, many tombs of Popes, and a wealth of chapels. One controversial tomb is that of Pope Celestine V who allegedly died at the hands of his overeager successor, Boniface VIII. Researchers were recently granted permission to x-ray the tomb and it clearly showed that a ten-inch nail was driven into Celestine's skull.

To complete your tour of St. Peters, head up to the top of the church for a view over outside over the piazza and the city. Truly spectacular vistas.

Evening
From St. Peters, to return to the area around the Spanish Steps for dinner, either take a taxi back to Piazza di Spagna, or head to the metro stop **Ottaviano** and catch the metro to the **Spagna** stop. From here it is a short walk to the amazing local restaurant **La Buca di Ripetta** (*see Best Eats*).

After dinner, take some time to amble through the best shopping area in Rome, called **Il Tridente**. So named because the three main roads that radiate out from the Piazza del Popolo look like a trident. This is one of the most popular areas for Italians and visitors alike, and is a perfect capstone to your day trip to Rome.

A FANTASTIC WEEKEND IN ROME

Even with a weekend, there are gems you can discover in Rome. In our jaunt through the Eternal City, we will mix together great restaurants, amazing sights, ancient ruins, relaxing cafes, outdoor markets, quality nightlife, and zest for life that Romans exude in their own special way.

Friday Evening
Start your Roman weekend at the Spanish Steps, soaking up the energy and ambiance, wandering with crowds down the **Via del Corso**, **Via Condotti** and other great shopping streets. Stop in my

favorite piazza just off the Corso, **Piazza San Lorenzo in Lucina**, grab a seat at the outdoor café **Teichner** (Piazza San Lorenzo in Lucina 17), and savor an apertivo before dinner. When your stomach starts rumbling, head over to the nearby **Vini e Buffet** (*see Best Eats*), my favorite *enotecha* (wine bar) in Rome. This is a fantastic place to grab a light meal and some great wine. The rustic and charming setting is authentically Roman and offers a unique dining experience.

If you prefer an upscale way to end your evening instead of wandering the streets or sitting in a piazza, you can sample the offerings at **Caffe Greco** (Via Condotti 86, Map A.), which since 1740 has been a stop on the grand tour of Rome. A unique and elegant café where you can get all sorts of drinks, snacks and pastries.

After the meal, your options are virtually endless as right here you are in the middle of everything. You can head over to the **Trevi Fountain** and elbow your way through the crowds to see the fountain lit up in all its glory. You can also make your way to the nearby **Piazza Navona** or **Pantheon** and savor the nightlife at those spots, or you can head back to the **Spanish Steps**, grab a seat there and watch the parade of Romans enjoying the evening. Or if you have the energy you can sample all four as they are well within walking distance of one another.

Saturday Morning
Start your day at Rome's best museums, those located in the Vatican. If you want to avoid standing in the long lines outside the **Vatican Museums**, you need to book a guided tour, either for individuals or groups. *Info:* Viale Vaticano, Tel. 06/6988-4466. €12. www.vatican.va. From November - March and June - August open 8:45am to 12:20pm. From March - June and September - October open 8:45am to 3:20pm. Closed most Sundays and all major religious holidays such as Christmas and Easter. Metro-Ottaviano.

The treasures you will see in the Vatican Museums have been conservatively estimated to be valued at between four and six billion dollars. Here you can find paintings by Giotto; many works by Raphael; ancient Roman and Greek statues; Etruscan bronzes, gold objects, glasswork, candelabra, necklaces, rings, funeral urns, and amphora; Egyptian art, wooden mummy cases and funeral steles, mummies of animals, and a collection of ancient papyri; and many, many more fine works of art.

To top off the tour is the private chapel of the popes, the **Sistine Chapel**, famous for ceiling painted by **Michelangelo**, which he started in 1508 and finished four years later. On the wall behind the altar is the fresco of the *Last Judgment* also by Michelangelo, who was over 60 years of age when he completed this project in 1542.

Saturday Afternoon
After visiting the Vatican Museums, stop at their snack bar/ restaurant for lunch. After which, it is onto the nearby **Saint Peter's**. This church resides on the site where Peter the saint is buried. Over the centuries the church was expanded by a number of different architects and artists, including **Michelangelo**. On November 1, 1626, Urbano VIII dedicated the Basilica as we know it today.

In the niches that support the arches are statues of the founders of many religious orders. In the last one on the right you'll find the seated bronze statue of Saint Peter. The statue's foot has been rubbed by so many people for good luck that its toes have all but disappeared.

Just past the statue is the grand **cupola** created by Michelangelo. It is held up by four colossal spires leading to a series of open chapels. Under the cupola, above the high altar rises the famous **Baldacchino** (Grand Canopy) made by Bernini, and constructed of bronze taken mainly from the roof of the Pantheon. In front of the altar is the **Chapel of Confessions** made by Maderno, around which are 95 perpetually lit lamps illuminating the **Tomb of Saint Peters**. In front of the shrine is the kneeling **Statue of Pius VI** made by Canova in 1822.

If you grow tired of the many beautiful works of art and wish to get a bird's eye view of everything, you can ascend into Michelangelo's Cupola either by stairs (537 of them) or by elevator. The views from the top over the city of Rome are magnificent.

After visiting St. Peters, we are on our way to the Colosseum. Either take a taxi or head to the metro stop Ottaviano and take it to Termini, and change from the Linea A to Linea B and take that to Colosseo. Here you will find the **Arch of Constantine**, a

Best Views Over Rome

• **Balloon Rides** – amazing views over Rome from the Borghese Gardens (*see Best Activities chapter.*
• **Top of the Vittorio Emanuele Monument**, Piazza Venezia
• **Top of St Peter's** – A trip to the top of dome offers stunning panoramic vistas over the city.
• **Gianicolo Hill** – From the Piazza Garibaldi are the best views over the city.
• **Aventine Hill** – Possibly the most unique view over Rome is through the keyhole in the door to the priory of the Knights of Malta at Piazza dei Cavalieri di Malta #3.

triumphal arch built in 312 CE to commemorate the Emperor's victory over Maxentius at the Ponte Milvio. This is the largest and best preserved in Rome.

Also here is the **Colosseum**, formally known as the *Flavian Amphitheater*, this structure remains the single most recognized

 monument surviving from ancient Rome. Its construction began in 72 CE by Vespasian on the site of the Stagnum Neronis, an artificial lake built by Emperor Nero near his house on the adjacent Oppian Hill. Over 500 exotic beasts and many hundreds of gladiators were slain in the arena during the building's opening ceremony in 80 CE, which lasted three months. These types of bloody spectacles continued until 405 CE, when they were abolished. *Info:* Piazza del Colosseo. €6. www.roma2000.it/zcoloss.html. Hours: summer - 9am-7pm; winter - 9am-5pm. Metro-Colosseo.

In its prime the Colosseum was covered with marble, and each portico was filled with a marble statue of some important Roman. Despite having seen better days, it is still wonderful sight for kids and adults to explore.

Saturday Evening
For dinner tonight we are going to head over to one of my all time favorites, **La Buca di Ripetta** (*see Best Eats*). This small, friendly local trattoria serves straightforward, tasty Roman cuisine. Only one room, its high walls covered with cooking and farming paraphernalia such as enormous bellows and copper pans. Remember to make reservations.

Afterwards take the time to wander the best shopping area in Rome, called **Il Tridente**. The main drag is the Via del Corso, with moderately priced shops, then there is the Via Condotti with its high end boutiques, and be sure to wander side streets to find all manner of little stores. This is one of the most popular areas for Italians and visitors alike.

Sunday Morning
You've tasted modern Rome in and around the Spanish Steps, religious Rome at the Vatican and Saint Peters, and Ancient Rome at the Colosseum. Now it's time to blend them all together by going to the **Pantheon**.

Deep in the heart of Rome's centro storico, it's old medieval core, the Pantheon was constructed in 27 BCE as a pagan temple and was converted to a Catholic church in 609 CE. After admiring the beauty and symmetry of the structure that inspired Brunelleschi to construct the dome of the Duomo in Florence, wander through the back streets to **Piazza Navona**. This is another example of ancient Roman architecture being incorporated in the flow of modern Roman life. Only more so in the case of Piazza Navona, as the stands for the ancient gladiatorial stadium were built upon by Medieval and Renaissance buildings which now front the square.

From here, head past the Campo dei Fiori and over one of Rome's pedestrian bridges, **Ponte Sisto** to Trastevere, the perfect place to

immerse yourself in Roman life. Trastevere literally means "across the river" and here you'll find interesting shops and boutiques, and plenty of excellent restaurants among the small narrow streets and *piazzette* (small squares). Our destination is the **Piazza Santa Maria in Trastevere** and the church of the same name.

This was one of Rome's earliest churches and the first to be dedicated to the Virgin Mary. It was built in the 4th century CE. Best known for its prized Byzantine-style mosaics, the interior

 consists of three naves separated by columns purloined from ancient Roman temples. *Info:* Piazza Santa Maria in Trastevere 1, Tel. 06/581-4802. www.roma2000.it/ztraste.html. Hours 7am-7pm.

From here we are going to head straight down the Via della Lungaretta to the Lungotevere, wait for the traffic to stop and cross over to the **Isola Tiberina**. This island used to be a dumping ground for dead and sick slaves. Also, at that time, in the 3rd century BCE, there was a sanctuary here to the Greek God of healing, Askleapios. Currently half the island is taken up by the hospital of Fatebene Fratelli showing that traditions do live on.

The whole island is a great place to relax with wide walkways along the river. The remains of the **Pons Aemilius**, the oldest bridge in Rome washed away by a flash floor in 1598, can be seen south of the island. The oldest surviving bridge in Rome is the **Ponte Fabricio** leading from the island to the Jewish Ghetto. It was built in 62 BCE.

Sunday Afternoon
Stop at the **Antico Caffe dell'Isola** (Via Ponte IV Capi 18, Map B) for some rest and light refreshment. This cafe is a great place to come on a warm, sunny day, and sit on their terrace far from the crowds of Rome.

From the island it is a short walk to the **Campidolgio**, the Capitoline Hill. This is one of the seven hills of Rome, home to the **Capitoline Museums**, second only to the Vatican Museums in quality, which includes the **Senatorial Palace**

ALTERNATE PLAN
If you want peace and solitude, wander down some steps next to the bridge over to Trastevere to the embankment by the river. Bring along some food you picked up from the café, toddle around admiring the tranquility of the running water, and settle down for a respite from Rome's hectic pace.

and the **Palace of the Conservatori**. Also located here is the bronze **statue of Marcus Aurelius**. The Capitoline Museums are the perfect place to see what ancient Romans looked like.

Different from Greek sculpture, which glorified the subject, Roman carvings captured every realistic flaw. Whether they were short, fat, thin, ugly, here they remain, warts and all. *Info:* Piazza del Campidoglio 1. Tel. 06/6710-2071. www.museicapitolini.it. €5. Hours 9am-7pm. Closed Mondays.

Besides the busts, you'll find a variety of celebrated pieces from antiquity including *Dying Gaul*, *Cupid and Psyche*, the *Faun*, and the nude and voluptuous *Capitoline Venice*. Then in the **Room of the Doves** you'll find two wonderful mosaics that were taken from Hadrian's Villa. One mosaic is of the doves drinking from a basin, and another is of the famous masks of comedy and tragedy.

Sunday Evening
For dinner this evening, we are going to head back to a restaurant in Campo dei Fiori, **La Carbonara** (*see Best Eats*). Some people find this place to be too touristy, but I ignore that because of the atmosphere and food. This lively piazza is a great way to end your weekend in *la bella Roma*. Their *spaghetti alla carbonara* is, as expected, really good, but also try their *spaghetti alla vongole verace*.

A WONDERFUL WEEK IN ROME

Ancient Roman ruins, great museums, Christian churches, pagan temples, superb restaurants, relaxing cafes, old port cities trapped in time (Ostia Antica), the Aurelian Wall, ancient aqueducts and subterranean catacombs: all this and more will be featured in this one-week tour of *la bella Roma*. The sights listed have been separated geographically and are itemized in order of those you should first. See the Metro map on page 34 if you want to get around town quickly!

RECOMMENDED PLAN: Spend a day in each of the four geographic sections (Spanish Steps/Via Veneto, Centro Storico, Around the Forum, and The Vatican), another day sampling those sights featured in the Best of the Rest section, a day in the ancient town of Ostia Antica, then a final day visiting the aqueducts and catacombs in and around the Parco Regionale dell'Appia Antica.

Spanish Steps/Via Veneto
This area starts at the Piazza del Popolo and radiates from there down the three streets that begin in that square. For our purposes, this area will absorb surrounding sites, and a few slightly beyond its specific geographic boundaries. All sites are listed in order they can best be viewed.

Let's begin our tour in the **Piazza di Spagna**. The accompanying

Spanish Steps are one of the most beautiful spots in Rome. Named after the old Spanish Embassy to the Holy See that used to stand on the site, the 137 steps are officially called the *Scalinata della Trinita dei Monti*, named for the church at the top. Even so most people just call them the **Span-**

ish Steps. The fountain in the middle of the piazza is known as the **Barcaccia** and was designed n 1628 by Pietro Bernini in commemoration of the big flood of 1598. This piazza is a favorite gathering spot for Italians and tourists alike.

Don't Miss ...

- Colosseum
- Roman Forum
- Pantheon
- St. Peter's Basilica
- Vatican Museums
- Castel Sant'Angelo
- Piazza Navona
- Campo dei Fiori
- Trevi Fountain
- Spanish Steps
- Il Tridente Shopping Streets

Why not start your day at **Babington's Tea Room** is not the most Italian place to break our fast, but it is a slice of Roman history nonetheless. This ancient café has been serving customers for several centuries, and is where Shelley, Lord Byron, Keats and other literary luminaries would congregate when in Rome. *Info:* 23 Piazza di Spagna, Tel. 06/678-6027. Closed Thursdays. Map A. End

The Spanish Steps is smack dab in the middle of Rome's best shopping area, **Il Tridente**. So named because the three main roads that radiate out from the Piazza del Popolo look like a trident. This is one of the most popular areas for Italians and

visitors alike, and it will likely take many hours of exploring to the do the area justice. If you're looking for high-end shopping, you'll find it on the Via dei Condotti or the Via del Corso.

Within this warren of streets is a wine bar called **Enotecantina** (*See Best Eats*). Opened in 1860, until a few years ago this was an old-fashioned wine store selling local vintages directly from large vats. Now it's a fern-filled wine bar with wooden stools and ceramic seats. Light meals and snacks of all sorts are served here, and wine by the glass.

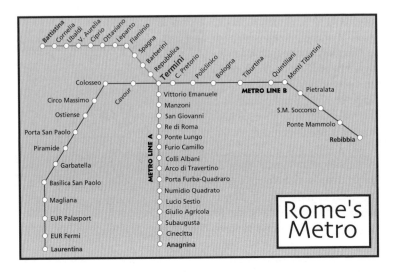

Rome's Metro

Another great location to visit, just off the Via del Corso, is the wonderfully relaxing **Piazza San Lorenzo in Lucina**. Though in the middle of everything, this piazza seems much less touristed than most. For a snack, sample **Teichner** (*Info:* Piazza San Lorenzo in Lucina 17, Map A, B & C.), a classic café. If it is closer to meal time, nearby is my favorite wine bar in all of Rome, **Vini e Buffet** (*see Best Eats*), a great place for lunch, dinner, snack, or just a glass of wine.

All around here are twisting winding streets to explore filled with great local shops, boutiques, and more. In your wanderings make sure to stumble upon the largest and most impressive of Rome's fountains, the **Trevi Fountain**. Built by Nicola Salvi in 1762 from a design borrowed from Bernini, the fountain takes up an entire exterior wall of the Palazzo Poli that was built in 1730. In the central niche is Neptune on his chariot drawn by marine horses preceded by two tritons. In the left niche is the statue representing Abundance, and to the right Health. The four statues up top depict the seasons, and the crest is of the family of Pope Clement XII, Corsini.

There is an ancient custom that guarantees that all who throw a coin into the fountain are destined to return to Rome. So turn your back to the fountain and throw a coin over your left shoulder, with your right hand, into the fountain and fate will carry you back. Please don't try and recreate Anita Ekberg's scene in the film *La Dolce Vita* when she waded through the fountain to taunt Marcello Mastroiani. It is illegal to walk in the Trevi fountain. *Info:* Piazza di Trevi. www.roma2000.it/ztrevi.html. Metro-Barberini.

Need an ice cream break? Stop in at **San Crispino**, for my money the best *gelateria* in Rome. *Info:* Via della Panetteria 42, Map A.

From the Trevi head over to the bottom of the Via Veneto and the macabre **Church of Bones**, more formally known as **Santa Maria della Concezione**. In the crypt of the church there is an eerie arrangement of the bones of over 4,000 skeletons of ancient friars that were exhumed and decoratively placed on the walls. The reason this display exists is that a law was passed many centuries ago stating that no graveyards or burial grounds could exist inside the walls of Rome. Rather than part with the remains of their brothers by re-burying them in a cemetery outside the walls, the Cappucin brothers exhumed the fraternal remains and decorated the crypt with them. *Info:* Via Veneto 27, Tel. 06/4871185. Open daily from 7am to noon and 4pm to 8pm. €3. Metro-Barberini.

After this funereal display, head up the **Via Veneto**. Though the allure of this street is rather faded today, it is still a great place to stroll and admire the high end hotels, stores, and cafés. At the bottom of the street is the **Piazza Barberini** where you'll find the graceful **Fontana delle Api** (Fountain of the Bees) as well as the **Fontana del Tritone**, both designed and sculpted by Bernini. In the middle of the  Via Veneto is the grandiose **Palazzo Margherita**, built by G. Koch in 1890, which is now the home of the **American Embassy**. At the top of the Via Veneto is the **Aurelian Wall**, through which you can access the **Borghese Gardens**. *Info:* www.roma2000.it/zveneto.html. Metro-Barberini.

Built from 272-279 CE, the **Aurelian Wall** was built to protect Rome from an incursion of Germanic tribes, and enclosed not only the old city of Rome but also some of the farmland that fed it. Today the walls extend a total length of about 12 miles, and consist of concrete rubble encased in brick almost 12 feet thick and 25 feet high. In some places the wall's height is nearly 50 feet. There are 380 square towers interspersed along its length, each are a distance of two arrow shots apart.

There were 18 main gates, many of which have been rebuilt to accommodate different defense strategies throughout the ages. Most recently they were adapted for the onslaught of automobile traffic. The ones that are the best preserved with most of their Roman features still intact are the **Porta San Sebastiano** (near San Giovanni in Laterano), **Porta Asinara** (next to Porta San Giovanni) and the **Porta Toscolana** (behind the train station).

After admiring the Aurelian Wall, walk through the gate at the top of the Via Veneto and enter the **Borghese Gardens**, the most

 picturesque park in Rome, complete with serene paths, a lake where you can rent boats, some wonderful museums, lush vegetation, expansive grass fields, a large riding ring, and more. If you want an afternoon's respite from the sights of the city, or you're tired of spending time in your hotel room during the siesta hours, escape to these luscious and spacious gardens. Besides the peace and tranquility, consider taking a **balloon ride** here! *See Best Activities for more details.*

In the Borghese Gardens is the **Villa Borghese**, an exemplary art collection. Housed in a beautiful villa constructed in the 17th century, the ground floor of this museum contains an exquisite sculpture collection, but the main draw is the gallery of paintings on the first floor. Before you abandon the sculptures, take note of the reclining *Pauline Borghese*, created by Antonio Canova in 1805. She was the sister of Napoleon, and looks quite enticing posed half naked on a lounge chair. Another work not to miss is *David and the Slingshot* by Bernini (1619) said to be a self-portrait of the sculptor. Other works by Bernini are spotlighted and intermixed with ancient Roman statuary. On the first floor the paintings not to miss include *Madonna and Child* by Bellini, *Young Lady with a Unicorn* by Raphael, *Madonna with Saints* by Lotto, and some wonderful works by Caravaggio. *Info:* Villa Borghese, Piazza dell'Uccelliera 5. Tel. 06/632-8101. €6. Reservations: www.ticketeria.it. Open 9am-9pm, until midnight on Saturdays, only until 8pm on Sundays. Closed Mondays. Metro-Spagna.

Also in the Borghese Gardens is the **Museo di Villa Giulia**, built in 1533 by Julius III, this incredible archaeological museum contains 34 rooms of ancient sculptures, sarcophagi, bas-reliefs, and more, mainly focusing on the Etruscan civilization. Items of interest include the statues created in the 5th century BCE of a *Centaur*, and *Man on a Marine Monster*; Etruscan clay sculptures of *Apollo*, *Hercules with a Deer*, and *Goddess with Child*; objects from the Necropoli at Cervetri including a terracotta work of *Amazons with Horses* created in the 6th century BCE and a sarcophagus of a "married couple," a masterpiece of Etruscan sculpture from the 6th century BCE. *Info:* Piazza di Villa Giulia 9. Tel. 06/332-6571. €5. Tickets: www.ticketeria.it. Hours 9am-6:30pm Tues-Fri, Sundays until 8pm and Saturdays in the summer open also from 9pm-midnight. Closed Mondays. Metro-Flaminio.

Rome's Best Parks

• **Borghese Gardens** – Peace and serenity among the vibrant urbanity of the Eternal City. Come here for balloon rides, great museums, or just a place to relax and have a picnic.
• **Parco Regionale dell'Appia Antica** – One of the best kept secrets in Rome. Contains ancient aquaducts, the Appia Antica, and the catacombs. (www.parcoappiaantica.org)
• **Villa Doria Pamphili** – An oasis of calm located out the Via Aurelia Antica just past Trastevere.

Centro Storico

This area, the historic center of Rome, or *centro storico* in Italian, is bordered by the Tiber river as it extends down to the Isola Tiberina, and abuts the area around Il Tridente. Much of the layout of this warren of streets comes from haphazard Medieval and Renaissance construction that overlaid existing Ancient Roman roads, sites and structures. This area is a veritable pastiche of architectural and historical influences.

The best place to start any exploration of the centro storico is right in the middle of it at the **Pantheon**. Constructed by Agrippa in 27

BCE, the Pantheon was restored after a fire in 80 CE and returned to its original rotunda shape by the Emperor Hadrian. In 609 CE, it was dedicated as a Christian Church and called Santa Maria Rotunda. In 1620 the building's bronze ceiling was removed and melted into the cannons for Castel Sant'Angelo and Bernini's Baldacchino in Saint Peter's.

You enter the building by way of the original bronze doors and the first thing you notice when you look up is that there is a hole in the ceiling!! Remember this used to be a pagan temple, Pantheon means "all the gods" in Latin, and this opening to the elements was an expression of that pagan connection to the natural world.

There are three niches in the building that contain the following tombs: **Victor Emmanuel II** (died 1878), one of Italy's few war heroes, **Umberto I** (died 1900), **Queen Margherita** (died 1926), and the tomb of renowned artist whose last name of **Sanzio** is not nearly as well known as his first, **Raphael** (died 1520). *Info:* Piazza della Rotonda. Tel. 06/6830-0230. www.roma2000.it/zpanthe.html. Open Monday-Saturday 9am-6:30pm, Sundays 9am-1pm. At 10am on Sundays is a mass. Tel. 06/6830-0230.

One of the best gelaterie in Rome is the **Cremeria Monteforte**, located on the right hand side of the Pantheon. Stop here for a bite of exquisite Roman ice cream. *Info:* Via della Rotonda 22, Map B & C.

Located behind the Pantheon, **Santa Maria Sopra Minerva** was also built on the pagan ruins of a temple, this one dedicated to Minerva. In this expansive church, you can find many tombs of famous 15th and 16th century personages as well as beautiful paintings, sculptures, frescoes and bas-relief work. One attraction is the remains of Saint Catherine of Siena — who died in Rome in 1380 — at the high altar.

Rome's Best Chocolates

Right around the corner from Santa Maria Sopra Minerva is this gem of a chocolate store, **Moriando & Gariglio**. Opened in 1886 it is the place to come for artisan-style chocolate. *Info:* Via del Pie di Marmo, Map A & B.

To the left of the altar is the statue of *Christ Carrying the Cross* created by Michelangelo in 1521. The bronze drapes were added later for modesty. If you compare this work to the one to the right of the altar, *John the Baptist* by Obici, you can easily see why Michelangelo is considered a master. His statue looks as if it could come to life, while the one by Obici simply appears carved out of stone.

Behind the altar are the tombs of Pope Clement VII and Leo X that were created by the Florentine sculptor Baccio Bandanelli. In front of the church is a wonderful sculpture of an elephant with an obelisk on his back called *Il Pulcino*, which was designed by Bernini. *Info:* Piazza della Minerva, Tel. 06/6990339. Hours 7am-7pm.

A short walk away is the famous **Piazza Navona**, located on the site of an ancient Roman stadium built in 86 CE. Before you come into the piazza, head over to the north entrance, where there is an excavation allowing us to see some original stone arches located 20 feet below the current street level, indicating how much silt has accumulated since the Roman Empire.

Located in the middle of the square is Bernini's exquisite **Fontana Dei Quattro Fiumi** (Fountain of Four Rivers), sculpted from 1647-51. The four figures supporting the large obelisk (a Bernini trademark) represent the four major rivers known at the time: the Danube, the Ganges, the Nile, and the Plata Rivers.

Within this statue Bernini has hidden a window back in time. Notice the figure representing the Nile shielding its eyes from the facade of the church it is facing, **Santa Agnese in Agone**. This church was designed by Bernini's rival at the time, Borromini. Bernini is playfully showed his disdain for his rival's design through the sculpted disgust in his statue.

At the south end of the piazza is the **Statue of Il Moro** (actually a replica) created by Bernini from 1652-54. To the north is a basin with a 19th century **Statue of Neptune** struggling with a sea monster.

If this is your first time to Rome, to savor the artistic and architectural beauty, as well as the vibrant nightlife of the piazza, choose a table at one of the local restaurants or cafés and sample some excellent Roman *gelato* (ice cream), grab a coffee, or have a meal and watch the people go by. Navona has been one of Rome's many gathering spots for people of all ages since the early 18th century.

If you looking for something a little more off the beaten path than what Piazza Navona has to offer, head down the Via Tor Mellina to the **Antico Caffe della Pace**, a nice vine-covered cafe. This is a scenic place to stop for sustenance and to savor the local ambiance of the area. *Info:* Via Tor Mellina #3-7, Map B & C.

Nearby is the **Campo dei Fiori**, which used to serve as the spot where heretics were burned at the stake and criminals were hanged. The monument in the middle is in memory of Giordano Bruno, a famous philosopher who was immolated here in 1600. Today, this typically Roman piazza hosts a lively flower and food market every morning until 1pm, except Sundays. Then in the evenings it moonlights as the party spot for the younger set. This entire area, from the Campo dei Fiori towards St. Peter's and bordered by the Lungotevere and Corso Vittorio Emanuele is filled with antique stores, artisans workshops, and more.

If you're in need of sustenance, **La Carbonara** (*see Best Eats*) in the Campo dei Fiori serves authentic Roman cuisine in a vibrant local atmosphere.

A short walk away is the **Jewish Ghetto**. This ancient Jewish quarter is a peaceful riverside neighborhood that looks much like any other section of Rome until closer inspection reveals Kosher food signs and men wearing skull caps. The official ghetto ceased to exist in 1846 when its walls were torn down, but the neighborhood remains home to one of Europe's oldest and proudest Jewish communities, housing as many as 40,000 Jews at one point. In 1556 Pope Paul IV confined all Jews to this small section of the city and enclosed it with high walls.

Located at the corner of the Via Portico d'Ottavia in the Jewish Ghetto are the remains of the **Teatro di Marcello**, one of greatest theaters in ancient Rome, able to hold around 15,000 spectators. Regrettably, as was the case with most ancient Roman monuments, it was used as a source of building materials after the fall of the Empire. Eventually it was transformed into a sumptuous Renaissance palazzo for the noble Savelli family. Today the  structure is a high-end apartment building. *Info:* www.roma2000.it/zmarce.html.

Rome's Best Pastries

There is no better place than the Jewish Ghetto to find pastries in Rome. Here are two places, almost next door to one another, where you can grab a quick snack and a coffee: **Dolceroma** (Via del Portico d'Ottavia 20b, Map B) and **Il Forno del Ghetto** (Via del Portico d'Ottavia 2, Map B).

In the middle of the Tiber River is the **Isola Tiberina**, which used to be a dumping ground for dead and sick slaves, as well as a place of worship to the Greek God of healing, Askleapios. Currently half the island is taken up by the hospital of Fatebene Fratelli showing that traditions do live on. Visible south of the Isola Tiberina are the remains of the ancient **Pons Aemilius**, the oldest bridge in Rome, washed away by a flash floor in 1598. The oldest surviving bridge in Rome is the **Ponte Fabricio** leading from the island to the Jewish Ghetto. It was built in 62 BCE.

Across the Tiber is the neighborhood of **Trastevere**, which literally means "across the river". It is a great place to end our day as it is filled with interesting shops and boutiques, and plenty of excellent restaurants among the small narrow streets and *piazzette* (small squares). The best sight to see in Trastevere is **Santa Maria in Trastevere**, one of Rome's earliest churches and the first to be dedicated to the Virgin Mary. Known for its exquisite Byzantine-style mosaics. *Info:* Piazza Santa Maria in Trastevere 1, Tel. 06/581-4802. www.roma2000.it/ztraste.html. Hours 7am-7pm.

Around the Forum
The city state of Rome emerged as a regional power 2,200 years ago built itself into a Republic and then and Empire that last over 600 years. At its core is the Roman Forum, Palatine Hill, Colosseum, Arch of Constantine and more. This area is where Rome's ancient glory comes to life.

On the other side of the Colosseum from the Arch of Constantine and down the Via Giovanni in Laterano is the amazing church of **San Clemente**. When you enter you are in the **Upper Church**, a simple basilica divided by two rows of columns. The **Lower**

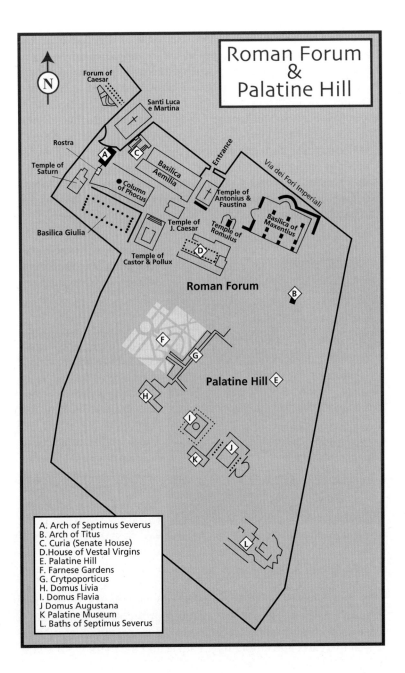

Roman Forum
&
Palatine Hill

A. Arch of Septimus Severus
B. Arch of Titus
C. Curia (Senate House)
D. House of Vestal Virgins
E. Palatine Hill
F. Farnese Gardens
G. Crytpoporticus
H. Domus Livia
I. Domus Flavia
J Domus Augustana
K Palatine Museum
L. Baths of Septimus Severus

Church was discovered in 1857 and contains subterranean passages that housed an early Christian place of worship from the days when Christians had to practice their religion below ground for fear of persecution. Even further below is the reason we are here, for the remains of a pagan temple dedicated to **Mithras**. Brought to Rome from Asia Minor in 67 BCE, where it had been the religion of Alexander the Great's army, this pagan religion was one of the most popular in all of the Roman Empire. Known for their ritual baptism by the blood of freshly killed bulls, Christianity adopted this practice of ritual baptism, but with water instead of blood, to lure Mithraic worshipers. *Info:* Via di San Giovanni Laterano. €2 (to the lower church). Hours to visit the basement 9am-1pm. Closed Sundays. Metro-Colosseo.

Also known as the Flavian Amphitheater, the **Colosseum** was opened in 80CE. Used as a public arena where exotic beasts were pitted against unarmed men, and thousands of gladiators lost their lives. These types of bloody spectacles continued until 405 CE, when they were abolished. At one point the arena could hold over 50,000 people. Each of the three tiers of seats is supported by a different set of columns: Doric for the base, Ionic for the middle and Corinthian for the top.

Inside, the first tier of seats was reserved for the tribunes and other dignitaries such as knights (which is where the Medieval Age got the term for their chivalric representatives. In fact, the plumed helmets, courteous manner, and colorful banners of Medieval knights were all based on ancient Roman officers, their behavior, garb, and emblems.). The second tier in the Colosseum was for citizens, and the third tier for the lower classes and slaves. The Emperor, Senators, Government Officials and Vestal Virgins sat on marble thrones on a raised platform that went around the entire arena.

Inside the arena, below where the floor once was, we can see vestiges of the subterranean passages that were used to transport the wild beasts. Human-powered pulley elevators were employed to get the animals up to the Colosseum floor. At times the arena was flooded to allow for the performance of mock naval battles. Unremarkable architecturally, the Colosseum is instead an engineering marvel from the past that deserves our admiration. *Info:* Piazza del Colosseo. €6. www.roma2000.it/zcoloss.html. Hours: summer - 9am-7pm; winter - 9am-5pm. Metro-Colosseo.

Located outside the Colosseum the **Arch of Constantine** was built in 312 CE to commemorate the Emperor's victory over Maxentius at the Ponte Milvio. Comprised of three archways, this is the largest and best-preserved in Rome.

After 15 years of excavations, the **Domus Aurea** is intermittently open to public viewing due to persistent water leakage. Also known as **Nero's Golden House**, this palace was built by Nero after the great fire of 64 CE destroyed his first abode, not to mention a great deal of Rome. Nero appropriated a huge amount of land in much of central Rome and had the finest craftsmen of the day work on this structure. You can view eight rooms today, all underground, and admire the vaulted ceilings, extant pieces of frescoes and stone reliefs, beautiful floor mosaics, and pieces of broken sculpture. *Info:* Viale della Domus Aurea. Tel. 06/399-67700. Metro-Colosseo.

Rome's Best Alimentari

Volpetti is the place to come to find great edibles to take home with you, bring back to your room, or nibble on the street. You can get tasty salami, delectable cheeses, hot and cold prepared food, and truly local cultural experience. *Info:* Via della Scrofa 31/32, Map B & C.

Hours: 9am to 7:45pm summer; 9am to 5pm winter; closed on Tuesdays. €5. To visit the Domus Aurea, you must make a reservation at *Centro Servizi per l'Archeologia* (Via Amendola 2, Metro-Colosseo, Mon-Sat 9am-1pm and 2-5pm). Book reservations in advance through Select Italy (Tel. 847/853-1661 in the U.S.; www.selectitaly.com, cost $19). Or, once you're in Rome, call 06/3974-9907.

From the Domus Aurea it is a short walk to the **Roman Forum**. The area initially emerged the center for the religious, commercial and political activities of the early settlers, then was greatly expanded in the Imperial era when Roman emperors began building self-contained *Fora* in their own honor. The entire area has been decimated by war, used as a quarry for other buildings in Rome, and has been haphazardly excavated, but is still a wonder to behold. *Info:* Largo Romolo e Remo 1, Tel. 06/699-0110, €6, www.roma2000.it/zforo.html, Open 9am-8pm and in the summers on Saturday until midnight, Metro-Colosseo.

In the Roman Forum you'll find a number of interesting sights, but these are the best (see map on page 43):

The **Arch of Septimus Severus (a)** was built in 203 CE to celebrate the tenth anniversary of the Emperor Septimus Severus' reign. Over the side arches are bas-reliefs depicting scenes from victorious battles fought by the Emperor against the Parthians and the Mesopotamians.

The **Arch of Titus (b)** was erected in 81 CE by Domitian to commemorate the conquering of Jerusalem by Titus. The arch contains bas-reliefs of the Emperor and of soldiers carrying away the spoils of Jerusalem. It is one of the most imposing structures remaining from ancient Rome, and a pilgrimage site for every Jewish tourist to the city.

The **Curia (c)** was founded by Tullus Hostilius and initially erected between 80 BCE and 44 BCE, it was completed in 29 BCE by Augustus. It was the house of the Senate, the government of Rome in the Republican period, and the puppet government during the empire. It was once covered with exquisite marble but is today a combination of stucco and brick. The structure was rebuilt after a fire in 283 CE, and converted into a church in the seventh century CE. The interior is still a large plain hall, with marble steps that were used as the senator's seats. Take the time to go inside and sit where the Roman Senators sat ages ago. This is where Julius Caesar was murdered.

The **House of the Vestal Virgins (d)** is where the vestal virgins lived who dedicated themselves to maintaining the sacred fires in the nearby **Temple of Vesta**. A portico of two stories adorned with statues of the Vestals surrounded a round open court that was decorated with flower beds and three cisterns. In the court you can still see the remains of some of the statues and the pedestals on which they sat.

Located in the Forum is the **Palatine Hill (e)**. Once the residence of the Roman emperors during the Golden Age and Imperial Period, it was here, in 754 BCE, that Romulus is said to have founded the city of Rome. However, actual records and not just myth have indicated that settlement was actually established in the 9th century BCE, 3000 years ago. Aristocratic families also resided here, leaving behind wonderful architectural relics most of which have been excavated today.

Entering the Palatine, you pass through the **Farnese Gardens (f)**. Originally called the Domus Tiberiana, these gardens were laid out in the sixteenth century and were full of orange trees and gurgling fountains. Underneath the gardens is the **Cryptoporticus (g)**, a subterranean tunnel built by Nero for hot-weather walks and as a secret route from the Palatine and his

Golden House across the valley on the Oppian Hill. Further up the hill is the **Domus Livia (h)** named after Augustus' wife. The wall paintings here date from the late Republic period. Nearby is the **Domus Flavia (i)** with the foundations of what appear to be a maze. Next to that is the **Domus Augustana (j)**, the emperor's private residence. The oval building may have been a garden or a theater for the emperor's private entertainment.

In between the Domus Flavia and Domus Augustana is the **Palatine Museum (k)**, a nondescript gray building which houses human remains and artifacts from the earliest communities in Rome. In the upstairs rooms are busts and other works from the fourth century CE.

Finally, at the farthest corner of the Palatine lie the remains of the small palace and **Baths of Septimus Severus (l)**. These are some of the best-preserved buildings on the hill, quite possibly because it was the most difficult point to reach, deterring the scavengers from looting its structure for building materials.

Located just outside of the Forum and on one of the seven hills of Rome are the second best set of museums in Rome, the **Capitoline Museums**. These include the **Senatorial Palace** and the **Palace of the Conservatori**, which was constructed by a design from Michelangelo. In the courtyard of the Palace you will find the famous large stone head, hand and foot that are fragments from a huge seated statue of Constantine.

Inside the museums, look for the famous *Boy with a Thorn*, a graceful Greek sculpture of a boy pulling a thorn out of his foot; the *She-Wolf of the Capitol*, an Etruscan work of Romulus and Remus being

Roma Pass

This **integrated ticket** gets you into the most important museums and archaeological sites of Rome. It allows free access to the first two museums/archaeological sites visited, after which you get reduced entry for the others. It also offers full access to Rome's public transport system for its duration. *Info:* €18 for three days. www.romapass.it. Tel. 39-06/8205-9127 (daily 9am-7:30pm), or 39-06/0606 (daily 24 hours).

suckled by the mythical wolf of Rome, the death mask bust of Michelangelo; the marble *Medusa* head by Bernini; the celebrated

painting *St. Sebastian* by Guido Reni that shows the saint with arrows shot into his body; and the famous Caravaggio work, *St. John the Baptist. Info:* Piazza del Campidoglio 1. Tel. 06/6710-2071, www.museicapitolini.it. €5. Hours 9am-7pm. Closed Mondays.

Vatican

Most people do not know that the Vatican is its own country, and it was not always confined within these few hundred acres in the center of Rome. It used to be a city-state extending up along the Adriatic, through Umbria and Le Marche, into the Po Valley north of Florence. Though reduced in size and stature, visiting the Vatican, it's museums, the Sistine Chapel, St. Peter's, and what used to be the castle of the Vatican, Castel Sant'Angelo are all must see destinations while in Rome.

Located in the monumental square Piazza San Pietro, **Saint Peter's** is the largest church in the world. The church rises on the site where Peter the saint is buried. Over the centuries the church began to expand and became incongruously, lavishly decorated, and structurally unsafe. Bramante worked on it, as did Raphael and Michelangelo, who graced the top with the pointed dome modeled after Brunelleschi's on the Duomo in Florence.

Surrounding the piazza above the oval structure are 140 **statues of saints**. In the center is an **obelisk** 25.5 meters high with four bronze lions at its base, all of which were brought from Heliopolis during the reign of Caligula (circa 40 CE) and which originally stood in the circus of Nero, which was on this site. If you stand on the two porphyries (disks) in the ground in St. Peter's Square, located on either side of the obelisk, and look at the **columns** (which run four deep) surrounding the square, only one column is visible from each row of four.

The **facade** is 115 meters long and 45 meters high, and is approached by a gradually sloping grand staircase. At the sides of this staircase are the statues of **Saint Peter** (by De Fabis) and **Saint Paul** (by Adamo Tadolini). On the balustrade, held up by eight Corinthian columns and four pilasters, are the colossal statues of the Savior and St. John the Baptist surrounded by the Apostles, excluding Saint Peter.

The church is more than 15,000 square meters in area, 211 meters long and 46 meters high. There are 44 altars and 229 marble columns. On the floor of the central nave you'll find lines drawn identifying where other churches in the world would fit if placed in Saint Peter's. Also on the floor, near the front entrance, is a red disk indicating the spot where **Charlemagne** was crowned Holy Roman Emperor by Leo III on Christmas Day in 800 CE. To the

right of this, in the first chapel, is the world-famous *Pieta* sculpted by Michelangelo in 1498, when he was only 24.

In the niches of the pilasters that support the arches are statues of the founders of many religious orders. In the last one on the right you'll find the seated bronze statue of Saint Peter. The statue's foot has been rubbed by so many people for good luck that its toes have all but disappeared.

Just past the statue is the grand **cupola** created by Michelangelo, held up by four colossal spires that lead to a number of open chapels. Under the cupola, above the high altar rises the famous **Baldacchino** (or Grand Canopy) made by Bernini, and built of bronze taken from the roof of the Pantheon. In front of the altar the **Chapel of Confessions** made by Maderno, around which are

95 perpetually lit lamps illuminating the **Tomb of Saint Peters**. In front of the shrine is the kneeling **Statue of Pius VI** made by Canova in 1822.

Throughout the rest of the Basilica you'll find a variety of superb statues and monuments, many tombs of Popes, and a wealth of chapels, not the least of which is the **Gregorian Chapel** designed by Michelangelo. One controversial tomb is that of Pope Celestine V who allegedly died at the hands of his over-eager successor, Boniface VIII. Researchers were recently granted permission to x-ray the tomb and it clearly shows a ten-inch nail driven into Celestine's skull.

> **ALTERNATE PLAN**
> If you are looking for a unique experience try the **Scavi (underground) tour below St. Peter's Basilica**. You'll find mysterious bones, uncovered graves, ancient foundations, and tons of archeological intrigue. But you need to reserve well in advance. *Info:* Fabbrica of St. Peter, 00120 Vatican City, Tel. 011-39-06-6987-3017, www.vatican.va. €10.

You can ascend into Michelangelo's Cupola either by stairs (537 of them) or by elevator. The views from the top over the city of Rome are magnificent. On the way down, if you are hungry or thirsty, there is a nice café at which to grab some sustenance. *Info:* Piazza San Pietro. Hours 8am-6pm, but only until 5pm in the winter. Tel. 06/6988-4466. www.vatican.va. Metro-Ottaviano.

Our next stop, the **Vatican Museums**, are close by St. Peter's. These museums are so extensive that they could easily take the better part of a day. Here you will find Egyptian, Greek & Roman artifacts, as well as the best collection of paintings and sculptures anywhere in the world. *Info:* Viale Vaticano, Tel. 06/6988-4466. €12. www.vatican.va. From November - March and June - August open 8:45am to 12:20pm. From March - June and September - October open 8:45am to 3:20pm. Closed most Sundays and all major religious holidays. Metro-Ottaviano.

There is a plethora of amazing collections to admire in the Vatican Museums, but these are the best:

Pinacoteca Vaticana - A wonderful collection of masterpieces from many periods, including works by Giotto and Raphael.

Pius Clementine Museum – Mainly known as a sculpture museum, you can also find mosaic work and sarcophagi from the 2nd, 3rd and 4th centuries. One mosaic in particular is worth noting, the *Battle between the Greeks and the Centaurs*, created in the first century CE. Also worth noting is the bronze statue of Hercules and the **Hall of the Muses** that contain statues of the Muses and the patrons of the arts.

Chiaramonti Museum - This museum includes a collection of over 5,000 Pagan and Christian works, including Roman Sarcophagi, *Silenus Nursing the Infant Bacchus*, busts of Caesar, the Statue of Demosthenes, the famous *Statue of the Nile*, as well as a magnificent Roman chariot recreated in marble by the sculptor Franzone in 1788.

Etruscan Museum - This museum contains objects excavated in the Southern part of Etruria from 1828-1836, as well as pieces from later excavations around Rome. Here you'll find an Etruscan tomb from Cervetri, as well as bronzes, gold objects, glasswork, candelabra, necklaces, rings, funeral urns, amphora and much more.

Egyptian Museum - A valuable documentary of the art and civilization of ancient Egypt; you can find sarcophagi, reproductions of portraits of famous Egyptian personalities, works by Roman artists who were inspired by Egyptian art, a collection of wooden mummy cases and funeral steles, mummies of animals, a collection of papyri with hieroglyphics, and much more.

Rooms of Raphael - Initially these rooms were decorated with the works of many 15th century artists, but because Pope Julius II loved the work of Raphael so much, he had the other paintings destroyed and commissioned Raphael to paint the entire room. Not nearly as stupendous as the Sistine Chapel by Michelangelo, but it still is one of the world's masterpieces.

Sistine Chapel - Last but not least is the private chapel of the popes, famous for the ceiling painted by **Michelangelo**.  Started in 1508 and finished four years later, the fresco has scenes from the Bible, among them the *Creation*, where God comes near Adam, who is lying down, and with a simple touch of his hand imparts the magic spark of life. On the wall behind the altar is the fresco of the *Last Judgment* also by Michelangelo and commissioned by Clement VII. Michelangelo was over 60 years of age when he started the project in 1535. He completed it seven years later in 1542.

Connected to that Vatican by a covered walkway, which was used more than once to whisk the Pope to protection from invading armies, is the **Castel Sant'Angelo** that houses a museum with a collection of armaments from the Stone Age to the modern era. There are also some art exhibits and luxuriously preserved Papal apartments. A great site for kids and adults to explore. *Info:* Lungotevere Castello 50, Tel. 06/3996-7600. www.roma2000.it/zmusange.html. €5. Open 9am-7pm. Closed Mondays. Metro-Lepanto.

Best of the Rest
This day is not confined to a geographic area and contains a collection of sights and churches all over Rome to visit. From Michelangelo's masterpiece in **San Pietro in Vincoli**, to evidence of female bishops in the early days of the church in **Santa Prassede**, to the museums at the **Baths of Diocletian**, to the ancient remains of the **Circus Maximus**, this day will bring you from one side of Rome to the other. Some of these sights are within walking distance from one another, but if not, please note the specific metro stop indicated for each sight.

Located near the Colosseum, **San Pietro in Vincoli** was founded in 442 CE as a shrine dedicated to preserving the chains with which Herod allegedly bound St. Peter in Jerusalem. These chains are in a crypt under the main altar and can be viewed through a glass partition. Chains aside, the reason to come to this church is the tomb of Julius II carved by Michelangelo. On it you will find the seated figure of *Moses*. The horns on Moses's head, by the way, symbolize divine inspiration, and are not meant to represent that Jews have horns, as many people throughout the ages interpreted them to mean. Flanking Moses are equally exquisite statues of *Leah* and *Rachel* also done by Michelangelo. *Info:* Piazza di San Pietro in Vincoli, Tel. 06/488-2865. Hours 7am-12:30pm and 3:30pm-6pm. Metro-Cavour.

Like St. Paul's Outside the Walls, St. Peter's, and St. John Lateran, **Santa Maria Maggiore** is one of the four patriarchal basilicas of Rome. Its name derives from the fact that it is the largest church (*maggiore*) in Rome dedicated to the Madonna. The interior is worth a visit mainly because of the 5th-century mosaics — definitely the best in Rome — its frescoes, and multi-colored marble. On the right wall of the **Papal Altar** is the funeral

 monument to Sixtus V and on the left wall the monument to Pius V. Opposite this is the **Borghese Chapel**, so called since the sepulchral vaults of the wealthy Borghese family lie beneath it. Here you'll view the beautiful bas-relief monumental tombs to Paul V and Clement VIII on its left and right walls. Towards the west end of the church is the **Sforza Chapel** with its intricately designed vault. Pius VI's eerie crypt is below and in front of the main altar. *Info:* Piazza di Santa Maria Maggiore. Tel. 06/483-195. www.roma2000.it/zschmar.html. Hours 8am-7pm. Metro-Termini.

In the small church of **Santa Prassede**, near Santa Maria Maggiore, you will find a mosaic of a female bishop from the early church, Episcopa Theodora, the most compelling evidence for the existence of women as priests and early leaders of the church. Located in the side chapel of St. Zeno directly to the left as you enter the church. Theodora lived around 850 CE and in the mosaic she is wearing the same kind of pectoral cross as worn by bishops today. There is clear evidence of an attempt to change her name from Theodora (the "r" and the "a" were clearly removed in the mosaic and replaced by other tiles) to Theodo, but her title "episcopa", the feminine form of the Latin word for bishop gives away this subterfuge. Though controversial, many theologians are finally delving into the evidence indicating equality of the sexes in the early church. However, most evidence is in more obscure locations around the world, while St. Prassede is walking distance from the central train station in Rome. *Info:* Via Santa Prassede 9a, 9am-noon; 3pm-5pm.

Most people don't realize that **San Giovanni in Laterano** (St. John Lateran), and not St. Peter's, is the cathedral of the Catholic world. It was established in 312 CE on land donated by Roman Emperor Constantine, the founder of the modern Catholic Church, who needed one unifying religion to try and tie his crumbling empire together. Today, the simple facade of the church — created by Allessandro Galiliei in 1735 — is topped by fourteen colossal statues of Christ, the Apostles, and saints.

To get inside, you must pass through the bronze door that used to be attached to the old Roman Senate house. A prime example of the pilferage from ancient Roman sites. The interior of the church, laid out in the form of a Latin cross, has five naves filled with historical and artistic objects. The wooden ceiling and the marble flooring are from the 15th century. The most beautiful artistic aspect of the church is the vast transept, richly decorated with marbles and frescoes portraying the *Leggenda Aurea* of Constantine. One item of historical interest is the simple wooden table, on which it is said that Saint Peter served mass. *Info:* Piazza San Giovanni in Laterano 4, Tel. 06/6988-6452. www.roma2000.it/zschgiov.html. Hours: Baptistery: 6am-12:30pm and 4-7pm; Cloisters 9am-5pm. Metro-San Giovanni.

The **Baths of Diocletian** were the most extensive baths of their times in which more than 3,000 bathers could be accommodated

simultaneously. Built by Maximilian and Diocletian from 196-306 CE, today the **Museo Nazionale delle Terme** is located here. If you like ancient sculpture you'll enjoy this collection of classical Greek and Roman works. Start with the *Hall of Masterpieces* where you'll find the *Pugilist*, a bronze work of a seated boxer, and the *Discobolus*, a partial sculpture of a discus thrower celebrated for its amazing muscle development. Another inspiring work is the celebrated *Dying Gaul and His Wife*, a colossal sculpture from Pergamon created in the third century BCE. Then there is the *Great Cloister*, a perfectly square space surrounded by an arcade of one hundred Doric columns. *Info:* Viale delle Terme. €1. www.roma2000.it/zdiocle.html. Hours 9am-2pm. Holidays until 1pm. Closed Mondays. Metro-Repubblica.

The **Circus Maximus** (or circuit, i.e. race-track) is located on the flat lands to the south of the Palatine Hill. It was erected in 309 CE by the Emperor Maxentius in honor of his deified son Romulus, whose temple is on the Palatine. Then in Imperial times it was expanded, destroyed, enlarged and ultimately in the Middle Ages, used as a quarry. Despite the lack of artistic accoutrements its shape is clearly visible underneath the contoured grass and earth, and some of the original seats remain at the turning circle of the southwestern end. The slight hump running through the center marks the location of the *spina*, around which the chariots, and at times runners, would race. In its prime the Circo Massimo could hold between 150,000-200,000 spectators, more than most modern stadiums. *Info:* Via del Circo Massimo. www.roma2000.it/zcircom.html. Metro-Circo Massimo.

Outside the west end of the track is the Church of **SM in Cosmedin,** famous for the **Bocca della Verita** (mouth of truth), an old Roman drain cover that now resides under the church's portico. Reputed to grab hold of the hand of the person who, with hand inserted, tells a lie. According to legend, it was once used by Roman husbands to test the their wives faithfulness.

Built in 217 CE by the Emperor Caracalla, the **Baths of Caracalla** were second in size only to the Baths of Diocletian. They were used until the sixth century at which time they were destroyed by the invasion of Visigoths. The baths were once rich with marble and statues and decorated with stucco and mosaic work. All that is left are the weathered remains of  the massive brick structure that offers an insight into the scale of the baths, but doesn't offer a glimpse of their beauty. *Info:* Via Terme di Caracalla 52, Tel. 06/3996-7700. www.roma2000.it/zcaracal.html. €5. Hours Monday-Saturday 9am until one hour before dark. Mondays and Holidays 9am-1pm. Metro-Circo Massimo.

Ostia Antica
Nothing compares to Pompeii's mesmerizing archeological tableau (see *The Bay of Naples & Amalfi Coast* section), but if you don't have the time to visit that ancient Roman town trapped in time by the eruption of Vesuvius in 79 CE, then just 15 miles southwest of Rome, Ostia Antica is the next best thing. It is a superb illustration of what life in Ancient Rome was like at the height of the Empire only a shade less vivid than that of Pompeii.

Founded in the fourth century BCE, **Ostia Antica** was once the bustling seaport of Ancient Rome. However, back in the fifth century CE the town was abandoned because its two harbors had completely silted up. The extent of the sediment accumulation is evidenced today by the modern shore being three miles beyond the ancient seawall of the town.

Though it was not covered by a storm of deadly ash as was Pompeii, being discarded and left as a ghost town allowed Ostia Antica to remain almost completely intact. The backbone of Ostia Antica is the *Decumanus Maximus*, nearly a mile long. Once colonnaded, it runs from the **Porta Romana** straight to the **Forum**. Along the way you pass the well-preserved old **Amphitheater** and the **Piazzale dei Corporazione** (Corporation Square), a tree-lined boulevard once filled with the bustle of over seventy commercial offices. All of these shops are worth a visit, but the laundry and wine store, with their tastefully decorated mosaic tiled floors representing their trades, are best. All around, the variety of mosaic-tile floors document the diversity of goods and services available in Ostia. Commodities included furs, wood, grain, beans, melons, oil, fish, wine, mirrors, flowers, ivory, gold, and silk. Among the services offered were caulkers, grain measurers, maintenance men, warehousing, shipwrights, barge men, carpenters, masons, mule drivers, stevedores and divers for sunken cargoes.

Farther down the *Decumanus Maximus* you arrive at the **Capitolium**, a temple dedicated to Jupiter and Minerva, located at the end of the **Forum**. The **insulae** (apartment blocks) offer a unique insight into where the average citizen and smaller merchants lived. These apartments were generally four to five stories tall, well lighted, had running water, as well as garbage removal and toilets on each floor. Two private homes, where wealthier merchants once lived are the **House of the Cupid and Psyche**, which is west of the Capitolium, and the **House of the Dioscuri**, which is at the southwest end of town. *Info:* The site is open daily 9am–6pm in summer, 9am–4pm in winter. €5. The museum is open one hour less. www.ostia-antica.org or www.ostiantica.info.

And it's not just the town itself that is worthwhile, getting here can be fun as well. By train, it is only 40 minutes from Stazione Ostiense, but not very scenic. However, arriving by boat via the Tiber River, though it takes around two and a quarter hours, offers a unique perspective from which to view the surrounding countryside and get an idea as to how ancient goods and passengers moved between Rome and Ostia. *Info:* Tickets cost €10 one-way and €11 return. www.battellidiroma.it.

Parco Regionale dell'Appia Antica

This is one of the best-kept secrets in Rome. Located just outside the ancient walls of Rome near San Giovanni Laterano, this is a must-see destination on a week-long trip to the Eternal City. The park covers an area of around 3,400 hectares within which are 16km of the **Via Appia Antica** and along which are impressive **ancient aqueducts** and **Christian catacombs**. There are also many other sights to see including numerous medieval, renaissance and baroque churches, medieval towers and fortifications, and ancient temples.

There is nothing quite like walking along cobblestones that were laid down by Roman legionnaires, passing by imposing ruins of the aqueducts that supplied the city with water, and entering catacombs scratched from the earth thousands of years ago. A stroll in the **Parco Regionale dell'Appia Antica** is quite literally taking a walk through history. *Info:* www.parcoappiaantica.org, Via Appia Antica 58/60, Mon-Sat, 9:30am-5:30pm (4:30pm Winter); Sunday and holidays 9:30am-5:30pm (4:30pm Winter).

The best way to get to the park is on the **Archeobus** service that runs from the Piazza Cinquecento outside of Termini Station, heads to Piazza Venezia, the Circus Maximus, Baths of Caracalla, then into the park, to the catacombs and the aqueducts. If you did not want to get off and wander around, the entire trip would take 2 hours. You are able to get on and off the bus at any stop throughout the day. *Info:* Tickets cost €8, which can be bought at the ticket office on island 'E' in Piazza Cinquecento, on board the bus, and at the park info offices. Your ticket allows entrance the Catacombs of S. Sebastiano and S.Callixtus for only €3, and allows you to rent a bike for only €2 at the Park headquarters.

Though located just outside the Parco Regionale dell'Appia Antica, the **Catacombs** are directly adjacent, so easily accessible, if you first enter the park then head over to the catacombs – especially if you use the stop & go feature of the dedicated bus service. These underground Christian tombs were originally an ancient Roman necropolis, a pagan place of burial. The early Christians took them over as clandestine meeting places, and were eventually turned into burial chambers for them. Here you can visit the **crypts of the Popes**, the crypt of Saint Cecilia, the crypt of Pope Eusebius, as well as frescoes dating back to the 3rd century CE.

St. Callixtus Catacombs, *Info:* Via Appia Antica 110, Monday - Sunday 8.30am-noon, 2:30pm-5pm until March; From March onwards 8:30am-12:30pm, 2:30pm-5:30pm; Closed on 1st January, 25th December, at Easter. Tel. 06/4465610 or 06/51301580. €5.

Basilica of St. Sebastian and Catacombs, *Info:* Via Appia Antica 136, Monday-Saturday 8:30am-noon, 2:30pm-5:30pm Closed on Sundays, Closed from 15th November to 13th December; Tel. 06/7850350. €5

4. FLORENCE & TUSCANY

A visit to Italy is not complete without a trip to **Florence**. The Renaissance achieved the bloom of artistic expression here when countless artists, writers, inventors, political theorists and artisans filled the world with the glow of their brilliance and the fruits of their labors. Michelangelo and Leonardo da Vinci may be the best known outside of Italy, but I'll wager you've also heard of Dante, Petrarch, Brunelleschi, Machiavelli, Giotto, Raphael as well as many other learned and talented Florentines.

Strolling through the cobblestone streets of Florence is like being in a history book come to life. This wonderful city must be experienced firsthand to appreciate and fully understand the magical atmosphere. So read on, and I'll guide you through the amazing city of Florence, and also Tuscany's other best spots — **Siena**, **Pisa**, **Lucca**, and **San Gimignano**

ONE GREAT DAY IN FLORENCE

If all you have is 24 hours, this tour will give you as meaningful an introduction to the city as you can possibly get. Along the way you will walk in the footsteps of such **artistic luminaries** as Michelangelo, Leunardo da Vinci, Raphael, Brunelleschi, Dante, Machiavell, plodding along the same cobblestoned streets that have remained unchanged for hundreds of years.

The best place to start is with the master himself, the man who is still considered the best sculpture the world has ever known, Michelangelo Buonarroti, and his renowned **statue of David** at the **Accademia**. Be sure to make reservations well in advance to visit here by going to www.firenze.net. Otherwise you will spend most of your morning waiting in a line to get in. *Info:* open 10:30am-1pm and 2-6pm in winter and 3-7pm in summer, Via Ricasoli 60, Tel. 055/214-375. www.polomuseale.firenze.it/accademia. Open 9am–7pm Tuesday–Saturday. Sundays 9am-1pm. €6.

The museum's main draw is a statue that is as close to perfection as can be achieved with a hammer and chisel. Started from a discarded block of marble that Michelangelo bought on his own – no one commissioned this work – he finished sculpting *David* at the age of 25 in the year 1504, after four years of labor. It was originally in front of the Palazzo della Signoria, but was brought here in 1873 to protect it from the elements, and a substitute put in its old spot. Having recently undergone a complete restoration, the *David* now truly shines.

After admiring these and other sculptures in the Accademia let's head over to the **San Lorenzo Market**, Florence's largest outdoor market. *Info:* open everyday from 8am-dark. Closed Sundays in the winter.

After you have found gifts and keepsakes to bring home, let's stop in the Mercato Centrale and grab lunch at **Nerbone** (*see Best Eats*). After lunch, or before, whatever your preference take the time to walk through the **Mercato Centrale**, Florence's main food market for fish, meat, vegetables, cheeses, oils, breads, and many

other delicacies. If you want to buy some salami, prosciutto, or cheese the best purveyor of these treats is **Perini** (www.periniitalia.it) inside the market; come here also to get gifts for home, snacks for the room, or picnic supplies. *Info:* Via dell Ariento, open Mon-

day–Friday, 7am-2pm and 4pm-8pm, Saturday 7am-12:15pm and 1pm-5pm. Sunday 3pm-5pm.

After lunch it's off to the world famous **Duomo**, known officially as **Santa Maria del Fiore** (Saint Mary of the Flowers). Consecrated in 1436 it was started in 1296 by Arnolfo di Cambio on the spot where the church of Santa Reparata existed. After di Cambio's death in 1301, the famous **Giotto** took over the direction of the work, but he dedicated most of his attention to the development of the Bell Tower (Campanile).

When Giotto died in 1337, Andrea Pisano took over until 1349. By 1421 everything else was finished except for the dome. Eventually **Brunelleschi** won a competition to design and build the dome, beating out his rival Ghiberti, the creator of the bronze panels on the east door of the Baptistery. Some say the artistic rivalry between these two helped spark the Renaissance itself.

Over the years, slight modifications and changes have been made, and in 1887, the current facade of the Duomo was finished by architect **Emilio de Fabris**. In the interior there are enormous

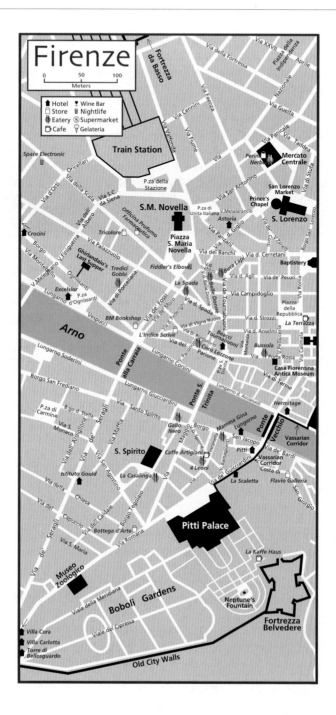

Firenze

0   50   100
Meters

🛏 Hotel   🍷 Wine Bar
🏠 Store   🎵 Nightlife
🍴 Eatery   Ⓢ Supermarket
☕ Cafe   🍦 Gelateria

Via XXVII
Via della Fortressa
Piazza della Indipendenza
Aprile
Via Nazionale
Via Guelfa

Fortrezza da Basso
Via Faenza
Via Cennini
Via Valfonda
Via Fiume

Train Station

Space Electronic
Oricellari
Via della Scala
Via d'Orti
Via S.C. da Siena
Via dell'Alloro
Tricolore

Perini Nerbo
Mercato Centrale
Via Panicale
Via Taddea
Via di Stufa

Via San Antonino
San Lorenzo Market
Prince's Chapel
S. Lorenzo
Via V.Zanelli
Borgo San Lorenzo

P.za della Stazione

S.M. Novella
P.za di Unità Italiana
V.Metalarancio
Astoria
Via Pana d. Giglio

Officina Profumo Farmaceutica
Piazza S. Maria Novella
Via dei Banchi
Via d. Cerretani
Baptistery

Crocini
Borgo
Via Montebello
V.Finiguerra
Via Palazzuolo

Ghirlandaio's Last Supper
Tredici Gobbi
Fiddler's Elbow
V.d. Trebbio
Luca Lapi
Via d. Agli
Via de' Pecori
Via Roma

V.Melegnano
Ognissanti
La Spada
Via delle Donne
Via Campidoglio
Piazza della Repubblica

Excelsior
P.za d'Ognissanti
Lungarno d'Ognissanti
Via d. Porcellana
Via de' Fossi
Via del Moro
Via d. Spada
Via de' Tournabuoni
Via d. Strozzi
La Terrazza

Vespucci
BM Bookshop
Via d. Federighi
Via di Vigna Nuova
Beacci Tournabuoni
Via d. Anselmi
Via Pellicceria
Bussola
Via Calimala

Arno

L'Indice Scrive
Via del Parione
Il Coco Lezzone
Via d. Purgatorio
Pza S. Trinita
Via Porta Rossa

Lungarno Soderini
Ponte alla Carraia
Lungarno Corsini
Lungarno d. Acciaioli
Casa Fiorentina Antica Museum
Via di Terme

Borgo San Frediano
Lungarno Giucciardini
Ponte S. Trinita
Hermitage

P.za di Carmine
B.go d. Stella
Via de' Serragli
Via Santo Spirito
Gallo Nero
Borgo
Mammo Gina
Lungarno
Ponte Vecchio
Vassarian Corridor

Via S. Monaco
Via d. Ardiglione
Via d. Maffia
Via San Agostino
Caffe Artigiani
Via d. Spronee
Coverelli
San Jacopo
Pitti
Via de' Bardi
Vassarian Corridor

S. Spirito
4 Leoni
Via d. Ramaglianti
Via de' Guicciardini
Costa di

Istituto Gould
La Casalinga
La Scaletta
Flavio Galleria

Via della Chiesa
Via d. Caldaie
Borgo Tegolaio
Via Giorgio

Via d. Capuccio
Bottega d'Arte
Via Romana

Via d. Serragli
Via S. Maria

Pitti Palace

Museo Zoologico

La Kaffe Haus

Viale della Meridiana
Boboli Gardens
Neptune's Fountain

Villa Cora
Villa Carlotta
Torre di Bellosguardo

Viale del Cipressa

Fortrezza Belvedere

Old City Walls

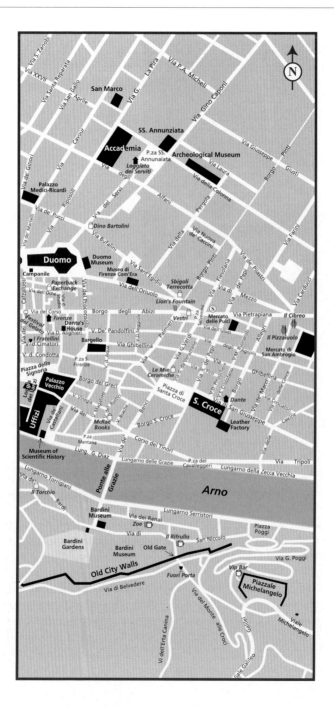

gothic arches supported by pillars. The dome itself is 90 meters high and 45.5 meters in diameter and is decorated with frescoes representing the Last Judgment done by Giorgio Vasari and Federico Zuccari at the end of the 16th century. In the niches of the pillars supporting the dome are statues of the Apostles.

The central chapel is home to the **Sarcophagus of San Zanobius** that contains the saint's relics. The bronze reliefs are the work of Lorenzo Ghiberti (1442). When you've finished wandering through the cathedral and admiring the art and stained glass windows, go to the top of the Duomo and get some great views of Florence. The way up is a little tiring, but the photo opportunities are fabulous. *Info:* Piazza del Duomo. Tel. 055/230-2885. Church open Monday-Saturday 10am–5pm, Sunday 1pm-5pm. Free. Admission to the dome €6.

After the Duomo, since time is fleeting, give passing glances to the Baptistery and Campanile while heading to the Piazza della Repubblica, where we are going to take a break at the roof top café, **La Terrazza** of the department store La Rinascente *(see sidebar)*.

After loading up on caffeine and pastries it's off to the **Piazza della Signoria** which

Florence's Best Cafe

La Terrazza is a tranquil spot with **panoramic vistas** over the terra cotta rooftops of the city. Located on the roof of the Rinascente department store, this is an ideal place to come for a break. *Info:* Piazza della Repubblica, Rinascente, 5th Floor, Open 10am-8pm.

consists of the Palazzo Vecchio, the Loggia della Signoria, the replica of the statue of David, and many cafes and *palazzi*. Over the centuries great historical and political occurrences, as well as the lives of average Florentines, have all flowed through this piazza. And one, the heretic monk, Savanorola, was burned alive here.

To the left of the Palazzo Vecchio is **Ammannati's Fountain** with the giant figure of *Neptune*. Commonly called *Biancone* (Whitey) by the locals. Just beyond that is the equestrian statue representing *Cosimo I dei Medici*.

In the piazza, on the right of the Palazzo as you face it is the expansive and airy **Loggia dei Lanzi**, a combination of Gothic and Renaissance architecture, built during the years 1376–1382. Inside the loggia are some wonderful sculptures: *Persius* by Cellini in 1553 under the left hand arch; *The Rape of the Sabines* by Giambologna in 1583 under the right arch; as is *Hercules and the Centaur* by Giambologna done in 1599.

To end the day we will be heading to the **Uffizi**. To be able to make this happen you should have made a reservation to enter the gallery by using the same website (www firenze.net) you used to reserve your entry into the Accademia. The **Uffizi Gallery** holds the most important and impressive display of art in Italy, and some would say the world. *Info:* Piazzale degli Uffizi. Tel. 055/238-8651. www.polomuseale.firenze.it/uffizi. Open Tuesday to Saturday 8:30am-6:30pm, Sundays and Holidays 9am-2pm. Closed Mondays. €6.5.

After being inundated with some of the world's most amazing art, let's head over to the world's most amazing bridge, the **Ponte Vecchio**, literally meaning Old Bridge.

After admiring the views from here, our day of touring is over, but a meal still awaits us in the maze of streets near Piazza Santa Maria Novella at **La Spada** (*see Best Sleeps & Eats*). Come here for superb local food, in a rustic ambiance, deep in the heart of the Florence.

A FANTASTIC WEEKEND IN FLORENCE

With a weekend, we can explore more of what we've already seen in-depth, and cover a lot more ground as well.

Friday Evening

Start your weekend in Florence on Friday evening by exploring the *centro storico* on foot. Begin by admiring the church that rests under that huge dome created by Brunelleschi, **Santa Maria del Fiore** (Saint Mary of the Flowers), commonly known as the **Duomo**. Contrary to a popular tourist misconception, the name Duomo does not refer to the dome itself, it means "cathedral." Every Italian city has a Duomo.

It took 14 years just to construct the gigantic dome, and until the Houston Astrodome was built in the 1960s, this was the largest free-standing dome in the world. As such it is an architectural masterpiece and engineering marvel. Brunelleschi had to invent countless machines, pulleys, and supports just to construct the dome. Many of the designs for machinery found in **Leonardo da Vinci's** notebooks are actually sketches of devices created by Brunelleschi.

When you've finished wandering through the cathedral and admiring the art and stained glass windows, if it is still open go to the top of the Duomo and get some great views of Florence. The way up is a trek, but its well worth it. *Info:* Piazza del Duomo. Tel. 055/230-2885. Church open Monday-Saturday 10am–5pm, Sunday 1pm-5pm. Free. Admission to the dome €6.

After the Duomo lets wander over to the famous **Baptistery**. Definitely considered one of the most important buildings in the city, the Baptistery was built in the 10th and 11th centuries and dedicated to Saint John the Baptist, the patron saint of Florence; and up until 1128, it was the cathedral of Florence. However, this small structure just didn't reflect the growing stature of the city, so the Duomo was built. *Info:* Piazza del Duomo. Tel. 055/230-2885. Open everyday 2pm–5:30pm. €2.

The interior is encrusted with stunning Byzantine style mosaics. The most famous of which is the demon eating the damned to the right of the large Christ figure. Outside the Baptistery, Ghiberti's doors are the real reason people come to see this sight. Michelangelo described the **East Door** by Ghiberti as "the door to paradise." When the originals were washed free during the flood of 1966 and almost lost, copies were made which is what you see now. The originals are in the Duomo Museum.

From the Baptistery it is only a short walk to the tall **Campanile**, which is covered in colored marble and adorned with bas-reliefs by Andrea Pisano and Luca della Robbia and Andrea Orcagna. Sculptures by Donatello, Nanni di Bartolo, and others used to be in the sixteen niches but are now in the Duomo Museum. *Info:* Piazza del Duomo. Tel. 055/230-2885. Open 8:30am–6:50pm (9am -4:20pm in off season). €6.

From here wander down Via del Calzaiuoli to the **Piazza della Signoria** which contains the **Palazzo Vecchio** (the old government seat), **Ammannati's Fountain** with the giant figure of Neptune, the equestrian statue of *Cosimo I dei Medici*, and the replica statue of David.

Also in the piazza is the **Loggia dei Lanzi** that contains some amazing statues including: *The Rape of the Sabines* by Giambologna in 1583 under the right arch and *Persius* by Cellini in 1553 under the left arch.

As it is getting on towards dinner time, head over to **La Bussola** (*see Best Eats*) where you can get superb pizza as well as pasta and other delicacies.

Saturday Morning
Let's start today off with a visit to Michelangelo's statue of **David** in the **Accademia**. If you don't want to spend the morning in a long line waiting to get in, be sure and make reservations at www.firenze.net. *Info:* Via Ricasoli 60, Tel. 055/214-375. www.polomuseale.firenze.it/accademia. Open 9am–7pm Tuesday–Saturday. Sundays 9am–1pm. €6.

Leading up to the *David* are *The Prisoners* also by Michelangelo, so called because the figures appear to be trapped in stone. Designed to hold the Tomb of Pope Julius II on their sculpted shoulders, Michelangelo died before he could bring the figures to life; and now they appear as if they are struggling to be freed from the marble's embrace.

Take the time to admire the *David* from every angle. This is one of the world's most famous statues, finished in 1504 when Michelangelo was only 25 years old.

Also in the Accademia is the **Sala Dell'Ottocento** (The 19th Century Hall) that is a gallery of plaster models and other works by students and prospective students of the Academy. Despite the medium, plaster, these works are exquisite. The holes you see in the casts are iron markings used as guides so that when carved into marble the figure can be recreated exactly.

From the Accademia it is only a short walk to the **Archeological Museum**. Here you will find an impressive array of Egyptian artifacts such as stelle, statues, coffins and more that make this collection a fine introduction to the splendor that was ancient Egypt. Also available here are a fine accumulation of Etruscan statuary and funereal urns as well as Greek artifacts. *Info:* Via della Colonaa 36, Tel. 055/23575. Mon-Sat 8:30am-2pm, Sun 8:30am-1pm. Closed alternate Sundays and Mondays. Admission.

Florence's Best Gelato

While there are plenty of places to get ice cream in Florence, with over 80 flavors, **Festival del Gelato** is the best. Just off Via Calzaiuoli, it is also conveniently located. *Info:* Via del Corso 75r.

Saturday Afternoon

After the Archeological Museum, let's head to the **Mercato Centrale**. Florence's main market is slowly being turned into a tourist center, but it still contains some of its old authenticity. The meat and fish section is on the ground floor, where you can find all sorts of offerings including baby pigs, whole chickens, cows hoofs, and more. If you're into healthy food, make your way upstairs to their the and vegetable market. While in the market, the best place to grab a bite to eat is **Nerbone**, a wonderfully authentic old time Florentine eatery where you can get great sandwiches, pasta, salad, and beer and wine. One of my favorite spots in all of Florence. *Info:* Via dell Ariento, open Monday–Friday, 7am–2pm and 4pm–8pm, Saturday 7am-12:15pm and 1pm-5pm. Sunday 3pm-5pm.

Now head to a great place to shop in Florence, the **San Lorenzo Market**. Here you can find all sorts of gifts and keepsakes to bring home. *Info:* open everyday from 8am-dark. Closed Sundays in the winter.

After shopping to your hearts content, head over to one of my favorite museums, the **Museo di Firenze Com'Era**. Literally translated it means the Museum of the Way Florence Was. A fabulous collection of paintings and prints of scenes of Florence in times gone by, as well as maps, scale models and more that help bring the past to life.

One of the most fascinating paintings is the famous *Pianta della Catena* a 19th century reproduction of a 15th century woodcut showing Florence's cityscape from vantage point of the hills in the Otrarno. A new exhibit illustrates the evolution of Florence from the earliest settlements to the Roman period. These displays help bring the city's past to life and show how much has remained the same over the centuries. *Info:* Via dell'Oriuolo 24, Open June-Sept Mon & Tues 9am-2pm; Sat 9am-7pm.Open Jan-May & Oct-Dec Mon, Tues, Wed 9am-2pm & Sat 9am-7pm. www.comune.firenze.it. Admission €3.

From here it's a short walk over to the Piazza della Repubblica and the roof top terrace café of the Rinasecente department store,

La Terrazza (*see Best Eats*). The perfect place to come for a pick me up. Very relaxing, great views, wonderful atmosphere. A hidden gem in Florence.

After being suitable nourished, head over to the nearby **Casa Fiorentina Antica Museum**. An excellent display of everyday artifacts used by rich Florentines from the 14th thought 18th centuries. The displays offer an intriguing insight into how the wealthy lived ages ago, helping us realize how amazingly luxurious our modern existence really is. Though this palazzo contains a private well and an ingenious pulley system to harvest the water, while most people back then had to use public fountain, its relative opulence pales in comparison to the everyday system of running water modern citizens enjoy. *Info:* Via Porta Rossa 13, Tel. 055/238-8610. Open Tues-Sun 8:30am-2pm, Closed alternate Sundays and Mondays. Admission.

Saturday Evening
To reward ourselves for a day well spent touring, let's head to the

tiniest wine bar in Florence, **I Frattellini**. No bigger than six feet wide by 4 feet deep, this popular mini-enotecha serves up small snacks and savory local vintages. So belly up to the bar, order a glass of vino, and enjoy an introduction to the authentic heart and soul of Florentine life. *Info:* Via dei Cimatori 38/r, Open noon-midnight.

Tonight we will have dinner in the Oltrarno at **4 Leoni** (*see Best Eats*). A popular local place, it is becoming increasingly well known with tourists, but it has lost none of its neighborhood charm.

Sunday Morning
Let's start the day at the **Uffizi Gallery**. Remember to have reserved a ticket in advance otherwise you will have to wait in an ungodly long line. *Info:* Piazzale degli Uffizi. Tel. 055/238-8651. www.polomuseale.firenze.it/uffizi. Open Tuesday to Saturday 8:30am-6:30pm, Sundays and Holidays 9am-2pm. Closed Mondays. €6.5.

This is one of the most magnificent collections of art found anywhere in the world. Some works were damaged in the great flood of 1966, and still others were damaged in 1993  when a terrorist car bomb ripped through parts of the Gallery. Even so, the Uffizi is still one of the finest galleries on the planet. I highly recommend taking your time and purchasing one of the audio tours so that you can get a more complete understanding of the magnificence of the works displayed here.

Once done with the your visit to the Uffizi Gallery, head over to the **Ponte Vecchio**. Literally meaning Old Bridge, the name came about because the bridge has been around since Etruscan times. The present bridge was rebuilt on the old one in the 14th century by **Neri di Fiorvanti**. In the middle of the bridge are two arched openings that offer wonderful views of the Arno.

Glancing up on the left hand side as you cross the bridge to the Oltrarno, you can see the **Vassarian Corridor** with it's circular, barred windows extending over the bridge from the Palazzo Signoria, through the Uffizi Gallery, and ultimately into the Boboli Gardens attached to the Pitti Palace. It was the private passage used by the Medici to get from their home in the Pitti Palace to the seat of government in the Palazzo Signoria.

Sunday Afternoon
After crossing the bridge, we are off on a jaunt to get some of the best views of Florence. Along the way we will pass through an **ancient gate in the old walls** of Florence just outside of which is one of Florence's best wine bars, **Fuori Porta**. It has a lovely atmosphere, with a terrace, and serves up tasty vintages complemented by a light menu. *Info:* Via Monte alle Croci 10r, www.fuoriporta.it. Open 12:30pm to 3:30pm and 7 pm to 12:30am everyday. Meal for two €30.

 Now you are fortified for the hike up the hill to **Piazzale Michelangelo**. From this piazza you have wonderful views over the city of Florence. At the center of the piazza is a replica of the statue of *David* by Michelangelo. Around the pedestal are replicas of four statues that adorn the tombs of famous Medici that Michelangelo also created.

Sunday Evening
On the way back, though it will be a bit of a hike, let's head over to the impressive church of **Santa Croce**. *Info:* Piazza Santa Croce. Tel. 055/246-6105. Open 10am -12:30pm and 2:30pm - 6:30pm (3-5pm in off-season). Closed Wednesdays. €4.

Surrounded by ancient palazzi, in the center of the Piazza Santa Croce is a statue of **Dante Aligheri**, he of *Divine Comedy* fame, sculpted by Enrico Pazzi in 1865. The church itself is ornate yet simple. Construction was begun in 1295 but its modern facade was created in 1863 by Nicolo Matas. It has a slim bell tower whose Gothic style doesn't seem to fit with this modern exterior. The interior, on the other hand, fits perfectly with the simple stonework of the bell tower.

Initially, the walls inside had been covered with exquisite frescoes created by Giotto but these were covered up for being too erotic by order of Cosimo I in the 16th century. What remains is a basic monastic church that conveys piety and beauty in its simplicity. Of the many Italian artistic, religious, and political geniuses that lie buried beneath Santa Croce, the most famous has to be that of **Michelangelo** himself. Other prominent Florentines buried here are **Niccolo Machiavelli, Galileo Galilei, Dante Aligheri** and **Lorenzo Ghiberti**.

After visiting the church and its cloisters it is time to find some sustenance for dinner. In this area of the city are many options, including **Il Pizzaiuolo**. If you want a real Florentine dining experience (eating Sicilian pizza) far away from the thundering herd of tourists, this simple little pizza place is for you. *Info:* Via de' Macci 113r, Tel. 055/241171. Closed Sundays and in August. No credit cards accepted. Meal for two €25.

A WONDERFUL WEEK IN FLORENCE & TUSCANY

Along with many artistic gems, Florence is bursting with savory restaurants, relaxing cafes, wonderful wine bars, and a vibrant community. In this section you will find all the ingredients to make a week-long visit to Florence rewarding and memorable. For your convenience the best sights in each section of town have been listed in order of importance, taking the guess work out of what to visit first. To cap the section, a short day trip to **Lucca** has been featured. More day trips are featured in the "Two Weeks in Tuscany" section.

RECOMMENDED PLAN: As the **Centro Storico**, Florence's old historic center, has the vast majority of sights that you want to see, spend your first three days exploring the artistic and architectural riches this section has to offer. Day four and five expand your range out into the Centro district and visit the **Accademia** with the Statue of David and the church of **Santa Croce**. Day six head over to the **Oltrarno**, the other side of the Arno river; and the final day head out to one of Tuscany's most amazing towns, **Lucca**.

Centro Storico – Part I

The *centro storico* (old historic center) is filled with the major sights that Florence has available: the Duomo, Baptistery, Campanile, and Uffizi Gallery. This area of the city is the heart and soul of Florence and is easily walkable.

When you're in Florence the one sight it is impossible to miss is the **Duomo**, Florence's cathedral, also known as **Santa Maria del Fiore** (Saint Mary of the Flowers). Construction began in 1296 and by 1421 everything was finished except for the dome. Eventually **Brunelleschi** won a competition to design and build the dome, beating out Ghiberti, the creator of the bronze panels on the east door of the Baptistery. This started a heated rivalry that some say helped spark the Renaissance itself.

It took 14 years just to construct the gigantic dome, and until the Houston Astrodome was erected in the 1960s, this was the largest free-standing (without internal supports) dome in the world. The dome is not only an architectural masterpiece but is a wonder of engineering as well. Brunelleschi had to invent countless machines, pulleys, and supports just to construct the dome. Many of the designs for machinery found in **Leonardo da Vinci's** notebooks are actually sketches of devices created by Brunelleschi.

Inside there are enormous gothic arches, supported by giant pillars. The dome is decorated with frescoes representing the Last Judgment done by Giorgio Vasari and Federico Zuccari at the end of the 16th century. In the niches of the pillars supporting the dome are statues of the Apostles.

The central chapel is home to the **Sarcophagus of San Zanobius** that contains the saint's relics. The bronze reliefs are the work of Lorenzo Ghiberti (1442). When you've finished wandering through the cathedral and admiring the art and stained glass windows, go to the top of the Duomo and get some great views of Florence. The way up is a little tiring, but the photo opportunities are ideal. *Info:* Piazza del Duomo. Tel. 055/230-2885. Church open Monday-Saturday 10am–5pm, Sunday 1pm-5pm. Free. Admission to the dome €6.

Nearby is the **Campanile**, the cathedral's bell tower, which is covered in colored marble and adorned with detailed bas-reliefs. The sculptures by Donatello, Nanni di Bartolo, and others that used to be in the sixteen niches but are now in the Duomo Museum. *Info:* Piazza del Duomo. Tel. 055/230-2885. Open 8:30am–6:50pm (9am -4:20pm in off season). Admission €6.

The main attraction of the **Baptistery** is the bronze paneled doors by **Ghiberti**. When the originals were washed free during the flood of 1966 and almost lost, copies were made and are what you see now. The original are in the Museum of the Duomo. On the **East Door** you'll find stories of the Old Testament.

The interior is encrusted with stunning Byzantine style mosaics, the most famous of which is the demon eating the damned to the right of the large Christ figure. Inside you'll also the tomb of Giovanni XXIII by Donatello and Michelozzo in 1427. Next to the altar, you'll see the *Angel Holding The Candlestick* by Agostino di Jacopo in 1320. To the left between the Roman sarcophagi is the wooden statue *Magdalen* by Donatello in 1560. *Info:* Piazza del Duomo. Tel. 055/230-2885. Open everyday 2pm–5:30pm. Admission €2.

The building housing the **Uffizi Gallery** was begun in 1560 and was originally designed to be government offices, but today holds the most important and impressive display of art in Italy, and some would say the world. The gallery mainly contains paintings of Florentine and Tuscan artists of the 13th and 14th

Reserve Tickets!

It is strongly recommended that you **reserve tickets in advance** for a specific day and a specific time of entry on the web through **www.firenze.net** so that you do not have to stand in the incredibly long lines common at the Uffizi, Accademia and other museums, especially in the summer. Alternately, if you do not want to wait in the Uffizi's huge line for general admission, but have not reserved tickets in advance on the web, go to door #2 and buy tickets for a specific date and time in the future, possibly even later that same day.

centuries, but you'll also find works from Venice, Emilia, and other Italian art centers as well as Flemish, French, and German studies. In conjunction there is a collection of ancient sculptures.

These fabulous works of art were first collected by the Medici family (Francesco de Medici started it off in 1581) then later by the Lorraine family. The last of the Medici, the final inheritor of that amassed wealth, Anna Maria Luisa donated the entire Gallery to the Tuscan state in 1737 so that the rich collection gathered by her ancestors would never leave Florence. Some items were damaged in the great flood of 1966, and still others were damaged in 1993 when a terrorist car bomb ripped through parts of the Gallery. Even so the Uffizi is still one of the finest galleries in the world. *Info:* Piazzale degli Uffizi. Tel. 055/238-8651. www.polomuseale.firenze.it/uffizi. Open Tuesday to Saturday 8:30am-6:30pm, Sundays and Holidays 9am-2pm. Closed Mondays. Admission €6.5.

On the next page I have compiled a list of the most important pieces in the Uffizi. If you want a more complete listing or an audio guided tour, you can get those as you enter.

ALTERNATE PLAN

Any day that you feel as if you have had enough of Renaissance art, there is a nearby golf course for you to try: **Circolo Golf dell'Ugolino**, 9 km from Florence. *Info:* Par 72, 18 holes, 5,728 meters. Open all year round except Mondays. Via Chiantigiano 3, 51005 Grassina, Tel. 055/320-1009, Fax 055/230-1141.

- *Duke and Duchess of Urbino* - Piero della Francesca, Room VII
- *Madonna of the Pomegranate, The Primavera, The Birth of Venus,* and *Annunciation* - Botticelli - Room X

- *Madonna of the Goldfinch* - Raphael - Room XXV
- *Holy Family* - Michelangelo - Room XXV
- *Venus of Urbino* - Titian - Room XXVIII
- *Young Bacchus* - Caravaggio - Room XXXVI
- *Portrait of an Old Man and Two Self Portraits* - Rembrandt - Room XXXVII
- *Portrait of Isabelle Brandt* - Peter Paul Rubens - Room XLI

Centro Storico – Part II
The continuation of the tour of the centro storico includes a stop at the **Bargello Museum**, a visit to the **Piazza della Signoria** and the sights there, then a shopping tour of the **Mercato Centrale** and **San Lorenzo Market**.

Located in the building that was the first seat of government in Florence, as well as the headquarters of the justice department, police, and customs departments, in the **Bargello Museum** you will find works by Michelangelo including *Bacco* (1496-97) *David-Apollo* (1530-32) which is the first large classical sculpture by the artist, and *Bruto* (1530), which means ugly, and is the only bust created by Michelangelo of Lorenzo de Medici. The other featured artist in the museum is Donatello including *S. Giorgio* (1416) accompanied by two statues of *David*, one younger in marble (1408-9) and the other more famous one in bronze (circa 1440), the *Bust of Niccolo of Uzzano* made of multi-colored terracotta, *Marzocco* (1418-20), a lion that symbolizes the Florentine Republic, *Atys-Amor*, a wonderful bronze, and the dramatic *Crucifixion*.

The Accademia and the Uffizi get all the press, but this is one of the best museums of sculpture anywhere in the world. *Info:* Via del Proconsolo, Tel 055/210-801. www.polomuseale.firenze.it/bargello. Open Tuesdays-Saturdays 9am-2pm and Sundays 9am-1pm. Holidays 8:30am-1:50pm. Closed Mondays. Admission €4.

The **Piazza della Signoria**, with the Palazzo, the Loggia, the fountain, the replica of the statue of David, the cafes and *palazzi* is incomparable in its beauty. Over the centuries great historical and political occurrences, as well as the lives of average Florentines, have all flowed through this piazza. This is a wonderful piazza in which to find a seat at a cafe and watch the people walk by.

The statue to the left of the Palazzo is **Ammannati's Fountain** with the giant figure of *Neptune*. Commonly called *Biancone* (Whitey) by the locals because of its bland appearance. Giambologna created the equestrian statue representing *Cosimo I dei Medici* on the left of the square.

In the Piazza della Signoria, on the right of the Palazzo as you face

it, is the expansive **Loggia dei Lanzi** that contains some wonderful sculptures: *Persius* by Cellini in 1553 under the left arch; *The Rape of the Sabines* by Giambologna in 1583 and *Hercules and the Centaur* by Giambologna in 1599 both under the right arch. There is also *Menelaus supporting Patroclus* and a few other less important works.

The most imposing structure in the square is the **Palazzo Vecchio** and the accompanying **Arnolfo's Tower**. Its construction began in the late 13th century and took hundreds of years to finish. In front of the building on the platform at the top of the steps, where the replica statue of *David* by Michelangelo now resides, orators used to harangue crowds, and for this reason this section of the building is called *Arringhiera* (The Haranguing Area). Located here are the *Marzocco* (a lion symbolizing the Florentine Republic; a stone copy of the original sits in the National Museum); *Judith and Holofernes* sculpted by Donatello in 1460, which is a record of the victory over the Duke of Athens; and *Hercules and Cacus* created by Baccio Bandinelli.

The interior is mainly filled with artwork glorifying the Medici family who ruled the Florentine Republic for centuries. Everything is elaborate and ornate, as befitting the former home of the richest family in the world at that time. The fountain in the center of the couryard, *Graceful Winged Cupid* was done by Verrochio in 1476.

The most splendid and artistic hall in Florence is the **Hall of the Five Hundred - Salone dei Cinquecento**. On the wall opposite the entrance you'll find three large magnificent paintings by Baccio D'Agnolo, Baccio Bandinelli and Giorgio Vassari: *The Conquest of Siena; The Conquest of Porto Ercole; The Battle of Marciano.* On the wall across from this you'll find *Maximilian Tries to Conquer Livorno; The Battle of Torre San Vincenzo; The Florentines Assault Pisa.* Underneath these painting are sculptures by Vincenzo de Rossi representing *Hercules' Labors.*

The ceiling is divided into 39 compartments with paintings by

Giorgio Vasari that represent *Stories of Florence and the Medici*. The coup de grace is in the niche of the right wall at the entrance. Here you'll find Michelangelo's unfinished work, *The Genius of Victory*, which was designed for the tomb of Pope Julius II.

Other rooms of note include: the **Study of Francesco I de Medici** where you'll find the work of many of Florence's finest artists crammed into as small a space as imaginable; the **Hall of the Two Hundred - Salone dei Duecento** where the Council of two hundred citizens met during the time of the Republic; and the

Monumental Quarters – Quartieri Monumentali which are a series of rooms that get their names from members of the Medici family. Each is elaborate in its own right, filled with paintings, sculptures, frescoes, and more. *Info:* Piazza della Signoria. Open Monday-Friday 9am-7pm, and Sundays 8am-1pm. www.comune.firenze.it/servizi_pubblici/arte/musei/a.htm. Closed on Saturdays. Admission €5 for upstairs galleries.

Located in a building in the midst of the outdoor Mercato di San Lorenzo, is the **Mercato Centrale**, Florence's main food market for fish, meat, vegetables, cheeses, oils, breads, and many other delicacies. The meat and fish section is on the ground floor, with the fruit and vegetable market upstairs. A truly authentic Florentine experience. Stop by **Perini** for salami and cheese and **Nerbone's** for some great food. *Info:* Via dell Ariento, open Monday–Friday, 7am–2pm and 4pm–8pm, Saturday 7am-12:15pm and 1pm-5pm. Sunday 3pm-5pm.

The **San Lorenzo Market** is Florence's largest and most frequented outdoor market. It completely dominates the church of San Lorenzo, its piazza, and many adjacent streets. You can find leather jackets, wallets, T-shirts, belts, and much more, most at prices close to half of what you would pay in a store. Remember to bargain, because usually the starting price is rather high. A trip to Florence is not complete with a shopping spree here. *Info:* Piazza San Lorenzo, everyday from 8am-dark. Closed Sundays in the winter.

Centro Storico – Part III
The third part of the jaunt around Florence's old historic center includes a visit to a number of smaller but important museums that offer an insightful perspective into the life and times of Renaissance Florence and more.

The **Firenze Com'Era Museum** is a fabulous little museum with paintings and prints of scenes of Florence in times gone by, as well as maps, scale models and more that help bring the city's past to life. One of the most fascinating paintings is the famous *Pianta della Catena,* a 19th century reproduction of a 15th century woodcut showing Florence's cityscape from vantage point of the hills in the Otrarno. A new exhibit illustrates the evolution of Florence from the earliest settlements to the Roman period. These displays help show how much has remained the same over the centuries. *Info:* Via dell'Oriuolo 24, Tel. 055/276-8224. Open June-Sept Mon & Tues 9am-2pm; Sat 9am-7pm.Open Jan-May & Oct-Dec Mon, Tues, Wed 9am-2pm & Sat 9am-7pm. www.comune.firenze.it. Admission €3.

Best Chocolates

Bring your sweet tooth to **Vestri** for freshly made chocolate, steaming hot chocolate and all sorts of tasty morsels. *Info:* Borgo degli Albizi 11/r, Tel. 055/234-0374.

The **Duomo Museum** contains the many works of art that used to be in the Cathedral, Campanile and Baptistery are now located. The most famous of which are Ghiberti's bronze doors, located near the exit, and Michelangelo's unfinished *Pieta* created when he was in his 80s. It contrasts sharply from the Pieta in St. Peter's he created in his 20s. Other works to keep an eye out for are *St. John* by Donatello, *Habakkuh* by Donatello, *Virgin with Infant Jesus* by Arnolfo, and *Choir Gallery* with many scenes by Donatello. There are also reliquaries containing the remains of a number of different saints, a finger bone here, an arm there. You can also find Brunelleschi's scale models of the Duomo, his death mask, and drawings for the facade of the Duomo begun in 1860 and completed in 1887. *Info:* Museo dell'Opera del Duomo, Piazza del Duomo 9. Tel. 055/230-2885, www.operaduomo.firenze.it. Closed Sundays. Apr thru Oct: Mon - Sat 9am-7:30pm. Until only 7pm in off-season. Holidays open 9am-1pm. Admission.

Attached to the church of San Lorenzo, but with the entrance just around the corner to the back of the church, the octagonal **Prince's Chapel** was begun in 1604 on a design by Prince Giovanni de Medici. It houses the tombs of a variety of Medici princes, hence the name. Up to 50 of the Medici tombs are being exhumed for a DNA testing of the entire family, to finally find out who was related to whom. The reason this is so significant is that some of the Medicis were Popes, and it is speculated that they were not as chaste as they claimed to be. The DNA tests will put the debate to an end.

The chapel is of interest to many tourists because of the tombs in the New Sacristy created by **Michelangelo**. *The Tomb of Lorenzo, Duke of Urbino* (created by Michelangelo) has a statue of the duke seated and absorbed in meditation as well as two reclining figures that represent Dawn and Dusk. On the opposite wall is the *Tomb of Giuliano, Duke of Nemours* (also created by Michelangelo) which shows a seated duke replete in armor, ready for action, as well as two reclining figures that represent night and day. Another Michelangelo work in the New Sacristy is the unfinished *Madonna and Child*. Don't miss the alien head coming out of the suit of armor in the hallway. *Info:* Piazza Madonna degli Aldobrandini. Tel. 055/238-8602. www.polomuseale.firenze.it/musei/cappellemedicee. Open Tuesday-Saturday 9am–2pm, Sundays and Holidays 9am–1pm. Closed 2nd and 4th Sunday, and 1st, 3rd and 5th Monday of every month. Admission €6.

One of the oldest basilicas in Florence, **San Lorenzo** was designed by **Filippo Brunelleschi** from 1421-1446. The facade was never completed even though Michelangelo himself submitted a variety of designs for its completion. The interior is made up of three naves with chapels lining the side walls. In the central nave at the far end are two pulpits that are the last two works of **Donatello** who died in 1466 after completing them. You'll find plenty of works by Donatello in this church, including: Stucco medallions in the Old Sacristy that represent the *Four Evangelists* and those in the spandrel of the cupola of *Stories of Saint John the Baptist;* Sarcophagus of the Martelli Family (between the left transept and the nave); and Bronze doors with panels representing the *Apostles and Fathers of the Church* in the Old Sacristy. *Info:* Piazza San Lorenzo. Tel. 055/216-634. Open Tuesday-Saturday 9am–2pm, Sundays and Holidays 9am-1pm. Closed Mondays. Admission €2.50.

The **Casa Fiorentina Antica Museum** is an insightful museum filled with everyday artifacts used by rich Florentines

English-Language Bookstores

- **Paperback Exchange,** Via delle Oche 4r
- **BM Bookshop**, Borgo Ognissanti 4r
- **McRae Books**, Via de' Neri 32r

from the 14th thought 18th centuries. The displays offer an intriguing perspective into how the wealthy lived back then, helping us realize how amazingly luxurious our modern existence really is. *Info:* Via Porta Rossa 13, Tel. 055/238-8610. Open Tues-Sun 8:30am-2pm, Closed alternate Sundays and Mondays. Admission.

Located behind the Uffizi is the **Museo di Storia della Scienza** (Museum of Scientific History) which is a collection of scientific instruments from the 16th and 17th centuries. There are astrolabs, solar clocks, architectural tools and more. Of great interest are the original instruments used by **Galileo** (rooms IV and V) as well the mummified index finger from his right hand. Also of note are the map-making materials and ancient geographical tools (room VII). There is also a splendid reconstruction of the map of the world made by Fra Mauro.

On the second floor you will find an **astronomical clock** from the 15th century (room XII) and many instruments created and used in the 17th century, including the amazing mechanical *mano che scrive* (hand that writes) and *l'orologia del moto perpetuo* (clock of perpetual motion). A great museum for those interested in scientific discovery, or for those who need a break from art. *Info:* Piazza dei Guidici 1, Tel. 055/239-493 auto info line; Tel. 055/265-311. www.imss.fi.it. Hours Monday, Wednesday, Thursday, Friday 9:30am-5pm. Tuesday, Saturday 9:30am-1pm. Closed Sundays and most holidays. Admission.

Centro – Part I
These sights are located around the main *centro storico* area but just slightly outside of it. The main attraction today is the famous **Statue of David** at the Accademia Museum; but if it is Mon, Tues, or Sat morning be sure and switch the order of sights to first visit Ghirlandaio's brilliant **Last Supper**, as this location is only open at those times.

The **Accademia Museum** is filled with paintings and sculptures by artists from the Tuscan school of the 13th and 14th centuries, but the museum's main draw is a statue that is as close to perfection as can be achieved with a hammer and a chisel,

Michelangelo's *David*. Started from a discarded block of marble that Michelangelo bought it on his own – no one commissioned this work – he finished sculpting *David* at the age of 25 in the year 1504, after four years of labor. It was originally in front of the Palazzo della Signoria, but was replaced with a substitute in 1873 to protect the original from the elements.

Leading up to the *David* are *The Prisoners* by Michelangelo, so called since the figures appear to be trapped in stone. Designed to hold the Tomb of Pope Giulio II on their sculpted shoulders, Michelangelo died before he could bring the figures to life; and now they appear as if they are struggling to be freed from the marble's embrace. *Info:* Via Ricasoli 60, Tel. 055/214-375. www.polomuseale.firenze.it/accademia. Open 9am–7pm Tuesday–Saturday. Sundays 9am-1pm. Closed Mondays. Admission €6.

The nearby **San Marco Museums** are a hidden treasure. Actually this 'place' is the church, the cloisters, the museum next to the church, and the Biblioteca de Michelozzo. The church has some incredible works by **Fra Bartolemeo** and **Michelozzo**, as well as from **Donatello's** workshop.

The museum has what could be the largest collection of **Fra (Beato) Angelico** paintings anywhere, all located in the cells

 where monks used to live. The library (*biblioteccha*) is a spartan presentation of old song books. Along with the monks cells, there is a memorial for **Savanorola**, the fundamentalist Christian who had the Medicis thrown out of the city, and enflamed citizens to start "Bonfires of the Vanities," where they burned the opulent possessions of the age. In this memorial is a cape Savanorola wore, a cross he used, as well as the cell in which he slept and worked. Near the exit of the museum is a vast display of ancient architectural elements removed from the rubble of Florentine buildings

caused by WW II and preserved here. *Info:* Piazza San Marco, Tel. 055/239-6950. www.polomuseale.firenze.it/sanmarco. Closed on the 2ⁿᵈ and 4ᵗʰ Monday of the Month. €6.

In the **Palazzo Medici Ricardi** are two major items of interest. The first is the garden on the ground floor where Michelangelo began his artistic career as a sculptor with the Medici family as his patron. The second is **Gozzoli's** *Journey of the Magi* in the Chapel of the Magi. Commissioned by Piero de Medici in 1459 to commemorate a visit in 1439 to Florence of Greek scholars from Constantinople that helped to propel Florence into being the leading center of European culture. Lorenzo di Medici, before he became known as The Magnificent, is fea-  tured in profile on a dark horse with the seven balls of the family emblem hanging from its harness. His younger brother Giuliano is to his left on a white horse facing out from the fresco. The artist is featured near the back of the figures between two bearded Greek scholars. And in case anyone had any doubt about his identity, Gozzoli inscribed his name into the brim of his hat. *Info:* Via Cavour 1, Tel. 055/234-0340. www.palazzo-medici.it/eng/home.htm. Open Mon, Tues, Thurs-Sat 9am-1pm, 3-5pm; Sun and holidays 9-1pm. Admission.

The exquisite church of **Santa Maria Novella** was started in 1278 and completed in 1470 in the Gothic style with green and white marble decorations that are typically Florentine in character. To the left and right of the facade are tombs of illustrious Florentines all created in the same Gothic style as the church. The interior of the church is in a "T" shape with the nave and aisles divided by clustered columns that support wide arches. Down the aisles are a variety of altars created by **Vasari** from 1565 to 1571. As an apprentice in Ghirlandaio's workshop, Michelangelo worked on many of the amazing frescoes in the chapel of the high altar, and is where he got the initial training that helped him create the now famous frescoes in the Sistine Chapel in Rome. You can spend hours in here admiring these magnificent frescoes created by many Florentine artists. *Info:* Piazza Santa Maria Novella. Tel. 055/210-113. Closed Fridays. Open 7am–11:30am and 3:30pm–6pm Mon–Thurs and Sat, and Sun 3:30pm–5pm. Admission €2.50.

Not as famous as Leonado da Vinci's *Last Supper* that resides in Milan, **Ghirlandaio's Last Supper** is nonetheless a treasure. With

an entrance to the left of the *Church of the Ognissanti*, down an entry way, through a cortile, past a small guard's desk, into an expansive room, resides this masterpiece by Ghirlandaio. Not only is the fresco sublime, but the atmosphere is serene. Without hordes of people or an array of competing artworks, this piece's impact is able to be fully appreciated. Make time to come see this piece. *Info:* Borgo Ognissanti 42, Tel. 348/645-0390. Open only Mon, Tues, and Sat 9am to noon. Free.

Centro – Part II
These sights are located around the main *centro storico* area but just slightly outside of it and include the amazing church of **Santa Croce** and a highly recommended **Archeological Museum**.

Most people come to Florence to see Renaissance architecture and art, and miss out on one of the best museums in the city, the **Archeological Museum**. Here you will find an impressive array of Egyptian artifacts such as stelle, statues, coffins and more that make this collection a fine introduction to the splendor that was ancient Egypt. Also available here are a fine accumulation of Etruscan statuary and funereal urns as well as Greek artifacts. Highly recommended. *Info:* Via della Colonaa 36, Tel. 055/23575. Mon-Sat 8:30am-2pm, Sun 8:30am-1pm. www.comune.firenze.it/soggetti/sat/didattica/museo.html. Closed alternate Sundays and Mondays. Admission.

SS. Annunziata is a hidden jewel in Florence. Erected in 1250, reconstructed in the middle of the 15th century by **Michelozzo**, when entering the Basilica you are instantly struck by the carved and gilded ceiling, and the profusion of marble and stucco. The church is particularly famous for a miracle thought to have taken place here. A certain painter named Bartolomeo was commissioned to paint a fresco in 1252 of the Annunciation. When he was about to paint the face of Mary in the painting, he fell asleep only to find the face painted for him, supposedly by angelic hands, after he awoke. The fresco is located inside the little chapel to the left of the entrance, and became the heart of the Basilica, which was subsequently dedicated to Our Lady Annunciate. *Info:* Piazza SS Annunziata, Tel. 055/239-8034. Open 7am-7pm. Free.

The church of **Santa Croce** sits in the Piazza Santa Croce, surrounded by ancient palazzi. On the steps of the cathedral is a statue of **Dante Aligheri**, he of *Divine Comedy* fame, sculpted by Enrico Pazzi in 1865. The church itself is ornate yet simple and was begun in 1295, though its modern facade was created in 1863. Legend has it that frescoes on the facade were created in only 20 days by 12 painters working non-stop. It has a slim bell tower whose Gothic style doesn't seem to fit with this modern exterior.

The interior, on the other hand, fits perfectly with the simple stonework of the bell tower. Initially, the walls inside had been covered with exquisite frescoes created by Giotto but these were covered up by order of Cosimo I in the 16th century as being too erotic. What remains is a basic monastic church that conveys piety and beauty in its simplicity. Of the many Italian artistic, religious, and political geniuses that lie buried beneath Santa Croce, the most famous has to be that of **Michelangelo** himself. Other prominent Florentines buried here are **Niccolo Machiavelli, Galileo Galilei, Dante Aligheri** and **Lorenzo Ghiberti**.

The cloisters are mainly known for their haven of calm., but you can also find the Pazzi Chapel, and a small museum with works by **Cimabue** and **Taddeo Gaddi**. *Info:* Piazza Santa Croce. Tel. 055/246-6105. Open 10am -12:30pm and 2:30pm - 6:30pm (3-5pm in off-season). Closed Wednesdays. Admission €4.

A great antique/junk market in the heart of one of Florence's blue collar neighborhoods is the **Mercato delle Pulci**. You can find all sorts of interesting collectibles here from flags to cutlery, to plates and more. *Info:* Piazzi dei Ciompi, Mon-Sat 9am-7pm.

Best Ceramics Shops

- **Le Mie Ceramiche** – ceramics artisans for three generations; truly wonderful pieces. *Info:* Via Verdi 8r.
- **Sbigoli Terrecotte** – buy their own work or world-famous Deruta pottery. *Info:* Via S. Egidio 4r.

After the Mercato Centrale, the **Mercato di Sant' Ambrogio** is the second most important produce, fish and meat market in Florence. Inside you can also find some typical eateries. Outside is a market for dry good, clothing, and other regular household stuff. *Info:* Piazza Sant' Ambrogio, Mon- Sat 7am-2pm.

Oltrarno
The other side of the Arno, the Oltrarno, has a more local feel than the *centro storico*. Here you can wander up some side streets on the way to the **Piazzale Michelangelo** and get lost in traditional neighborhoods. My favorite part of Florence, I am sure you will enjoy it as well.

Literally meaning Old Bridge, the **Ponte Vecchio** has been around in one form or another since Etruscan times. The present bridge was rebuilt on the old one in the 14th century by **Neri di Fiorvanti**. Thankfully this beautiful bridge with its gold and silver shops was

spared German destruction during World War II. In the middle of the bridge are two arched openings that offer wonderful views of the Arno.

Stefano Bardini was a 19th century collector of antiques and architectural elements. Today in the **Bardini Museum** you can find the many salvaged

Best Stationery Shop

Florence is known for its artisan stationery, and **Il Torchio** is the best by far. Located about 200 meters east of the Ponte Vecchio here you'll find books, pens, paper, and more. *Info:* Via de Bardi 17.

pieces he accumulated from the churches and palazzi demolished to build the Piazza della Repubblica in the 1860s to commemorate the creation of the Italian state. This building itself was built in 1883 from many of the excavated medieval and Renaissance masonry, including doorways, straircases, archways, and painted ceilings. The rooms are crowded with all sorts of statues, paintings, armor, musical instruments, ceramics and furniture. Upon his death in 1922, this eclectic collection was bequeathed to the city of Florence. *Info:* Piazza de'Mozzi, Tel. 055/234-2447. Open Mon, Tues, Thurs-Sat 9am-2pm; Sun 8am-1pm. Closed Jan 1, Easter Sunday, May 1, Aug 15, and Dec 25. Admission.

From here take a short but strenuous hike up to the nearby **Piazzale Michelangelo** where you have a wonderful view over the city of Florence. At the center of the square is a replica of the statue of *David* by Michelangelo, around which are replicas of four statues that adorn the tombs of famous Medici which Michelangelo also created.

While up here, if it is March through October, you can find the **Vip Bar**, a cafe that has outside seating just below the main level of the Piazzale Michelangelo with the same absolutely stunning views over the city of Florence. *Info:* Piazzale Michelangelo, Open March – October, not when it rains. Cell: 335/845-4745.

The latest addition to the plethora of Florentine sights is the **Bardini Gardens**. With spectacular vistas of Florence and 4 hectares of relaxing park space, this is a ideal place to get some peace and quiet with Florence spread out before you as a backdrop. Dating from medieval times, the garden is full of unexpected and wonderful surprises, such as hidden statues, a magnificent baroque staircase, fountains, grottoes, a small amphitheatre and breathtaking views. *Info:* Tel. 055.294883 - 055.290112. Two entrances, one on Via dei Bardi 1r, the other at Costa San Giorgio 4. Open Mon-Sun 8:15-sunset. Admission €8. Includes entrance to the Porcelain and Silver Museum in the Pitti Palace, the Fortrezza Belvedere, and the Boboli Gardens. www.bardinipeyron.it/sito_EN/bardini/index.htm.

Hidden behind the Pitti Palace is your respite from the Florentine summer heat and the hordes of tourists, the **Boboli Gardens**.

Begun in 1549 by Cosimo I, the Boboli gardens went through many changes, additions, and alterations before they reached their present design. Among the many pathways, well-placed fields and groves you can find plenty of spots to sit and enjoy a picnic lunch, or you can simply enjoy the platoons of statuary lining the walks. Some of the most famous works here include: *Pietro Barbino Riding a Tortoise* (located near the exit); a Roman amphitheater ascending in tiers from the Palazzo Pitti, designed as a miniature Roman circus to hold Medici court spectacles; and *Neptune's Fountain* at the top of the terrace, created in 1565 by Stoldo Lorenzi.

Best Wireless Wifi Spots

- **Zoe** – a thoroughly local café in the Oltrarno; a popular nightspot. *Info:* Via dei Renai 13/c, Open 7am-midnight everyday.
- **Lions' Fountain** – authentic Irish-style pub; the place to come for televised sports events. *Info:* Borgo Albizi 34r, Open from 6pm-2:30am everyday.

From Neptune's Fountain a path to the left leads to the wonderful **Kaffehaus**. This little cafe offers superb views of Florence as well as light snacks and drinks.

Built for the rich merchant **Luca Pitti** in 1440, the **Pitti Palace** was designed by Filippo Brunelleschi. Due to the financial ruin of the Pitti family, the construction was interrupted until the palace was bought by **Eleonora da Toledo**, the wife of Cosimo I. It was then enlarged to its present size. And from that time until the end of the 17th century, it was the family home for the Medici. Currently it is divided into six different museums; and since the upkeep and security for this building is so expensive, each museum charges their own separate entrance fee. *Info:* Piazza dei Pitti. Tel. 055/287-096. Building hours: Tuesday-Saturday 9am-7pm. Most museums only open until 2pm. Sundays and Holidays 9am-1pm. Closed on Mondays. Admission.

The best museums in the Palazzo Pitti are:

The **Museo degli Argenti** (www.polomuseale.firenze.it/ english/musei/argenti) contains works in amber, ivory, silver, crystal, precious woods and enamel collected by the Medici and Lorraine families. *Info:* The 1st, 3rd, and 5th Mondays and 2nd, and 4th Sundays of the month closed. Admission €6.

The **Pitti Gallery** runs the length of the facade of the building and includes paintings, sculptures, frescoes and furnishings of the Medici and Lorraine families (in Italian, it is the **Galleria Palatina e Apartamenti Reali**). This gallery has some fine works from the 16th and 17th centuries and the most extensive collection of works by Raphael anywhere in the world. Other artists included here are Andrea del Sarto, Fra' Bartolomeo, Titian and Tintoretto, Velasquez, Murillo, Rubens, Van Dyke and Ruisdal. The royal apartments feature an elaborate display of furnishings, carpets, wonderful silks covering the walls, as well as some fine paintings collected and displayed by the house of Savoy – the most notable of which is a series of portraits of the family of Louis XV of France. *Info:* Admission €6 includes entrance to the Museo delle Carozze. www.polomuseale.firenze.it/english/musei/palatina.

The **Museo delle Carrozze** (www.polomuseale.firenze.it/english/musei/carrozze) houses carriages used by the court of Lorraine and Savoy when they ruled Florence. The carriages are extremely elaborate and detailed, especially the silver decorated carriage owned by King Ferdinand II of the Two Sicilies. *Info:* Admission €6 includes entrance to the Galleria Palatina.

The **Galleria del Costume** (www.polomuseale.firenze.it/english/musei/costume) contains clothing from the 16th century to modern day. All are exhibited in 13 rooms of the Meridiana Wing. It is an excellent way to discern the changes in fashion from the 18th century to the 1920s. Also included are historical theater costumes created by the workshop of Umberto Tirelli. *Info:* Admission €4.

On our way to the Zoological Museum, as we head down the Via Romana, stop in what I consider to be the best art store in all of Florence, Stefano Ramunno's Bottega d'Arte Firenze (*see sidebar*).

After a brief interlude picking out some art to bring home, the **Zoological Museum** is just down the street. Here you can find a collection of stuffed animals from all over the world, some extinct, as well as bugs, fish, crustaceans, and more. Then there is the best part of the exhibit, the collection of over 500 anatomical figures in very life-like colored wax, made between 1175 and 1814. One exhibit you may not want your kids to see is the part on reproduction, which gets pretty graphic. The last room has miniature wax scenes that are realistic depictions of the toll taken by the Black Death. One particular tiny image of a rat pulling on a dead man's entrails is quite intense. The museum is used by many art students to study anatomy and you will find them discreetly sketching throughout. *Info:* Via Romana 17, Tel. 055/222-451. www3.unifi.it/msn. Closed Wednesdays. Open 9am–noon and until 1pm on Sundays. Admission.

Best Art Store in Florence

If you are looking for classic scenes of Florence, precisely etched and printed, or unique and colorful perspectives of familiar montages, the **Bottega d'Arte Firenze** has both. *Info:* Via Romana 20r, cell: 338/978-1478.

Begun in 1444 by Brunelleschi the church of **Santa Spirito** has a simple, plain, seemingly unfinished facade. Divided into three naves flanked by splendid capped Corinthian columns, this church looks very similar to San Lorenzo. There is a central cupola with two small naves in the wings of the cross that have small chapels just off of them. Lining the walls are small chapels capped by semi-circular arches are adorned with elaborate carvings. The main altar, created by Giovanni Caccini (1599-1607), is Baroque in style and intricately displayed. In the chapels off the wings of the cross to the right and left of the main altar are many fine works of art to be enjoyed (two of which are *Madonna con Bambino* by Fillipino Lippi and *San Giovanni and Madonna with Baby Jesus and Four Saints* by Masi di Banco). *Info:* Piazza Santo Spirito, Tel. 055/210-030. Open 8am-Noon and 4pm-6pm. Closed Wednesday afternoons. Free.

Lucca

There is so much to see and do in Florence alone that getting the chance to take a day trip outside the city may not even be feasible in a week-long trip. But in case you find the time, visit **Lucca**, only an hour and half from Florence by train. Its fully preserved Medieval ramparts and maze of medieval streets make for an amazing experience.

In case I haven't made it clear, Lucca is absolutely beautiful! If you have the time you simply must come here. Its main attractions are the complete walled fortifications surrounding the city, one of only two sets of complete Medieval battlements left anywhere in Europe. Originally designed to keep marauding Florentines at bay, these ramparts are now the site of a tree-lined greenbelt around the city and is the perfect place for a romantic *passegiatta* (slow stroll).

At the battlements, of which there are 10, each coincidentally shaped like a heart, there are plenty of places to cuddle with your loved one,

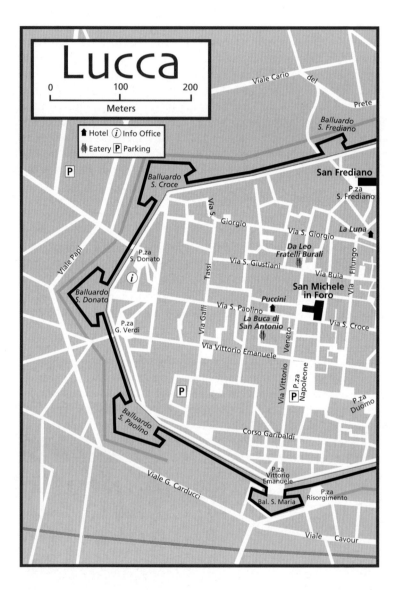

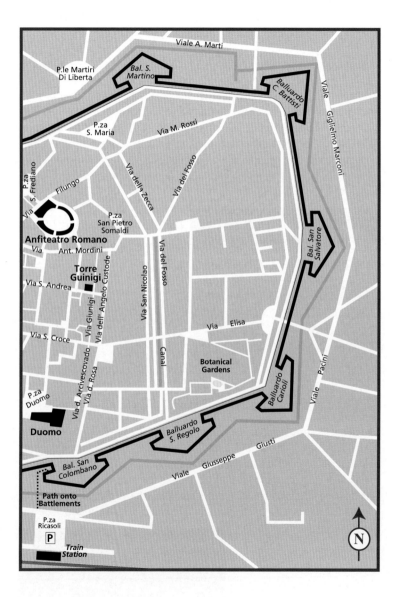

or sit at a wooden table and have a relaxing afternoon picnic. If you're with a family, the kids can roam free, exploring the nooks and crannies of the walls, while you and your spouse enjoy brief interludes of serenity. *Info:* www.luccatourist.it or www.lucca.info.

Besides the walls, which with Ferrarra's are the best preserved in Italy, Lucca offers a tight grid road pattern, a remnant of its Roman occupation, which with the cobble-stoned streets and ancient palazzi invoke an ambiance of Medieval charm. In this labyrinth is **San Michel in Foro** (*Info:* Piazza San Michele. Open 7am-7pm), located on what used to be Lucca's ancient Roman Forum, with its multitude of different columns, some intertwined like corkscrews, others doubled, and some carved with medieval grotesques.

Lucca's Best Eats

Don't miss **Da Leo Fratelli Buralli**. Rustic and local, this is a tasty serving of authentic Lucca. *Info:* Via Tegrimi 1, Closed Sundays. Meal for two €30.

Lucca's **Duomo** (*Info:* Piazza del Duomo. Open 7am-7pm), sits at the end of the Via Duomo in Piazza San Martino. This structure is perhaps the most outstanding example of the Pisan style of architecture outside of Pisa.

Exploring Lucca's labyrinth of tiny streets you will be entranced by the busy shopping area around Via Fillungo, the 12th century church of **San Frediano** (*Info:* Piazza del Collegio. Open 7am-7pm), the old Roman **amphitheater** that is now a circular series of apartments, and the **Torre Giungi** (*Info:* Via Giunigi. Open 9am-7pm in the summer and 10am-4pm in the winter. Admission €3.). On the top of this tower is a garden complete with full-grown trees and some fine panoramic views over the city. Lucca is an amazing city to visit, a little off the beaten path, helping to make a visit here authentically Italian.

TWO WEEKS IN FLORENCE & TUSCANY

For your first magical week in the land of Machiavelli, Michelangelo, Leonardo da Vinci, the Medicis and more, please refer to the previous section, *One Week in Florence & Tuscany*. In your second week it is time to discover those places where the true local heart of Tuscany beats even more strongly, in the hill towns of **San Gimignano**, **Cortona** and **Montepulciano**, and the cities of **Siena** and **Pisa**.

RECOMMENDED PLAN: This second week is about a combination of sightseeing and relaxing. On the first day of your second week go to **Pisa** as it is easily accessible by train from Lucca (see previous section *One Week in Florence & Tuscany*) and Florence. That same day, head back to Florence and down to **Siena** by train. Stay two or more nights, using your last day in Siena to rent a car and drive to **San Gimignano**. Keeping the rental car, the next day head down to **Cortona,** where you will stay for an additional two or more nights visiting **Montepulciano** with one of your days.

Pisa

Best known for the **Leaning Tower of Pisa**, the campanile to the city's **Duomo** located in the **Campo dei Miracoli**, Pisa also has a pleasant Medieval core and relaxing pedestrian shopping streets extending from the Tower to the train station.

Pisa's finest era was back in the 12th century, when its population was greater than 300,000. (Today it hovers around 100,000.) At that time Pisa was considered a city of marvels because its merchants and navy had traveled all over the Mediterranean, bringing back not only new products but also new ideas and styles in art. Pisa's decline began in earnest when the silt from the Arno gradually filled in the port and the cost of dredging was too great for the city to bear. From that point on Pisa became a pawn

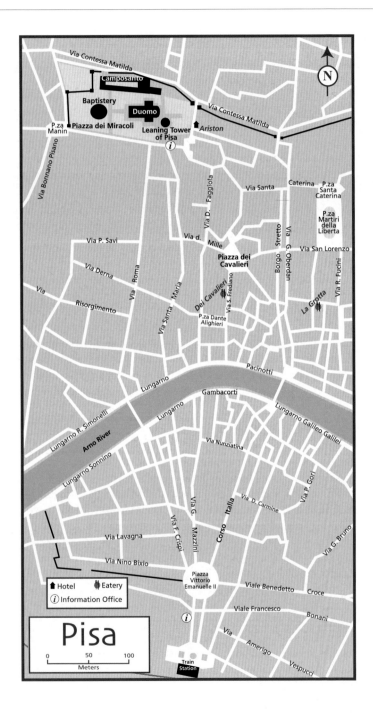

Via Contessa Matilda

Camposanto

Baptistery

Duomo

P.za Manin

Piazza dei Miracoli

Leaning Tower of Pisa

Ariston

Via Contessa Matilda

Via Bonnano Pisano

Via D. Faggiola

Via Santa

Caterina

P.za Santa Caterina

P.za Martiri della Liberta

Via P. Savi

Via d. Mille

Piazza dei Cavalieri

Via San Lorenzo

Borgo Stretto

Via G. Oberdan

Via Derna

Via Roma

Via

Risorgimento

Via Santa Maria

Dei Cavalieri

Via S. Frediano

La Grotta

Via R. Fucini

P.za Dante Alighieri

Pacinotti

Lungarno

Gambacorti

Lungarno Galileo Galilei

Lungarno R. Simonelli

Lungarno

Arno River

Lungarno Sonnino

Via Nunziatina

Via G. Gori

Via D. Carmine

Via Lavagna

Via F. Crispi

Via G. Mazzini

Corso Italia

Via Nino Bixio

Via G. Bruno

Piazza Vittorio Emanuelle II

Viale Benedetto

Croce

Viale Francesco

Bonani

Via

Amerigo

Vespucci

Train Station

♦ Hotel   ♙ Eatery
ⓘ Information Office

Pisa

0   50   100
Meters

that other Italian city-states traded back and forth. And today, all most tourists want to know about is the city's biggest mistake, the Leaning Tower, not any of its triumphs. *Info:* www.pisaonline.it.

The **Leaning Tower of Pisa** is located in the **Piazza dei Miracoli**, so named because of the stupendous architectural masterpieces filling the square. These are living testimony to the greatness the city of Pisa reached at the height of its glory. The square is surrounded by imposing walls, which in turn are surrounded by vendors selling a wide variety of tourist trinkets.

The tower itself is the most unique in the world as a result of its lean, which was not planned, but did start almost immediately, when the tower reached a height of 11 meters. However, the builders continued to work even though they realized that the foundation was unstable. This angle had been increasing at almost a millimeter a year until serious measures were undertaken in the 1990s to reduce the lean. First, cables were attached around the outside to keep the tower from leaning any further. Next a drilling rig removed soil from underneath the side of the foundation opposite the list. Pressure was exerted on the cable to pull the tower into the space vacated by the drilled soil, and the tower's lean has been corrected one-half a degree, or about 16 inches. Today you can wander up into the structure that **Galileo Galilei** supposedly used to conduct experiments concerning the laws of gravity. *Info:* Tickets €15. www.duomo.pisa.it.

Started in 1063, the **Duomo** was finally consecrated in 1118. The facade is covered with many columns and arches in what has become known as the Pisan style. The interior contains numerous sculptures and mosaics, among which is the famous mosaic *Christ and the Madonna* started by Francesco of Pisa and continued by Cimabue. The celebrated pulpit is the work of Giovanni Pisano, of the same family that built the Campanile.

There is also the lamp that hangs in the center of the nave that was created by Stolto Lorenzi. It is called the **Lamp of Galileo**, who, as rumor has it, discovered through observation and experimentation the oscillation of pendulum movements. Last but not least is the statuette in ivory by Giovanni Pisano of the *Madonna and Child. Info:* Open 8am–12:30pm and 3pm–6:30pm. In January only open until 4:30pm.

Begun in 1153 by the architect Diotisalvi, the **Baptistery** it is circular in form with a conical covering. The interior has five baptismal fonts created by Guido Bigarelli of Como in 1246 and the masterpiece of a pulpit created by Nicola Pisano in 1260. *Info:* Open 9am–1pm and 3pm–6:30pm. In January only open until 4:30pm.

The **Camposanto** is a rather serene and unpretentious cemetery started in 1278 by Giovanni di Simone. It was enlarged in the 14th century and stands today like an open-air basilica with three aisles. The soil in the center is rumored to have been brought from the Holy Land. The corridor around the earth is formed by 62 arches in a Gothic style of white and blue marble. You'll also find some beautiful frescoes along the walls and floors that were partially destroyed during World War II but have since been restored. *Info:* Open 8am–6:30pm. In January open from 9am–4:30pm. Admission €3.

Pisa's Best Eats

• **Dei Cavalieri** is in a great location and serves tasty local cuisine. *Info:* Via San Frediano 16, Meal for two €32.

• **La Grotta** is atmospheric, typically local, and serves great food. *Info:* Via San Francesco 103, Meal for two €35.

The **Piazza dei Cavalieri** is the most harmonious piazza in the city after the famous Piazza dei Miracoli. Literally translated the name means square of the knights, and it is named for the Knights of St. Stephen, an order established by Cosimo I de Medici to defend Florence and her holdings from pirates. The statue above the fountain by Francavilla in 1596 that is opposite the **Palazzo dei Cavalieri** (Knights Palace) is dedicated to this order. On its facade you'll find floral displays, symbols, coats of arms as well as sacred and profane images in the graffito style. In niches above the second row of windows you'll find six busts of Tuscan grand  dukes, from Cosimo I to Cosimo III de Medici.

The other buildings in this irregularly shaped piazza were built in the 16th and 17th centuries and include the **Church of St. Stephen's**, next to the Palazzo dei Cavalieri on the eastern side. On the western sides is the **Palazzo del Collegio Puteano** built in 1605. The southern side is occupied by the **Palazzo del Consiglio** (Council Chambers) of the order of the Knights of St. Stephen. On the northern side is the **Palazzo dell'Orologio** (Clock Palace).

The **Corso Italia** is the main pedestrian shopping street in Pisa and leads from the station to the Arno. A great place to get a feel for the life of this wonderful Tuscan city.

Just a short stroll from the Leaning Tower archaeologists are unearthing at least ten **Roman ships**, many complete with cargoes, that sank some 2,000 years ago in a rediscovered harbor in Pisa. Merchant vessels, a warship, and a ceremonial boat are all being excavated, and which contain coins, lamps, amphorae and more. These artifacts, and the boats themselves, are being readied for removal to the nearby Arsenali Mediciei, a large warehouse structure that is being transformed into a temporary laboratory and museum where the final phases of restoration will occur. *Info:* www.navipisa.it.

Siena

Generally described as the feminine counterpart to the masculine Florence, and even its nickname, **City of the Virgin**, belies **Siena's** fairer quality. Located 42 miles south of Florence, this picturesque walled city is known for its many impressive *palazzi*, expansive Campo, narrow and steep streets, immense churches, and delightful restaurants.

Siena is a great place to visit, with plenty to see and do, not the least of which is a chance to be absorbed into the Tuscan pace of life. One unique feature of Siena is that right inside the old cities walls, in the valleys between the ridges of the town, rural life still thrives, complete with roosters crowing and plants being tended and harvested. All of which lends a peaceful and serene quality to the city. *Info:* www.terresiena.it.

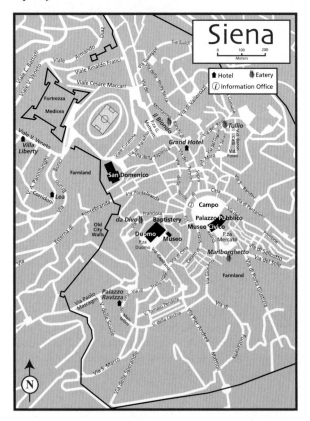

The heart of Siena is the **Campo**. Eleven streets lead into this picturesque square where, in the past, the people of Siena used to assemble at the sound of the **Sunto bell** to learn the latest news. The piazza is concave and irregular with a ring of rather austere buildings surrounding it, but even so it is a marvel of architectural harmony. On the curved side of the Campo sits the **Fonte Gaia** (Gay Fountain), the water for which comes here from 30 km away through a series of ancient pipes and aqueducts.

In the Campo is the **Palazzo Pubblico**. one of the most attractive and imposing Gothic buildings in all of Tuscany. Most of it was built between 1297 and 1340, with the top story being erected in 1639.

The Palio Race

The **Palio**, held in July and August, is a festival awash in period costumes, colorful banners, historic events, and a wild bareback horse race around the **Piazza del Campo**. The contestants in the Palio race are jockeys from the seventeen neighborhood parishes or *contrade* in Siena. More than a horse race, the Palio is also a community-wide expression of Siena's medieval roots, with flag-throwing displays and other period events.

This building reflected the wealth and success of Siena, which was almost the same size as London and Paris during the fourteenth century. The best part of this building is the **Torre del Mangia** with its amazing views over the rooftops of Siena. Built in 1334, the clock was added in 1360 and the huge bell was raised

to its present position in 1666. *Info:* In the Campo. Tower open 10am–dusk. In the winter open only until 1:30pm. Admission €3.

Inside the Palazzo Pubblico is the **Museo Civico**, which is filled with many wonderful paintings, frescoes, mosaics, tapestries, and sculptures. One of which is *Dolore* (Sadness) that features a seated man caught in the throes of that emotion. Upstairs is the famous **Sala del Mappamondo** (Hall of the Map of the World). From its large windows you can look out onto the market square. The other three walls are frescoed with scenes of the religious and civil life of the Siena Republic. In this museum you'll find many examples of the some of the finest Sienese art available. *Info:* Open 9:30am–7:30pm Monday–Saturday. Open Sunday 9:30am–1:30pm. Admission.

The combination of Gothic and Romanesque architectural elements in the **Duomo** of Siena is a result of the large amount of

time spent working on it. It was started in 1200 and what you see today was finished in the 1400s. There were plans to have made this cathedral a much larger place of worship; however, today, to the right of the Duomo as you face it, near the rear, only a few pillars and walls remain from the plans for that grandiose church.

Inside the cathedral the walls are covered with white and black stripes complemented by a row of 172 busts of popes, from Christ to Lucius III, all made in 1400. Beneath them are 36 busts of Roman Emperors. The inlaid floor contains a succession of scenes from the Old Testament, which took from 1372 to 1551 to complete. The earlier ones are done in black and white, and the later scenes have a touch of gray and red in them.

You can't miss the intricate and elaborate pulpit made by **Nicola Pisano** from 1265 to 1268. It is made of off-white marble and supported by nine darker marble columns resting on four lions. Besides the pulpit there are countless remarkable paintings, sculptures, reliefs, and stone coffins all throughout the church. The statues on the Piccolo altar have been attributed to **Michelangelo**. In the **Piccolomini Library** you'll find beautiful frescoes of the life of Pope Pius II made by the master Pinturicchio (Admission €2). As you leave the library you'll see the monument to Archbishop Bandini's nephews made in 1570 by Michelangelo. *Info:* Piazza del Duomo. 7:30am–1:30pm and 3pm to dusk from December to March. From March to November open 9am–7:30pm.

Siena's Best Eats

• **Il Biondo** has a relaxing terrace, in a great location, and serves tasty local and Italian specialties. *Info:* Vicolo del Rustichetto 10, Meal for two €40.

• **Marlborghetto** is my favorite place in Siena. *Info:* Via di Porta Giustizia 6, Meal for two €50.

• **Tullio** is completely local, boisterously Italian, and serves great local cuisine. *Info:* Vicolo di Provenzano 1, Meal for two €50.

In the **Museo dell'Opera del Duomo** is a valuable collection of paintings, statues, and fragments once displayed in the cathedral. One of the best paintings is Duccio di Buoninsegna's *Maestra* (1308-1311) that was originally on the high altar. You'll find a group of three sculptures, the *Three Graces*, which are Greek works of the 2nd century BCE that were once in the Piccolomini Library. You can't miss the exquisitely beautiful goldsmith's work, *Rosa d'Oro* (Golden Rose). Another work of interest is the plan of the unfinished facade of the Baptistery by Giacomo di Mino del Pelliciaio. *Info:* Piazza del Duomo. 7:30am–1:30pm and 3pm to dusk from December to March. From March to November open 9am–7:30pm. Admission €3.

In the **Baptistery of San Giovanni** you can find the baptismal fonts by Jacopo della Quercia, the bronze bas-relief of Bishop Pecci by Donatello, and many bronze reliefs of the Old and New Testament. The Baptistery was begun in 1315, but its facade has never been finished. *Info:* Piazza del Duomo. Open 9am–1pm and 3pm–5pm. In the summer open until 7pm.

The **Church of San Domenico** is a monumental and solitary structure overlooking the surrounding landscape and city. Its simple brick architecture of the 13th century was modified in the 14th and 15th centuries but still remains more like the walls of a convent than a church. Next to the sacristy is the **chapel of St. Caterina** where the saint's head is preserved in a silver reliquary. In the other chapels of the church, and along the walls, you'll find paintings by Sienese artists of the 14th through 16th centuries. *Info:* Costa San Antonio. Church is open from 9am–6pm. The Sanctuary is closed 12:30pm–3:30pm Monday–Saturday and all day Sundays.

San Gimignano

San Gimignano sits majestically on a hill overlooking the Elsa valley. Its earthen-colored walls contrast favorably with the surrounding green countryside. The most distinctive feature of this town is its amazing medieval towers. These structures help to create a magical atmosphere of timelessness, despite the hordes of tourists filling the tiny streets in the summer.

Don't get me wrong, San Gimignano is beautiful. Stunning actually. But if you come here in the summer, the peak of the high season, your experience will be tempered by a pushy polyglot ensemble of camera-toting tourists. But even then, this town is wonderful, as is Venice, Florence and other towns in Italy that also face an annual tourist infestation. *Info:* www.sangimignano.com.

San Gimignano's Best Eats

• **Bel Soggiorno** – refined ambiance, traditional Tuscan cuisine. *Info:* Via S. Giovanni 91, Meal for two €60.
• **Osteria delle Catene** – arched brick ceilings and white walls complement rustic Tuscan cuisine. *Info:* Via Mainardi 18, Meal for two €50.

The **Duomo** of San Gimignano is a remarkable monument to Tuscan Romanesque architecture. Though the exterior is nothing to write home about, the interior is resplendent with many fine frescos. Along the walls and in the left aisle, Bartolo di Fredi painted *Scenes from the Old Testament*. In the right aisle are displayed frescoes representing *Scenes from the New Testament*. In the

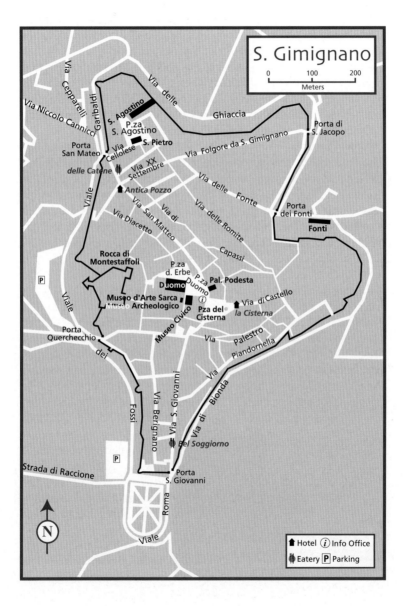

S. Gimignano

0   100   200
Meters

Via Cepparelli

Via Niccolo Cannicci

Via delle

S. Agostino

P.za
S. Agostino

Ghiaccia

Porta di
S. Jacopo

Porta
San Mateo

Via
Cellolese

S. Pietro

Via XX
Settembre

Via Folgore da S. Gimignano

delle Catene

Antica Pozzo

Via San Matteo

Via di

Via delle Fonte

Via delle Romite

Porta
dei Fonti

Fonti

Via Diacetto

Rocca di
Montestaffoli

Capassi

P.za
d. Erbe

P.za
Duomo

Pal. Podesta

P

Duomo

Museo d'Arte Sacra
Museo Archeologico

Museo Civico

Pza del
Cisterna

Via di Castello

la Cisterna

Porta
Querchecchio

dei

Via

Palestro

Piandornella

Via S. Giovanni

Via di Bionda

Via

Fossi

Via Berignano

Strada di Raccione

P

Bel Soggiorno

Porta
S. Giovanni

Roma

Viale

N

♠ Hotel ⓘ Info Office
♟ Eatery P Parking

central nave, on both sides of a fresco illustrating the *Martyrdom of St. Sebastiano* by Benozzo Gozzoli, there are two wooden statues by Jacopo della Quercia. On the upper part of the central nave between the two doors are Taddeo di Bartolo's frescoes showing *The Last Judgment*. But all of this is only prelude for what we find in the right aisle, next to the transept: the famous Chapel of St. Fina built in 1468. With the elegant altar by Benedetto da Maiano and the frescoes by Domenico Ghirlandaio, this entire chapel is a wonderful work of art. *Info:* Piazza del Duomo. March 1-Oct. 31: 9:30am-7pm; Nov 1-Feb 28: 10am-6pm.

The Palazzo del Popolo (People's Palace) is home to the **Museo Civico** (Civic Museum) and is situated on the left hand side of the Piazza del Duomo. It is one of the most important monuments in San Gimignano. The museum is rich in paintings from the Florentine and Sienese schools, such as the *Crucifix* by Coppo di Marcovaldo, triptyches by Niccolò Tegliacci and Taddeo di Bartolo, and other works painted by Domenico Michelino, Pinturicchio and Filippino Lippi. On the right hand side of the Palace is the **Torre Grosso** (Great Tower) erected in 1300 from which you can take in commanding views. *Info:* Piazza del Duomo, Tel. 0577/940-340. March 1-Oct. 31: 9:30am-7:20pm; Nov 1-Feb 28: 10am-5:50pm. Admission €6.

Just outside of the Piazza del Duomo is the triangular-shaped **Piazza del Cisterna** arrayed with brick pavement in a fish scale pattern. Constructed in 1273 and enlarged in 1346, the square is

circled by medieval homes and towers, and is a wonderful place to absorb the town's ambiance and charm. As you pass through the passageway from the Piazza del Duomo, you will go by the **Torri Gemelle degli Ardinghello**, constructed in the 1200s.

The **Museo d'Arte Sacra** includes material from local convents, the Duomo, and artifacts donated by private citizens and the Town Council. Some of the most valuable objects include the wooden sculptures from the 14th century; and the two statues of *The Annunciation*, one representing *The Angel* and the other *The Madonna*, of which only the head and the shoulders still exist. Then there is *The Crucifix*, a figure of Christ, which is handless.

There are also splendid psalm books as well as works from the 14th century. In the Silverware room, you will find intricate examples of silversmith's and goldsmith's art, most of which date back to the 17th and 18th centuries. You will also find some exceptional works in silk and satin with gold and silver braids. *Info:* Piazza Pecori, Tel. 0577/940-316. March 1 - March 31 & Nov. 1 - Jan. 20: 9:30am - 5pm; April 1 - Oct. 31: 9:30am - 7:30pm. From Jan 21 to Feb 28, the museum is closed. €6.

The **Museo Archeologico** has simple but instructive exhibits of Etruscan, Roman and medieval artifacts from the city and the surrounding area. Besides the objects of more common use (plates, bowls, vases, buckles and necklaces), which help to reveal the day-to-day lives of the ancients, the funeral urns consist of an elongated figure of the deceased holding a plate containing a small offering to pay for their passage to the afterlife. *Info:* Jan. 1-9: 11.00am - 6pm, Closed Thursdays; Jan 10 - Feb 28: Open only Thurs, Sat, Sun, Mon 11.00am-6pm; March 1 - Oct 31: Open every day 11.00am - 6pm; Nov 1 Dec 31: 11.00am - 6pm, Closed Thursdays. €6.

Located in the northernmost quadrant of the town, near the Porta St. Matteo, the construction of **Chiesa di San Agostino** began in 1280 and was completed in 1298. Its facade retains the simplicity of its original architectural style. The interior of the church is in a Romanesque style with Gothic elements and consists of a single great nave with three apses. The roof is supported by a rustic wooden framework. The *Chapel of the Blessed Bartolo* contains the saint's mortal remains in a marble monument sculpted by Benedetto da Maiano in 1495. The chapel's walls and vaults were frescoed by Sebastiano Mainardi in 1500. Its terracotta floor is work of Andrea della Robbia. Above the High Altar is *The*

Coronation of the Madonna and the Saints painted in 1483 by Piero del Pollaiolo. *Info:* Piazza San Agostino.

Cortona

Until *Under the Tuscan Sun* by Frances Mayes was released, **Cortona** was a sleepy little town. Since the book and subsequent movie, the town's charm and ambiance have been introduced to the world. Now if you come in the high season, Cortona will be filled with tourists. However, regardless of the tourist influx, the town is still a wonderful place to visit.

Cortona is commandingly situated with magnificent views over the Val di Chiana, the most extensive valley in the Apennine chain, which stretches to the hills of Siena. The **Sanctuary of Santa Margherita** towers above the town and is in turn overshadowed by the powerful defenses of the **Medici fortress**.

In conjunction, **Lago Trasimeno**, the largest lake in central Italy is just 9 kilometers away. A short drive from its shores brings you to the Umbrian capital of Perugia. And some important towns, such as Florence, Rome and Siena, are within easy reach by either train or car. *Info:* www.cortonaweb.net

Though there is not too much in the way of cultural sights in town, this being Italy there is always something to see. The **Etruscan Museum** exhibits a chandelier known as the Lamp of Cortona, one of the most celebrated bronzes from that time period. In the **Diocesan Museum** can be found the work of such minor masters as Luca Signorelli and Fra Angelico. The important medieval churches are those of **S. Francesco** and **S. Domenico**. Renaissance splendor is on display in the **Palazzo Casale** and in the churches of **S. Maria Nuova** and **S. Niccolò**.

Cortona's Best Eats

A refined yet down to earth eatery in Cortona, **Del Teatro** is filled with classical music softly wafting through the rooms tiled in terra cotta, supported with wood beams, and arrayed with quality art. Best of all, the food is superb and the prices are reasonable. *Info:* Via Maffei 2, Meal for two €45.

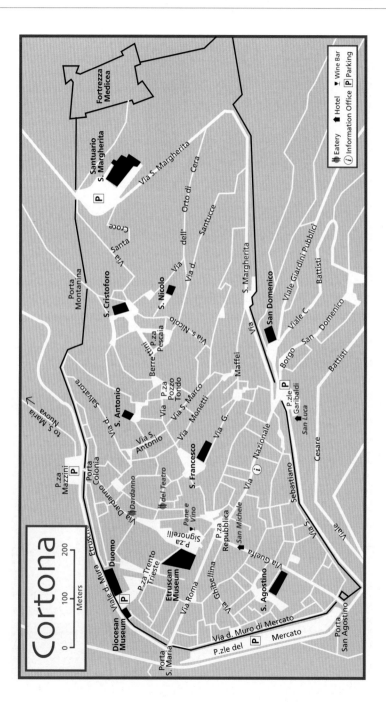

Cortona

Meters
0   100   200

Legend:
- Eatery
- ▲ Hotel
- ♥ Wine Bar
- Ⓘ Information Office
- Ⓟ Parking

Fortezza Medicea

Santuario S. Margherita

Via S. Margherita

Orto di Cera

Santa Croce

Via Santa Croce

Santucce

Via dell'

Orto di Cera

Porta Montanina

S. Cristoforo

S. Nicolo

Via S. Nicolo

San Domenico

Via S. Margherita

Viale Giardini Pubblici

Battisti

Viale C. San Domenico

Via d.

P.za Pescaia

Berrettini

S. Antonio

P.za Pozzo Tondo

Via S. Marco

Via S. Monetti

Via Maffei

Via S. Antonio

Via G.

Borgo

P.zle Garibaldi

San Luca

Battisti

Cesare

Porta Colonia

to S. Maria → to S. Nuova

P.za Mazzini

Via Salvatore

del Teatro

S. Francesco

Via Nazionale

Ⓘ

Sebastiano

Via Dardanno

Pane e Vino

P.za Signorelli

San Michele

P.za Repubblica

Via S.

Via Ghibellina

Via Guelfa

S. Agostino

Duomo

P.za Trento Trieste

Etruscan Museum

Via Roma

Viale d. Mura Etrusca

Diocesan Museum

Porta S. Maria

Via d. Muro di Mercato

P.zle del Mercato

Porta San Agostino

Viale

Take a break at a gracious wine bar in the main piazza across from the theater, **Pane e Vino**. You'll find rustic charm, great wine list, friendly service, and traditional, simple, and organic food. *Info:* Piazza Signorelli 27, www.pane-vino.it, Meal for two €25.

If you can, arrange your trip around the **Archidado Games** (circa May 12th to 19th each year), a fierce cross-bow competition between ancient neighborhoods, which compete for the prize of the Golden Dart (Verretta d'Oro). More than 250 townspeople dress in period garb and participate in religious ceremonies commemorating the marriage between Francesco Casali and Antonia Salimberi, which took place in 1397.

Montepulciano

This is a stunningly beautiful little town perched along a narrow limestone ridge high above the verdant plains that surround it. Enclosed by medieval fortifications, the tiny streets are bordered with attractive Renaissance palazzi and churches. Today **Montepulciano** is nearly identical to what it was five centuries ago. The beauty and majesty of the Renaissance and Medieval buildings have remained intact, allowing the town to live up to its moniker as the "Pearl of the 1500s." And it will most likely remain such a jewel since it is not that convenient to get to.

It is also a little different from most hill towns in that it does not have a geographic center. While Siena has its Campo, and other towns have a similar piazza that draws the community together, Montepulciano is spread along a ridge. Because of that the life of the town tends to get dissipated along the Corso, and funneled into individual restaurants or cafes. Despite this anomaly, come to Montepulcian, one of my favorite towns in all of Italy. *Info:* www.ctnet.it/montepulciano.

The **Church of St. Augustine** is one of the most beautiful and interesting buildings in Montepulciano. Its facade was designed by Michelozzo Michelozzi (1396-1472) in the first decade of the 15th century. As Brunelleschi's collaborator in architecture and

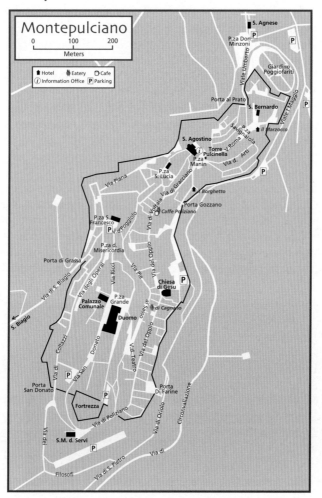

Donatello's disciple in sculpture, Michelozzi used simple and elegant Renaissance forms. On the high altar there is a wooden crucifix attributed to Donatello. In front of the church you will see the characteristic 16th century **Pulcinella**, a bell-tower which strikes the hours sonorously.

Montepulciano's Best Eats

Trattoria di Cagnano is replete with rustic charm and superb culinary offerings and is where the locals eat in Montepulciano. *Info:* Via del' Oppio ne Corso 30, Meal for two €40.

The **Madonna di San Biagio** on the Via di San Biagio on the outskirts of Montepulciano is also worth a visit. Built of honey and cream-colored stones it is **Sangallo's** masterpiece, a Renaissance gem begun in 1518, and which occupied him until his death in 1534.

Ready for a coffee or tea break? An elegant art nouveau café upstairs and refined restaurant below, **Caffé Poliziano**, is an upscale option while in Montepulciano. *Info:* Via di Voltaia ne Corso 27, Tel. 0578/758-615.

In the Piazza Grande you will find the **Palazzo Comunale**, onto which, in the 15th century, Michelozzo added a tower and facade to the original structure. On a clear day, the views that can be seen from the tower are superb. Also in the Piazza Grande is the **Duomo** built between 1592 and 1630. The facade is unfinished and plain, but the interior is elegant and tastefully adorned.

5. VENICE

Venice is one of the most frequented cultural centers in Europe, attracting over 20 million tourists each year. With its scenic canals, ornate bridges, gondoliers singing, grandiose palazzi, and charming local squares, it is easy to see why Venice is adored the world over.

The historic center of Venice is built on a group of small islands and earthen tidal banks in the middle of **Laguna Veneta**, a crescent-shaped lagoon separated from the Adriatic Sea by a barrier of narrow strips of islands and peninsulas. Some of Venice's islands include **Murano**, noted for its glassworks; colorful **Burano**, known for its lace; **San Giorgio Maggiore**, with the 16th century church of the same name; **La Guidecca** with its floating cafés and restaurants; and **Lido**, a beach resort built in the 19th century with casinos, golf course, beaches and nightlife.

Altogether there are more than 200 canals including the **Grand Canal**, and crossing the waterways there are around 400 bridges, the most famous of which is the **Rialto**

ONE GREAT DAY IN VENICE

If a day is all you have in this incredible place, then follow this plan for the best that the city has to offer, from the **Grand Canal** to **Piazza San Marco**.

You are either going to arrive at the Piazzale Roma by car or bus, or at the train station. Either way, for each location locate the nearest *vaporetto* (waterbus) stop for the #82 and take a ride down the **Grand Canal** to the **Rialto Bridge**. As you will be using the vaporetto system periodically today it is advised to buy a one-day pass instead of individual tickets to save yourself some money.

The **Ponte di Rialto**, completed in 1592, and the surrounding area

are filled with tourist-related shops. But before we start our grazing, let's go to the top of the bridge and admire the view out either side onto the Grand Canal.

If you can fight the urge to get distracted and buy something, we will have plenty of opportunities to purchase trinkets on this trip, let's muscle our way through the swarms of tourists to a pair of contiguous local markets, **Pesceria & Erberia**. This is where many Venetians and restaurants find their daily produce, fish, cheese and meats. Take some time to wander around, pull out your camera and capture some images of authentic Venetian life.

Grab some fruit to eat, or if you really want to get in the swing of things, stop at a local wine bar **Al Marca** for a taste of a local vintage to fortify you for the rest of the morning. Yes, you will see folks grabbing a quick *aperitivo* even early in the morning. *Info:* Campo della Vienna 213, open M-Sat 9am-3pm & 6-9:30pm. Map–Santa Croce & San Polo II.

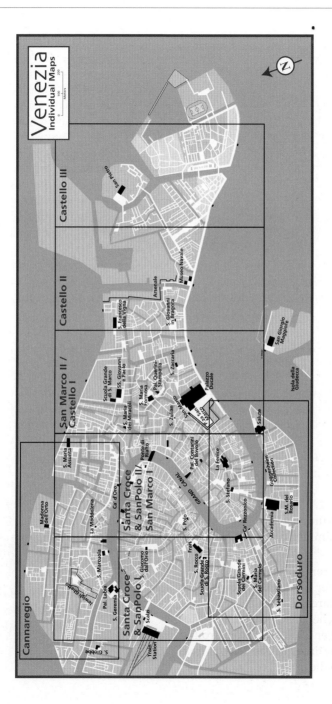

Venezia
Individual Maps

0 100 200
Meters

N

Cannaregio
Santa Croce & SanPolo I
Santa Croce & SanPolo II / San Marco I
San Marco II / Castello I
Castello II
Castello III
Dorsoduro

S. Giobbe
Jewish Ghetto
S. Geremia
Pal. Labia
S. Marcuola
Ferrovia Station
Scalzi
S. Giacomo dall'Orio
Frari
S. Rocco
Scuola Grande di S. Rocco
S. Maria del Carmelo
Scuola Grande dei Carmini
S. Sebastiano
La Maddalena
Madonna dell'Orto
Ca' d'Oro
S. Polo
Ponte di Rialto
Pal. Contarini del Bovolo
La Fenice
S. Stefano
Ca' Rezzonico
Accademia
S.M. del Rosario
Guggenheim Collection
S. Maria Assunta
S. Maria dei Miracoli
Scuola Grande di S. Marco
SS. Giovanni e Paolo
S. Maria Formosa
Pal. Querini Stampalia
S. Zulian
S. Marco
S. Zaccaria
Palazzo Ducale
Salute
S. Francesco della Vigna
S. Giovanni in Bragora
Arsenale
Museo Navale
San Pietro
San Giorgio Maggiore
Isola della Giudecca
GRAND CANAL

After whatever refreshment you chose to indulge in, it's back to the vaporetto for a ride down the rest of the Grand Canal to the **Piazza San Marco**. This is the epicenter of the city. Within this piazza are some of the main sights to see, starting with the piazza itself, which is the only open space in Venice allowed that appellation, *piazza*. All the rest are *campi*, fields. Wander around admiring the piazza from every angle to find the photo you want to take home with you. Along the way you can stop in one of the cafes for refreshment, just be aware that they are very expensive.

To start our tour of this piazza, let's get a bird's eye view at the top of the **Campanile**, the bell tower. The original bell tower collapsed in 1902, which lit a fire under the Italian government to do something about another tower in the country that had the potential of collapsing, the Leaning Tower of Pisa. In typically efficient Italian manner, work got underway on that project ... 90 years later. *Info:* Piazza San Marco, Tel. 041/5271-5911. Open November to March 9:30am-4:15pm, April to June and September to October 9am-7pm. €6. Vaporetto–San Marco.

Today, fear not, this tower is structurally sound, and offers you an unforgettable tableau of piercing spires, sloping rooftops, and shimmering canals.

After the campanile, head over to the **Basilica di San Marco**. Begun in 883 – the Venetian Republic thrived for over 1,000 years from around the time this basilica was built to the arrival of Napoleon in

Best Views Over Venice

These two **Campaniles** have the best panoramic views over Venice: **San Giorgio Maggiore** and the one in **Piazza San Marco**.

the 1800s – today the church is a mix of Byzantine, Gothic, Islamic and Renaissance materials. *Info:* Piazza San Marco, www.basilicasanmarco.it. Open 9:30am–5:30pm. Vaporetto–San Marco.

After all this, it is time for lunch. To do that, let's hop on another vaporetto over to the San Toma stop. Through this maze of streets let's locate the sumptuous restaurant **San Toma**, in the Campo San Toma. Pizza is their specialty, but they serve many other dishes as well. *Info:* Campo San Toma, Credit cards accepted. Closed Tuesdays. Meal for two €30. Vaporetto – San Toma.

After lunch it's time to head over to the magnificent Frari church. More formally known as **Santa Maria Gloriosa dei Frari**, this place is truly glorious, with some of the greatest works by Bellini, Titian, Donatello, and more. *Info:* Campo dei Frari, Tel. 041/275-0462, www.chorusvenezia.org. Open Mon-Sat 9am-6pm & Sun 1pm-6pm. €2.50. Vaporetto–San Toma.

Next up is the absolutely amazing **Scuola Grande di San Rocco**. In Italy there are buildings which house the best of specific artists: the Arena Chapel in Padua (Giotto), San Marco in Florence (Fra Angelico), Sistine Chapel in Rome (Michelangelo) and here in Venice the Scuola Grande di San Rocco (Tintoretto). *Info:* Campo San Rocco, 041/523-4864, www.scuolagrandesanrocco.it. April-Oct 9am–5.30pm, Nov-Mar 10am–4pm. €5.50. Vaporetto-San Toma.

After a healthy dose of all this art, it's time for a rest. And the best place to do that in all of Venice is the **Campo Santa Margherita**. Here you will find local shops and restaurants, and healthy community life. Choose a spot to sit for a mid-afternoon snack or drink. One suggestion is **Margaret Duchamp** with their expansive patio seating, excellent bar snacks and a wide variety of beverages. *Info:* Campo Santa Margherita 3019, Open 8am to 2pm. Closed Sundays.

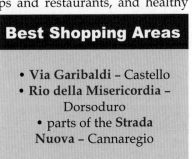

Best Shopping Areas

- **Via Garibaldi** – Castello
- **Rio della Misericordia** – Dorsoduro
- parts of the **Strada Nuova** – Cannaregio

After you have had your rest and savored the community life a bit, if you still want to do a little touring, head over to the **Accademia**, Venice's most famous art museum. Five hundred years of unequaled Venetian art are on display here. *Info:* Campo della Carita, Tel. 041/522-2247, www.gallerieaccademia.org. Monday 8:15am - 2pm, Tuesday to Sunday 8:15am - 7:15pm. €6.50. Vaporetto–Accademia.

After which, for dinner let's try the nearby **San Trovaso** (*see Best Eats*). Before dinner, however, while there may still be some light, head down the canal away from the restaurant. On your right hand side near the end is one of the last working gondola boatyards in Venice, the **Squero della Toffola**. *Info:* Dorsoduro #1097, Tel. 338/345-1116.

After your meal, head back to the Accademia Bridge, one of only three spans over the Grand Canal. Cross it into the expansive **Campo Santa Stefano** and grab an after-dinner drink at one of the cafes there and soak up the last remaining taste of Venetian life before you leave.

To head back to the train station or Piazzale Roma, go back across the Accademia Bridge and catch the vaporetto #82. At which time, as it is likely dark, you will be able to experience the entire Grand Canal twinkling with the lights of the many magnificent palazzi lining its expanse.

A FANTASTIC WEEKEND IN VENICE

A weekend in Venice will give you a glimpse of the city's beauty and charm. On this tour of Venice, we will visit the most important sites, wander through colorful neighborhoods, stop at local wine bars and restaurants, and sample the best that Venice has to offer.

Friday Evening
The place to start any visit to Venice is at the **Piazza San Marco**.

That being said, it is also the first place to leave. This square is the epicenter of mass tourism in the island city. For good reason. Many of the important sights to see are here. As a result it can get rather crowded.

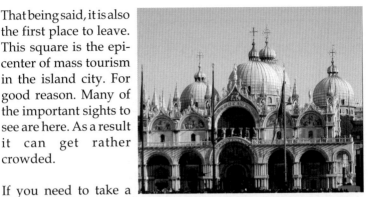

If you need to take a vaporetto from your hotel to get here, remember to buy a 3-day pass as this will be more convenient and inexpensive for you.

To start our tour of Venice, let's get a bird's eye view of the city at the top of the **Campanile**, the bell tower, in the center of the piazza. Rebuilt after a collapse in 1902, the original bell tower had a cage protruding from it that was used to hold criminals as punishment. Another tradition during feast days was to stretch a rope between the tower and the Doge's Palace and have an acrobat walk the span. *Info:* Piazza San Marco, Tel. 041/5271-5911. Open November to March 9:30am-4:15pm, April to June and September to October 9am-7pm. €6. Vaporetto–San Marco.

Afterwards, stroll around the square, enjoying the dueling musical ensembles cafes have set up to lure in tourists. If you choose to have a meal or a drink at one of cafes, be aware that it will be rather expensive. Instead of getting sucked in one of these atmospheric tourist traps, however, why not sample some more authentic Venetian cuisine.

A small walk away, through some of Venice's famously narrow streets, over some bridges, through some campi, is **Da Alberto**. A distinctly local place, in an off the beaten path neighborhood, come here for the *spaghetti can seppia nera* (with squid ink), a Venetian specialty, and all manner of tasty local dishes. *Info:* Calle Larga G. Gallina 5401, Tel. 041/523-8153, open M-Sat 10am-3pm & 4pm-11pm. Meal for two €40. Reservations needed. Map–Castello I.

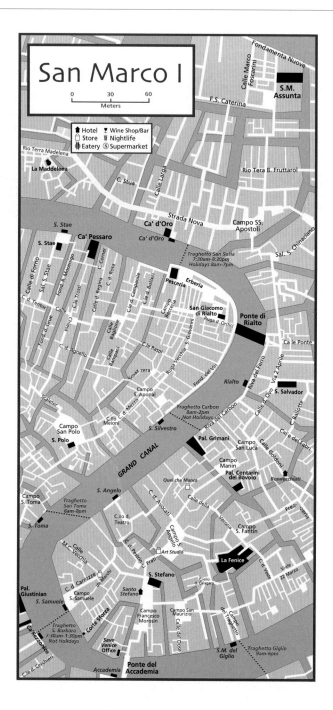

San Marco I

0   30   60
Meters

Hotel ♟ Wine Shop/Bar
Store ♟ Nightlife
Eatery ⓈSupermarket

Fondamenta Nuove
Calle Marco Foscarini
S.M. Assunta
F.S. Caterina
Rio Terra Madelena
La Maddelena
C. Stua
Calle Larga
Rio Tera B. Fruttarol
Strada Nova
S. Stae
Ca' d'Oro
Campo SS. Apostoli
Ca' Pessaro
Ca' d'Oro
S. Stae
Traghetto San Sofia
7:30am-8:30pm
Holidays 8am-7pm
Sal. S. Chinaciano
Calle di Forno
Sal. S. Stae
Fond. R. Mocenigo
C. d. Conner
Calle d. Regina
C. d. Rosa
Calle d. Campanile
Calle d. Bottieri
Pesceria
Erberia
C. d. Tentor
C. d. Gnoe
Calle
Chiesa
Campo Beccaria
San Giacomo di Rialto
Ruga d. Orifici
Ponte di Rialto
Calle Basilione
Ruga Vecchia S. Giovanni
Ca le Ponte
Fond. d. Gnoe
C. d. Agnello
Calle Rampani
C.le Raspi
Skoar zera
Fond. del Vin
Rialto
Riva del Ferro
Calle d. Oro Via 2 Aprile
S. Salvador
Scaleter
Campo S. Aponal
C. d. Mezzo
Traghetto Carbon
8am-2pm
Not Holidays
Riva del Carbon
Calle d. Oro
C. Ballotte
Campo San Polo
C.llo Meloni
S. Silvestro
Pal. Grimani
Campo San Luca
Calle Goldoni
Cal e del Fabri.
S. Polo
GRAND CANAL
Campo Manin
Pal. Contarini del Bovolo
Bonvecchiati
Campo S. Toma
Traghetto San Toma
8am-8pm
S. Angelo
Quel che Manca
C. d. Avocati
Calle della
Verona
Frez zeria
S. Toma
C.llo d. Teatro
Campo S. Fantin
Calle M.C. Vecchia
Campo S. Angelo
Art Studio
C. d. Pestin C. Frati
La Fenice
Viale 22 Marzo
Pal. Giustinian
C. d. Carrozze
de Mandsi
Campo S. Samuele
Santo Stefano
S. Stefano
C.llo d. Calagaro
C. d. Veste
S. Samuele
Campo Francesco Morosin
Campo San Maurizio
Calle del Dose
Campo del Traghetto
Traghetto
S. Barbara
7:30am-1:30pm
Not Holidays
Corte Sforza
Save Venice Office
Traghetto Giglio
9am-6pm
Ca' Rezzonico
C.lle d. Cerchieri
Accademia
Ponte del Accademia
S.M. del Giglio

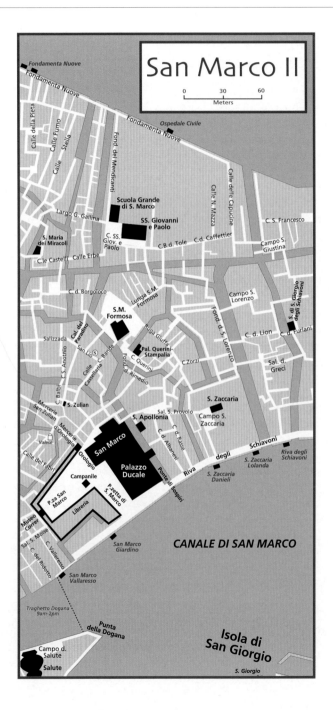

San Marco II

0   30   60
Meters

Best Wine Bars in Venice

- **Ae do Marie** – a true local neghborhood. *Info:* Calle dell'Ogio 3129, Map–Castello II.
- **Al Marca** – a hole in the wall near the Rialto. *Info:* Campo della Vienna 213, Map–Santa Croce & San Polo II.
- **Al Ponte** – great little place in an out of the way location. *Info:* Ponte del Cavallo 6378, Map–Castello I.
- **Do Mori** – a well-hidden *enotecha* near the Rialto. *Info:* Calle 2 Mori, Map–Santa Croce & San Polo II.

After your meal let's go for a walk. Despite the dark feel to the city, Venice is actually a very safe city in which to walk at night, especially when compared to US cities. Even so, use common sense. Stay on the well-trodden, well-lit pathways through Venice.

So take a stroll, get a sense of the city, because during the evenings is when Venice is least crowded with tourists and when you can feel most like a local. If you are looking for nightlife, you will find it around the Rialto bridge, in Campo Santa Margherita, and along the Corso Nuova.

Saturday
Start the day back in tourist central, **Piazza San Marco**. After visiting the basilica here, the Doge's palace, and the Museo Correr, this will be the last time we venture here.

The original **Basilica di San Marco** was begun in 883, but the church we see today was started in 1063. It was finished in 1073 and then for centuries it was sporadically adorned with superb mosaics, precious marbles, and war spoils brought back by merchants, travelers, and soldiers, so that today the church is a mix of Byzantine, Gothic, Islamic and Renaissance materials. *Info:* Piazza San Marco, www.basilicasanmarco.it. Open 9:30am–5:30pm. Vaporetto–San Marco.

Next stop is the **Palazzo Ducale**. One impressive sight is *The Staircase of the Giants*, so named because of the two colossal statues of Mars and Neptune on either side of the landing. Each new Doge of the Republic of Venice was officially crowned on the landing at the top of the stairs. You will also find some of the most beautiful plaster relief ceilings, marble fireplaces, paintings, sculptures, tapestries, medieval weapons rooms and ancient dungeons anywhere in Europe. Keep your eye out for the medieval chastity belt on display in the pistol room. Yikes! *Info:* Piazza San Marco, Tel. 041/271-5911, www.museicivicoveneziani.it. Open April to October 9am-7pm and November to March 9am-5pm. €11. Vaporetto–San Marco.

Next stop, the **Museo Correr**, which contains a comprehensive overview of the old Venetian Serenissima Republic. On display are coins, old maps, prints, drawings, paintings, instruments, seriously high heeled shoes, globes, bronze figurines, ships models, muskets, powder horns, cannons, swords, pikes, backgammon boards, playing cards, jigsaw puzzles, and yoyos, as well as documents, artifacts and mementos from the Venetian Republic. An incredible collection of art and history. *Info:* Piazza S. Marco 13/a. San Marco 52, Tel. 041/240-5211, www.museicivicoveneziani.it. Open from April to October 9am-7pm. From November to March 9am-5pm. €11. Price includes entrance to Doge's Palace, Museo Archeologico Nazionale, and the Torre dell'Orologio. Vaporetti–San Marco.

Hungry? If so, wander up the **Riva degli Schiavoni** and grab a seat at any of the tempting cafes you see there. Though rather touristy they are on an ideal place to grab a bite with incredible views of the Venetian Lagoon.

After your lunch break, take a vaporetto over to the Accademia stop and head to the **Accademia Museum**, filled with hundred years of unequaled Venetian art. *Info:* Campo della Carita,

Tel. 041/522-2247, www.gallerieaccademia.org. Monday 8:15am - 2pm, Tuesday to Sunday 8:15am - 7:15pm. €6.50. Vaporetto–Accademia.

Now, either take a vaporetto over to San Toma and wander over to Frari, or snake your way through Venice's warren of streets from the Accademia. After the Basilica of St. Mark's, **Santa Maria Gloriosa dei Frari** is the most remarkable ecclesiastical complex in Venice. Begun in 1250 it was finally finished in 1443.

Today the unadorned facade is not much to look at but the interior is simply magnificent. The main draw for this church is the **tomb of Titian**, the grand master of painting who died of plague in 1576. There are number of Titians featured inside including *Assumption of the Virgin* done in 1518 hanging over the main altar. *Info:* Campo dei Frari, Tel. 041/275-0462, www.chorusvenezia.org. Open Mon-Sat 9am-6pm & Sun 1pm-6pm. €2.50. Vaporetto–San Toma.

Next up is the **Scuola Grande di San Rocco**, which contains an absolutely amazing collection of Tintoretto's. In conjunction, along the walls of the upper hall are some incredibly ornate carved wooden benches.

After this tough day of touring, before we head out to dinner, it's time for a relaxing aperitivo in the **Campo Santa Margherita**. This local piazza has evolved to contain some great cafes and pubs, and is a place many younger Venetians come for a night out on the town. For our purposes, we are going to grab a seat at

Traghetto Rides

Traghetti are gondolas powered by two men and are used by commuters to get across the **Grand Canal**. For visitors, traghetti are a great way to get that gondola experience without paying the rapacious prices gondoliers charge. The traghetti locations across the Grand Canal are featured on the maps in this book.

a cafe, and chill out, possibly at **Margaret Duchamp** with its expansive patio seating, excellent bar snacks and a wide variety of beverages. *Info:* Campo Santa Margherita 3019, Open 8am to 2pm. Closed Sundays.

For dinner tonight, we are going to try something a little out of the ordinary. An absolutely fabulous and completely local place to dine, well off the beaten tourist path, yet still easily accessible is **Ristorante Mistra**. Hidden in a boatyard on the top floor of a warehouse overlooking the lagoon, to get here disembark from the vaporetto on the island of **Giudecca** at the Redentore stop, walk to your right, enter a white entryway to the boatyard, follow signs to the restaurant past old brick warehouses and dry docked boats to the far end on the right. At the rear of the building, up a flight of metal stairs is a wonderfully unique Venetian dining experience. *Info:* Tel. 041/522-0743, Giudecca 212a, closed Monday Evenings and Tuesdays.

Sunday
Though we do not have much time today, as the weekend draws to a close, we can still squeeze in a trip to the amazing island of **Murano**, where Venice's delicate glass artwork is created. Only a five-minute vaporetto ride away, Murano reminds me of the way Venice used to be 30 years ago. *Info:* Vaporetto **41**, **42**, **13**, or **LN** from Fondamente Nuove.

This town consists of five interconnected islands and is world-renowned for its **glass blowing** industry, which dates back to 1291 when the furnaces were banned from Venice as a precaution against fire and industrial espionage. At its height in the 16th century, Murano had 37 glass factories and a population of 30,000. Today there are only around 10 factories and the population is a little under 8,000.

ALTERNATE PLAN
If it's summer and you want to swim, head out to the **Lido**. There is also a golf course open year round, or you can rent a bike. See *Best Activities* chapter for details. To get to Lido from Venice catch the Vaporetto 1 or 82.

What used to be the closely guarded industrial secret of glass

 manufacture is today common knowledge, but Murano glass is still in demand all over the world because of the skilled artisans that prepare these fine works of art.

Check out the **glass factories** on Fondamenta dei Vetrai, three of which offer glass blowing exhibitions. If you don't want to take the time to get to these places, **Civam** is convenient to the Vaporetto. *Info:* Viale Garibaldi 24, Tel. 041/739-323.

To witness the history of Venice's glass blowing industry, visit the **Museo dell'Arte Vetraria**, the glass museum. *Info:* Fondamenta Giustiniano and Fondamenta Manin. Tel. 041/739-586. Open Mondays, Tuesdays, Thursdays and Saturdays 10am–4pm, Sundays 9am–12:30pm. Closed Wednesdays.

For lunch head over to the Fondamenta Manin and take in one of the following two restaurants: **Dalla Mora** - *Info:* Fondamenta Manin 75, Tel. 041/736-344. www.ristorantedallamora.com. Open every day. Meal for two €35; or **Da Tanduo** - *Info:* Fondamenta Manin 67-68, Tel. 041/739-310. www.datanduo.it. Closed Tuesdays. Meal for two €30.

A WONDERFUL WEEK IN VENICE

Spending one week in Venice will allow you to savor the sumptuous delights offered at a leisurely pace. For your convenience, the sights have been separated geographically by *siestiere* (district), then within each *siestiere* the sights have been listed according to their significance with an eye to making sure it was easy to get from one to the other.

RECOMMENDED PLAN: With the material separated by *siestieri*, days one through five will be spent visiting each local neighborhood of Venice; leaving days six and seven free to visit the Islands in the lagoon. After which you will have seen all the best that Venice has to offer.

Canale Grande

There is one sight that winds through all the *siestieri* – the **Grand Canal**. Shaped like a large upside down "S" bisecting the city, lining this wonderful waterway are tremendous old buildings, palaces, and homes epitomizing every architectural style that graced the thousand-year reign of the Venetian republic.

You'll also see small canals thrusting off into the interior, and beautiful gateways and entrances some beginning to be covered by the water. The best way to see the canal is to take the *vaporetto* **No. 1** or the **No. 82**. Take one trip during the day, as well as another at night when the palazzi are illuminated.

Cannaregio

Cannaregio is a *siestieri* of contrasts. It contains a densely populated

Don't Miss ...

These are the best sights to see in Venice by *siestieri*:

• **Canareggio**: Santa Maria Assunta
• **San Marco**: Piazza San Marco, Basilica di San Marco, Museo Correr & Biblioteca Nazionale, Palazzo Ducale, Ponte di Rialto
• **San Polo & Santa Croce**: Mercati di Erberia e Pesceria, Santa Maria Gloriosa dei Frari, Scuola Grande di San Rocco
• **Castello**: Santa Maria dei Miracoli, Santi Giovanni e Paolo, Museo Navale Storico
• **Dorsoduro**: Ca' Rezzonico, Galleria dell'Accademia
• **Islands**: San Giorgio Maggiore, Burano, Murano

commercial street, the **Strada Nuova** and only a few major tourists attractions; but it also is home to areas of unexpected tranquility. With its small grocery shops and simple local taverns, many areas of this neighborhood feel far removed from the hustle and bustle of mass tourism that floods Venice every year. One of the prettiest and most remote quarters is in the north, near the church of **Madonna dell'Orto** and around **Campo Mori**. Listed below, as in each of the different *siestieri*, are the best sights to see, in order of significance.

Close to the train station and just off the Strada Nuova is the first **Jewish Ghetto** in the world, created by an edict of the Venetian Senate in 1516. The reason behind its creation was that the Jews were being punished for their perceived role in the loss of trade that had once flowed into the Venetian lagoon from Byzantium and beyond the Black Sea. Even though history has clearly shown that it was Vasco de Gama's discovery of a route around the Cape of Good Hope in Africa to the spice lands in the east that caused Venice's economic decline, instead of the city father's blaming their own shortsightedness or the dramatic shift in world economics, the Venetian rulers found a ready scapegoat in the Jews.

Removed from their homes and packed behind the walls of a newly constructed cannon foundry — which in the Venetian

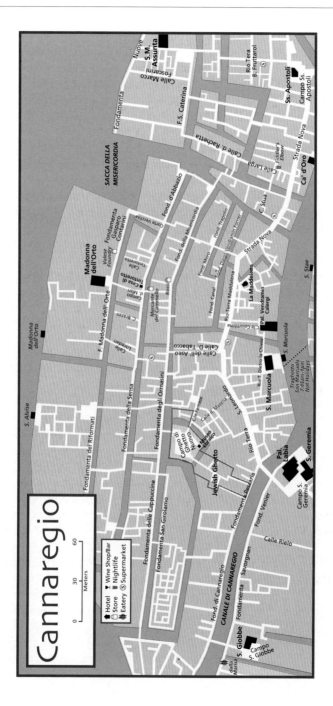

tongue is called a *getto* — not yet put to use, the Jews were locked in every night. As forced relocation of Jews spread to other cities during the economic turmoil of the next couple of centuries caused by this era of discovery, the name *getto* stuck and came to describe the places where Jews all over Christendom were henceforth to be confined.

In Venice, the Jewish incarceration space originally encompassing only the *Ghetto Nuovo* (new cannon foundry), but eventually expanded beyond that border as a result of population pressure. This first Jewish Ghetto remained an enforced enclave until 1797, ending when Napoleon conquered the Venetian Republic and disbanded it.

In this area you'll find five synagogues, three of which are open to the public: **Sinagoga Grande Tedesca**, **Sinagoga Spagnole**, and **Levantina**. The small museum, **Museo Ebraica** contains information about the five centuries of Jewish presence in Venice. Not as dramatic architecturally as other sights, or as significant artistically, but in terms of history, there is no more important spot in Venice. *Info:* Museum - Campo Ghetto Nuovo, Tel. 041/715-359, www.museoebraico.it. Open October to May 10am-5.30pm; June to September 10am-7pm. Closed Saturdays and Jewish holidays. Museum €3. Vaporetto–San Marcuola.

A short walk away is the austere Gothic church of **Madonna dell'Orto** is located in one of the quieter sides of Venice. Founded in the mid-14th-century it was initially dedicated to St. Christopher, patron saint of travelers. A dedication that was changed and the church reconstructed in the early 15th century when a statue of the Virgin Mary, said to have miraculous powers, was discovered nearby.

To the far right of the main altar, inside the chapel of San Mauro, is **Statue of the Madonna**, which inspired the re-dedication of the church. Some still claim miraculous cures stemming from prayer in the statues presence, making it as a good enough excuse as any to visit this church.

The interior, faced almost entirely in brick, is filled with light and uncluttered. Inside to the right of the entrance is Cima da Conegliano's painting, *St John the Baptist and Other Saints*. The empty space opposite once contained Giovanni Bellini's *Madonna with Child* but thieves purloined it not too long ago, and it has yet to be recovered.

Come here to see some magnificent paintings by **Tintoretto**, who was a parishioner of the church. His tomb, which is marked with a plaque, lies in the chapel to the right of the main altar. The most dramatic of his works here are the towering paintings in the main altar. On the right wall is *The Last Judgment*. In *The Adoration of the Golden Calf* on the left wall, the figure carrying the calf, fourth from the left, glancing out from the painting, is said to depict Tintoretto himself. *Info:* Campo Madonna dell'Orto, Tel. 041/275-0462. Open 9am–5pm, Sun 1pm-5pm. Tel. 0412750462. www.chorusvenezia.org. €2.50. Vaporetto–Madonna dell'Orto.

A little further afield is the impressively grandiose church, **Santa Maria Assunta**, also known as **Gesuiti**, which was built in the 12th century. After the original order of monks who owned the structure were suppressed by the Pope as their morals had become too lax (it appears that they were running a brothel out of the cloisters), the Jesuits (Gesuiti) bought the structure in 1656. It was remodeled between 1715 and 1730 with a Baroque facade that contains statues of the 12 Apostles.

This is a single-aisled church laid out in a Latin Cross Style and is decorated with a variety of colored marble inlays including attractive curly-cued columns around the main altar. The main attractions to this church are two outstanding paintings: the *Assumption of the Virgin* by Tintoretto (on the left before you get to the main altar) and the *Martyrdom of St. Lawrence* by Titian (on the left as you enter). To the right as

Chorus Church Pass

To buy a pass to see some of the best preserved churches in Venice, all at a low group rate of €9, simply visit one of the churches in question and opt to buy the **Chorus Pass** rather than the individual ticket. Otherwise each individual church costs €2.50 to enter. *Info:* www.chorusvenezia.org.

you enter is a fine work by Palma il Giovane. Having Venice's three master painters in one church offers you an opportunity to compare their styles. *Info:* Campo dei Gesuiti 4905. Open 10am-noon & 4-6pm. Vaporetto–Fondamenta Nuova.

The jewel of Cannareggio is the church of **Santa Maria dei Miracoli**. Any knowledgeable visitor to Venice should not miss

this amazingly restored little church. An exquisite masterpiece of the early Renaissance, Miracoli is a popular church with Venetians and is where many of them choose to get married. Tucked away in a picturesque maze of alleys and waterways in far eastern Cannaregio, it is often likened to a jewel box, as the facade is decorated with various shades of marble, fine bas-reliefs and sculptures. It was built in 1481 to 1489 to enshrine *The Virgin and Child* a painting believed to have miraculous powers, which now resides above the altar.

The interior of the church is best visited when piercing shafts of sunlight stream in through the windows, embellishing the pink, white and grey marble and reflecting onto the barrel vaulted ceiling housing 50 portraits of saints and prophets. *Info:* Campiello dei Miracoli, Tel. 041/275-0462, www.chorusvenezia.org. Open Mon-Sat 10am-5pm, Sun 1pm-5pm. €2.50. Vaporetto-Rialto.

An American Gondola Maker

There are few *squeri* (gondola boatyards) left in Venice, six to be precise, and one is owned and operated by an American transplant, **Tom Price** from North Carolina. If you want to learn about gondola-making from an American in Venice, visit **Canaletto**, Tom's boatyard. *Info:* Rio dei Mendicanti #6301, Cannaregio, Tel. 041/241-3963, Open M-F 9am-1pm & 2-6pm. Map-Castello.

Castello

Castello is the largest *siestieri* in the city and contains the famed **Arsenale**, where the great shipyards produced the Republic's indomitable fleet of warships, and the **Riva degli Schiavoni** promenade that starts by the Doge's Palace. Behind this bustling promenade is a warren of narrow alleys, neighborhood main streets, and almost forgotten squares with elegantly faded palazzi and fine churches.

The large Gothic Dominican church of **Santi Giovanni e Paolo**, also known as **San Zanipolo**, contains an abundance of art. Unfortunately, the facade was never finished, but it is still beautiful in its simplicity. The second church of the Republic after San Marco, San Zanipolo has a great number of important Venetians, including 25 doges, buried here. Artistic highlights include an outstanding work by Giovanni Bellini in the right aisle, second altar; Alvise Vivarini's *Christ Carrying the Cross* in the sacristy; and Lorenzo Lotto's *Charity of St. Antonino* in the right transept.

Don't miss the *Cappella del Rosario* (Rosary Chapel), off the left transept. It was built in the 16th century to commemorate the 1571 victory of Lepanto, when Venice led a combined European fleet to defeat the Turkish navy. The chapel was devastated by a fire in 1867 and restored in the early years of the 20th century with works from other churches, among them some beautiful Veronese ceiling paintings. Also don't miss the Pietro Mocenigo tomb to the right of the main entrance, a monument built by Pietro Lombardo and his sons. Outside the church is the expansive **Campo dei SS Giovanni e Paolo**, which contains the **Statue of Bartolomeo Colleoni**, an Italian soldier of fortune, or condottiere, who served the Republic from 1450–1475. *Info:* Campo Santi Giovanni e Paolo, Tel. 041/523-5913. Open everyday 7:30am-12:30am and 3:30pm-7:30pm. Vaporetto–Ospedale.

In the same piazza as San Zanipolo is the **Scuola Grande di San Marco**, founded in 1260 for religious and humanitarian purposes. Today it is part of the Ospedale Civile, Venice's main hospital. This structure was built 1437 and rebuilt 1485-95 from plans by Giovanni Buora, Mauro Docussi, and Pietro Lombardo. The facade is one of the most harmonious and significant Vene-

The Scuole of Venice

The **Scuole** of Venice were started centuries ago to help relieve the burden of poverty for Venice's most underprivileged citizens. These institutions still operate today above and beyond everything modern Italian society does for its citizens (universal health care, universal pension plans, free day care, inexpensive university study, and extensive and inexpensive public transit), showing that there is always a need for a kind heart.

tian Renaissance architectural displays. Asymmetrical in design it is still one of the most prized and original Venetian buildings with rich polychrome marble decorations and curvilinear crowning. As this building is now a working hospital, sightseeing is by appointment only. *Info:* Campo dei Santi Giovanni e Paolo. Open 8:30am-2pm. To make an appointment to visit the library call 041/529-4323 or 041/529-4111. Vaporetto–Rialto or Fondamente Nuove.

Just off the expansive Campo Santa Maria Formosa is the **Palazzo Querini–Stampalia**. A museum, research library, bookshop, cafe, garden, restaurant and a foundation dedicated to the preservation of art and knowledge in Venice. This palazzo is a wonderful introduction to the way Venetian nobility lived during the Serrenissima. Built in the 1500s it contains many of the original carpets, furnishings, sculptures, porcelain, musical instruments, scale models, paintings and more. The entrance however, is completely modern, offering a counterpoint of architectural styles. *Info:* Santa Maria Formosa 5252, Tel. 041/271-1411 Open 10am-6pm Tues-Sun. On Friday and Saturdays, open until 10pm. Closed Mondays. www.querinistampalia.it. €6. Vaporetto-Rialto.

Down by the Riva degli Schiavoni is the church of **San Zaccaria**. Dedicated to the father of Saint John the Baptist, Saint Zacharias, the body of that saint purportedly resides here, as do the remains of 8 doges (rulers of Venice). The present church was built between 1444 and 1515 and is a mixture of Gothic and Romanesque architecture. The walls of the aisles are covered in paintings by Tintoretto, Bellini, Van Dyke, and others. The church,

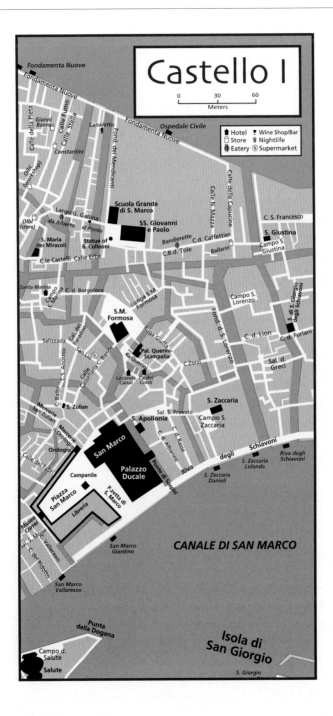

Castello I

0 30 60
Meters

Hotel ♟ Wine Shop/Bar
🗋 Store ♟ Nightlife
🍴 Eatery Ⓢ Supermarket

Fondamenta Nuove

Fondamenta Nuove

Calle della Pieta

Calle Fumo

Calle Stella

Gianni Basso

Canaletto

Fond. dei Mendicanti

Fondamenta Nuove

Ospedale Civile

Constantini

Olbi (workshop)

Scuola Grande di S. Marco

Largo G. Gallina

Olbi (store)

da Alberto

al Ponte

SS. Giovanni e Paolo

Calle N. Mazza

Calle delle Capucine

C. S. Francesco

S. Giustina

S. Maria dei Miracoli

Statue of B. Colleoni

Bandierette

C.d. Caffettier

Campo S. Giustina

C.le Castelli

Calle Erbe

C.B.d. Tole

Ballarin

Santa Marina

Campo S. Marina

C. d. Borgoloco

Lunga S.M. Formosa

Campo S. Lorenzo

S. di S. Giorgio degli Schiavoni

S.M. Formosa

Ruga Giuffa

Fond. d. S. Lorenzo

C. d. Lion

C. d. Furlani

Salizzada

Cal. del Paradiso

San Lio

Pal. Querini-Stampalia

C. Querini

C. Zorzi

Sal. d. Greci

C.S Apollonio

Calle Casellaria

C. Bande

Locanda Canal

Ca dei Conti

C. Balbi

S. Zaccaria

Mercerie San Zulian

S. Zulian

Sal. S. Provolo

Campo S. Zaccaria

Mercerie dell'Orologio

S. Apollonia

C. d. Rasse

Orologio

San Marco

C. d. Albanesi

Ponte di Sospiri

degli

Schiavoni

Riva degli Schiavoni

Calle del Fabbri

Campanile

Palazzo Ducale

Riva

S. Zaccaria Lolanda

S. Zaccaria Danieli

Museo Correr

Piazza San Marco

P.zetta di S. Marco

Libreria

Sal. S. Moise

C. Vallaresso

C. del Ridotto

San Marco Giardino

CANALE DI SAN MARCO

San Marco Vallaresso

Punta della Dogana

Campo d. Salute

Salute

Isola di San Giorgio

S. Giorgio

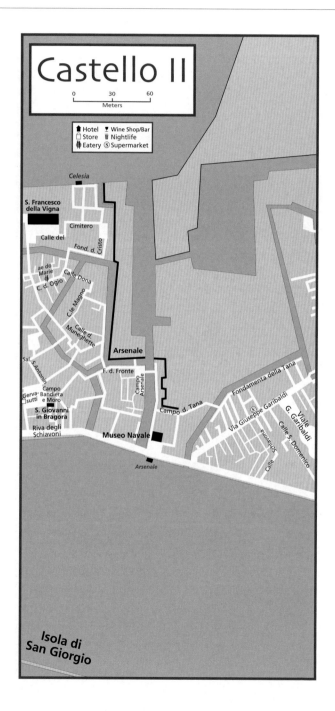

Castello II

0   30   60
Meters

♠ Hotel   ♟ Wine Shop/Bar
⌂ Store   ♝ Nightlife
♛ Eatery Ⓢ Supermarket

Celesia

S. Francesco
della Vigna

Cimitero

Calle del

Fond. d. Cristo

ae do
Marie
C. d. Ogio

Calle Dona

C.lle Magno

Calle d.
Muneghette

Arsenale

Sal. S. Antonin

F. d. Fronte

Campo
Arsenale

Campo
Gerva- Bandiera
sutti e Moro

**S. Giovanni
in Bragora**

Riva degli
Schiavoni

Campo d. Tana

Fondamenta della Tana

Via Giuseppe Garibaldi

Viale
G. Garibaldi

Calle S. Domenico

Schiavona

Calle

Museo Navale

Arsenale

Isola di
San Giorgio

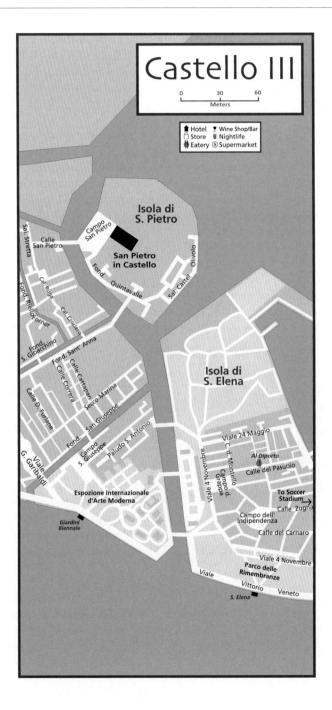

Castello III

0   30   60
Meters

♠ Hotel   ▼ Wine Shop/Bar
🏠 Store   🍷 Nightlife
🍴 Eatery   Ⓢ Supermarket

Isola di
S. Pietro

Campo
San Pietro

Sal. Stretta

Calle
San Pietro

San Pietro
in Castello

Fond. Quintavalle

Sal. Castel Olivolo

Fond. Rielo Corner

Cal. Ruga

Cal. Crocera

Fond.
S. Gioacchino

Fond. Sant' Anna

Calle Catapano

Calle Correra

Secco Marina

Calle D. Furlane

Fond. San Giuseppe

Campo
S. Giuseppe

Paludo S. Antonio

Viale
G. Garibaldi

Espozione Internazionale
d'Arte Moderna

Giardini
Biennale

Isola di
S. Elena

Viale 24 Maggio

Viale 4 Novembre

C. d. Montello

Campo d.
Grappa

Al Diporto

Calle del Pasubio

To Soccer
Stadium →

Calle Zugna

Campo dell'
Indipendenza

Calle del Carnaro

Viale 4 Novembre

Parco delle
Rimembranze

Viale

Vittorio

Veneto

S. Elena

however, is mainly known for its 1505 altarpiece by Bellini, a magnificent *Madonna and Child Enthroned* with Saints Peter, Catherine, Lucia and Jerome. *Info:* Campo S. Zaccaria 4693, Tel. 041/522-1257. Open Mon-Sat 10am-12am and 4pm-6pm; Sun 4pm-6pm. Vaporetto-S. Zaccaria.

Further along the Riva degli Schiavoni is the **Museo Navale Storico**, my favorite museum in Venice. This is an incredible collection of scale models of ancient ships and forts, uniforms and trophies of the modern Italian Navy, a wonderfully detailed model of the last *Bucintoro* (the vessel in which the Doge of Venice celebrated the "Wedding of the Sea" between Venice and the sea by throwing a ring into the Adriatic) and much more. *Info:* Riva San Biagio 2148, Tel. 041/520-0276. Open 9am–1:30pm Monday–Saturday. €1.55. Vaporetto–Arsenale.

Nearby the Museo Navale Storico you'll find the **Arsenale**, an imposing group of buildings, landing stages, workshops, ship-

yards and more from which the Venetian Navy was built. Begun in 1100, it has been continually enlarged over the years. Surrounded by towers and walls, the Arsenale has an imposing Renaissance entrance built in 1460. In the front of the entrance is a terrace with statues that symbolize the victory of the Battle of Lepanto. At the sides are four lions, the symbol of the Venetian city-state. Stop by to see this façade as the Arsenale is still a military base and you cannot enter.

At the extreme eastern point of the Venice is the small island of San Pietro, upon which sits the imposing church, **San Pietro di Castello**. The Latin-cross interior has a central nave and two side aisles and is surmounted by an impressive cupola. Most of the decoration is 17th century. Note the high altar of inlaid polychrome marble designed in 1649. On the right hand side of the church, between the altarpiece by Tizianello, nephew of the more famous Titian, and the next altar is the *Throne of St. Peter*, an assemblage of parts (probably compiled in the 13th century and not really old enough to be St. Peter's throne) including an old Arab funeral stele. The *Vendramin and Lando Chapels* in the north transept to the left of the main altar are of particular importance. A canvas by Veronese hangs above the entrance to the chapels. *Info:* Campo San Pietro 70, Tel. 041/275-0462, www.chorusvenezia.org. Open Monday-Saturday 10am-5pm, Sunday 1pm-5pm. €2.50. Vaporetto-Arsenale.

San Marco
Note: see maps on pages 124-125 earlier in this chapter.

This *siestieri* has been the heart of Venetian life since the early days of *La Serrenissima* (the Serene Republic of Venice), which lasted for almost 1,000 years. The San Marco area is home to the more refined gentry of Venice and contains the *Mercerie* – Venice's popular shopping streets. Heavily touristed and very crowded, San Marco is nonetheless a great *siestieri* to visit. But don't stay here. If you want a more authentic Venetian experience, find a hotel in a quieter corner of Venice. See *Best Sleeps* for suggestions.

When the Basilica of St. Mark and the Doge's Palace were being erected, the grassy field in front of them was filled in and paved over (between 1172-1178). This became the **Piazza San Marco**. On either side of the pavement, elegant houses were built with arcades running the length of them. Many were taken over by government magistrates, *Procurati*, which gives these buildings their name today, *Procuratie*. In 1723 the square was paved with gray trachyte and white marble. Alive at night with orchestra music being played by competing cafés this piazza is a wonderful place to stroll and people watch.

In the Piazza San Marco is the **Basilica di San Marco**, a large church seemingly covered in gold leaf. It was built to house the remains of the republic's patron saint, **St. Mark**, as well as to glorify the strength of Venice's sea power. The first structure was begun in 829. The church we see today was started in 1063 and was originally a Byzantine plan. It was finished in 1073, but then for centuries it was adorned with superb mosaics, precious marbles, and war spoils brought back by merchants, travelers, and soldiers, so that today the church is a mix of Byzantine, Gothic, Islamic and Renaissance materials. As such it is garishly and eclectically magnificent inside and out. *Info:* Piazza San Marco, www.basilicasanmarco.it. Open 9:30am–5:30pm. Vaporetto–San Marco.

Also in the Piazza San Marco is the **Campanile di San Marco** (bell

tower) built in 888 and finally collapsed on July 14, 1902. Reconstructed and re-opened to the public in 1912, it is one of the most convenient places to get a bird's-eye view of the city and the lagoon. The best place is the bell tower of the church of *San Giorgio Maggiore. Info:* Piazza San Marco, Tel. 041/5271-5911. Open November to March 9:30am-4:15pm, April to June and September to October 9am-7pm. €6. Vaporetto–San Marco.

Containing probably the most comprehensive overview of the old Venetian Serenissima Republic is the **Museo Correr & Biblioteca Nazionale**. On display are coins, old maps, prints, drawings, paintings, instruments, seriously high heeled shoes, globes, bronze figurines, ships models, muskets, powder horns, cannons, swords, pikes, backgammon boards, playing cards, jigsaw puzzles, yoyos as well as documents, artifacts and mementos from the Venetian Republic. Also included here is a valuable collection of Byzantine and Venetian bound books, as well as illuminated manuscripts, early printed books, illuminated codices, Greek and Latin codices, manuscripts and early printed books. *Info:* Piazza S. Marco 13/a. San Marco 52, Tel. 041/240-5211, www.museiciviciveneziani.it. Open from April to October

9am-7pm. From November to March 9am-5pm. €11. Price includes entrance to Doge's Palace, Museo Archeologico Nazionale, and the Torre dell'Orologio. Vaporetti-San Marco.

The **Palazzo Ducale**, also in the Piazza San Marco is must-see sight while in Venice. Finished in the 1400s after being started in  the 9th century, this was the seat of the government and the residence of the **Doge**, Venice's supreme head of state. You enter the flamboyant Gothic facade through the **Porta della Carta**, where you'll see the statue of *Doge Frascari*.

After passing through you'll enter the courtyard of the Palace, which has a pair of imposing bronze wells in the middle. Note *The Staircase of the Giants*, so named because of the two colossal statues of Mars and Neptune on either side of the landing made by Sansovino and his pupils. Each new Doge of the Republic of Venice was officially crowned on the landing at the top of the stairs. In this museum you will find some of the most beautiful plaster relief ceilings, marble fireplaces, paintings, sculptures, tapestries, medieval weapons rooms and ancient dungeons anywhere in Europe. Keep your eye out for the medieval chastity belt on display in the pistol room. *Info:* Piazza San Marco, Tel. 041/271-5911, www.museicivicivenezio.it. Open April to October 9am-7pm and November to March 9am-5pm. €11,00. Vaporetto–San Marco.

The **Bridge of Sighs** (Ponte dei Sospiri) connects the Doges Palace and *Prigione Nuovo* (New Prison) and was built in the 17th century to transport convicts from the palace to the prison to face their punishment. The name presumably derives from the sighs of despair from prisoners as they crossed the bridge. When you tour the Palazzo Ducale you get the

opportunity to walk through the bridge to the prison cells where prisoners were kept. *Info:* Vaporetto–San Marco.

Built between 1496 and 1499 the **Torre dell'Orologio** (Clock Tower) has an open terrace upon which stands a bell with two male figures on either side that hammer the bell to indicate the time. These figures have been performing their faithful service for over 500 years. Beneath the terrace that houses these figures is the symbol of Venice, a golden winged lion. Below the lion is a niche that contains a statue of the Virgin and Child. In addition to just telling the time, the clock also indicates the changing of the seasons, the movements of the sun, as well as the phases of the moon. *Info:* Piazza San Marco, Tel. 041/527-15911. €3. Vaporetto–San Marco.

On the other side of the *siestieri* of San Marco from Piazza San

Marco is the oldest of the three bridges spanning the canal, the **Rialto Bridge**, which was originally made of wood. In the 16th century the Doges decided to build a more stable bridge, and Michelangelo himself submitted a design but a local boy, Antonio Da Ponte, was awarded the contract. The bridge was finished in 1592. There are shops lining the span separated by a double arcade from which you can walk out onto the terraces and take some photos over the Grand Canal. *Info:* Vaporetto–Rialto.

In between Piazza San Marco and the Rialto is the opera house, **La Fenice** (The Phoenix). So named because it rose like a phoenix from the ashes of its predecessor, Teatro San Benedetto, burnt down in 1773. More recently it was destroyed by fire on the night of January 29, 1996, and it took almost a decade to resurrect it to its former glory. Now open again, this is one of the most beautiful and famous opera houses in the world. *Info:* Campo San Fantin, Tel. 041/24-24. www.teatrolafenice.it. €7. Vaporetto-Santa Maria del Giglio.

Near La Fenice is the **Palazzo Contarini del Bovolo** with its impressive white marble gothic staircase. The word *bovolo* in Venetian means snail shell, and is aptly named, since the external staircase is spiral-shaped, like a shell. Contarini is the name of the owner who had the tower built around 1499. *Info:* Corte dei Risi o del Bovolo, Tel. 041/270-2464, www.scalabovolo.org. €3.50. Apr-Oct everyday 10am-6pm. Nov-Mar Sat & Sun only10am-4pm. Holidays and Carnevale everyday 10am-4pm. Vaporetto-Rialto or San Marco.

San Polo & Santa Croce
The *siestieri* of San Polo and Santa Croce are both named after churches that stand within their boundaries. San Polo is still one of the liveliest *siestieri* in the city with its small shops and local bars. The bustle of the Erberia and Pescaria markets gives way to a maze of narrow alleys opening onto small squares and serene canals. Sights to see include the spacious **Campo San Polo**, the **Frari Church** and the **Scuola Grande di San Rocco**.

The Santa Croce district lies to the north of San Polo and while it presents an impressive facade to the Grand Canal with its palazzos, the warren of alleys that lie behind them display a humbler side to the city. For the most part, this district is a tangle of tightly packed streets and squares that are fun to explore and offer an insight into the local side of Venice.

There is no better place to start a visit to these two *siestieri* than at the **Frari**. Formally known as the church of **Santa Maria Gloriosa dei Frari** this place is truly glorious, with some of the greatest works by Bellini, Titian, Donatello, and more. This Romanesque-Gothic style Franciscan church was finished in 1443 and the unadorned facade is beautiful in its simplicity. The interior, in contrast, is magnificent. It is laid out in a Latin cross with single aisles set off by twelve huge columns. The main draw for this church is the **tomb of Titian**, the grand master of painting who died of plague in 1576. There are number of Titian's pieces featured inside including *Assumption of the Virgin* done in 1518 hanging over the main altar. *Info:* Campo dei Frari, Tel. 041/275-0462, www.chorusvenezia.org. Open Mon-Sat 9am-6pm & Sun 1pm-6pm. €2.50. Vaporetto–San Toma.

Nearby Frari is the absolutely amazing art collection in the **Scuola Grande di San Rocco**. In Italy there are buildings which house the best of specific artists: the Arena Chapel in Padua (Giotto), San Marco in Florence (Fra Angelico), Sistine Chapel in Rome (Michelangelo) and here in Venice the Scuola Grande di San Rocco (**Tintoretto**). In 1564 Tintoretto was commissioned to decorate the walls and ceilings of the Scuola, and now the Guildhall of San Rocco is home to an extraordinary series of canvases by that amazing artist. The eight on the ground floor portray scenes from the New Testament, while on the ceiling of the Upper Hall, Tintoretto created scenes taken from the Old Testament. On the walls of the Upper Hall are some stunningly detailed carved wooden benches. The building itself was founded in honor of San Rocco, the patron saint of contagious diseases, and it was hoped that the construction of this Scuola would save Venice from the plague. *Info:* Campo San Rocco, 041/523-4864, www.scuolagrandesanrocco.it. April-Oct 9am–5.30pm, Nov-Mar 10am–4pm. €5.50. Vaporetto-San Toma.

If you're getting tired of all the classic art in Venice, visit the **Galleria d'Arte Moderna** in the **Cà Pesaro** for a breath of fresh artistic air. All genres popular after the early 1900s are featured here included some absolutely sublime impressionist works. The artists most recognized in the permanent exhibit are Klimt, Chagall, Matisse, Gaugin, and Kandisky. Also located here is a museum on Oriental art. *Info:* Fondamenta Pesaro, Tel. 041/524-0662, www.museicivicivenziani.it. Open April to October 10am-6pm, November to March 10am-5pm. €5.50. Vaporetto-San Stae.

A leisurely walk away is the opulent Grand Canal façade of **San Stae**, adorned with many beautiful sculptures. Giovanni Grassi's late 17th-century interior reveals the clear influence of Palladio with a single nave flanked on each side by three open chapels.

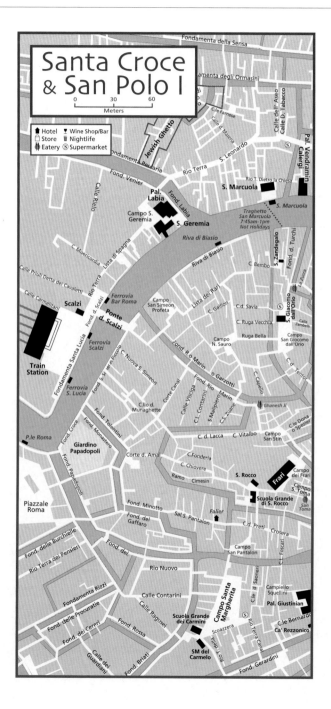

Santa Croce
& San Polo I

0   30   60
Meters

♠ Hotel   ♥ Wine Shop/Bar
♤ Store   ♪ Nightlife
♣ Eatery   Ⓢ Supermarket

Fondamenta della Sensa

amenta degli Ormasini

C.le Farnese

Calle dell' Aseo
Calle D. Tabacco

Jewish Ghetto

Calle di Maiena

Pal. Vendramin Calergi

Ondamenta Pescaria

S. Leonardo

Rio Terra

Rio T. Dietro la Chiesa

S. Marcuola

Calle Riello

Fond. Venier

Pal. Labia

Fond. Labia

Campo S. Geremia

S. Geremia

Traghetto San Marcuola
7:45am-1pm
Not Holidays

S. Marcuola

Fond. d. Turchi

Riva di Biasio

S. Zandegalo

La Zucca

C. Misericordia

Lista di Spagna

Riva di Biasio

C. Bembo

Calle Priuli Detta dei Cavaletti

Rio Terra

S. Giacomo dall'Orio

Calle Carmelitani

Ferrovia Bar Roma

Campo San Simeon Profeta

Lista del Bari

C. Gallion

C.d. Savia

Calle Zambelli

Scalzi

Fond. d. Scalzi

Ponte d. Scalzi

C. Ruga Vecchia

Campo San Giocomo dall'Orio

Ferrovia Scalzi

Fondamenta Santa Lucia

C. Nuova S. Simeon

Ruga Bella

Fond. R o Marin

C.d. Terriol

Train Station

Ferrovia S. Lucia

Fond. Rio Marin o Garzotti

C. Capella

Fond. Tolentini

Corte Canal

Calle Visciga

C.T. Contarini

S. Malpiero

C.S. Zuane

Ghanesh Ji

P.le Roma

Fond. Croce

Fond. Monastero

C.llo d. Munaghette

C. d. Lacca

C. Vitalbo

Campo San Stin

C.le Dona o Spezier

Giardino Papadopoli

Corte d. Amai

C.Fonderia

C. Chiovere

S. Rocco

Campo dei Frari

Frari

Piazzale Roma

Fond. Papadopoli

Ramo

Cimesin

Scuola Grande di S. Rocco

Campo S. Toma

San Toma

Fond. Minotto

Falier

Sal S. Pantalon

C.d. Preti

Crosera

Fond. del Gaffaro

C.t. Foscari

Fond. delle Burchielle

Fond. dei

Campo San Pantalon

Rio Terra dei Pensieri

Rio Nuovo

Campiello Squellini

Fondamenta Rizzi

Calle Contarini

Calle Ragusei

Campo Santa Margherita

C.le d. Saoneri

Pal. Giustinian

Fond. delle Procuratie

Fond. Rossa

Scuola Grande dei Carmini

Scoazzera

Rio Terra Canal

C.le Bernardo

Ca' Rezzonico

Fond. dei Cereri

SM del Carmelo

Calle dei Guardiani

Fond. Briati

Fond. Gerardini

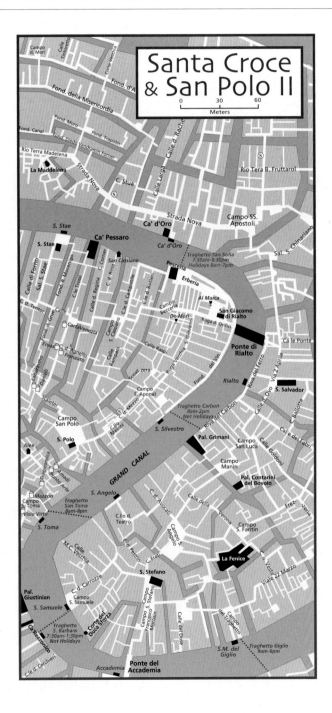

Santa Croce
& San Polo II

0   30   60
Meters

Passing in order along the altars of the south wall, you can see works by Nicolò Bambini, Giuseppe Camerata and Antonio Balestra. On the north wall, the chapels contain works by Torretto, Migliori and Amigoni respectively. The ceiling of the presbytery is decorated with a large canvas by Bartolomeo Letterini, and on the two side walls – above and below the two works by Giuseppe Angeli – are twelve smaller canvasses depicting the *Apostles*. By various artists, these works include such masterpieces as *The Martyrdom of St. Bartholomew* by the young Giambattista Tiepolo, *The Martyrdom of St. James* by Giambattista Piazzetta and *The Liberation of St. Peter* by Sebastiano Ricci. *Info:* Campo di San Stae 1981, Tel. 041275-0462, www.chorusvenezia.org. Monday-Saturday 10am-5pm, Sunday 1pm-5pm. €2.50. Vaporetto-San Stae.

In the large Campo and the adjoining streets near the Rialto bridge in the **Mercati di Erberia & Pesceria** is where Venetians find their daily produce, cheese, fish, and meats. It is a bustling, crowded, fun introduction to authentic Venetian life. *Info:* Vegetable market: Monday - Saturday 8am-1pm; Fish market: Tuesday - Saturday 8am-1pm. Vaporetto-Rialto.

Dorsoduro
Dorsoduro is the *siestieri* first settled when fisherman fled the Germanic tribes swarming across the Alps into Italy during the 5th century CE. Dorsoduro is a quiet neighborhood with shaded squares, serene canals and picturesque residences belonging to Venice's wealthy. Among the attractions are the wide views of the Lagoon both from the eastern tip near the **Santa Maria della Salute** and from the Zattere that run along the southern edge of the *siestieri*. Dorsoduro has a more vibrant side focused around the **Campo Santa Margherita**, which is relatively close to the train station and Piazzale Roma, the entry points for the city.

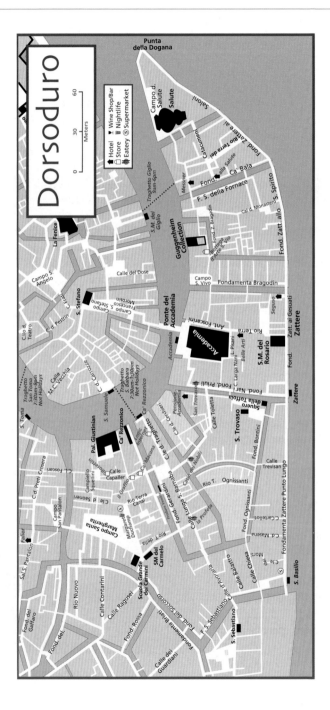

There is no better place to start a tour of this *siestieri* than with Five hundred years of unequaled Venetian art are on display at the **Galleria dell'Accademia**. The collection began in 1750 when the Republic of St. Mark's decided to endow the city with an academy to feature local painters and sculptors (*Accademia di Pittori e Scultori*). Since then it has grown and expanded immensely and is a must-see for anyone visiting Venice who is interested in art. *Info:* Campo della Carita, Tel. 041/522-2247, www.gallerieaccademia.org. Monday 8:15am - 2pm, Tuesday to Sunday 8:15am - 7:15pm. €6.50. Vaporetto–Accademia.

Keep an eye out for the following masterpieces:
- *St. George* – Montegna (Room 4)
- *The Madonna degli Alberelli* – Giovanni Bellini (Room 5)
- *The Tempest* – Giorgione (Room 5)
- *The Miracle of the Slave* – Jacopo Tintoretto (Room 10)
- *Banquet in the House of Levi* – Veronese (Room 10)
- *The Pieta* – Titian (Room 10). The last work of this amazing artist.
- *Legend of St. Ursula* – Vittore Carpaccio (Room 21)
- *Detail of the Arrival of The Ambassadors* – Vittore Carpaccio (Room 21)
- *Presentation at the Temple* – Titian (Room 24)

Best Open Spaces

- **Riva degli Schiavoni** – Castello
- **Riva dei 7 Martiri** – Castello
- **Zattere** – Dorsoduro

Nearby is the **Peggy Guggenheim Collection**. A magnificent 20th century art collection put together by the intriguing American heiress and art aficionado Peggy Guggenheim. It is exhibited in her old home, where she lived until her death in 1979. Here

you'll find all the 20th century art movements including cubism, surrealism, futurism, expressionism, and abstract art. There are works by Dali, Chagall, Klee, Moore, Picasso, Pollock and many others. If you love modern art you have to come here. *Info:* Calle San

Cristoforo, Tel. 041/240-5411, www.guggenheim-venice.it. Open 10am-6pm Mon-Sun. Closed Tuesdays. €10. Vaporetto–Accademia.

One of the sights you'll see from St. Mark's Square across the canal is the truly magnificent church of **Santa Maria della Salute**. Adorned with many statues sitting atop simple flying buttresses, this octagonal church is crowned with a large dome, and a smaller one directly above it. It was erected as thanksgiving for the cessation of a plague that struck Venice in 1630. Inside are six chapels all ornately adorned. On the main altar you'll find a sculpture by Giusto Le Court that represents *The Plague Fleeing The Virgin*. The church is replete with Titian's work, including *The Pentecost* to the left of the third altar, *Death of Abel* on the sacristy ceiling, *Sacrifice of Abraham* in the sacristy, *David and Goliath* on the sacristy ceiling, and an early work *St. Mark and The Other Saints* over the altar in the sacristy. *Info:* Campo della Salute, Tel. 041 522-5558, www.marcianum.it/salute. Open 9am-12am and 3pm-6pm everyday. Vaporetto–Salute.

The **Squero della Toffola** near the Zattere is one of the last working gondola boatyards in Venice. Not much to see really, other than gondolas place keel side up and periodically someone refurbishing them. But still this is a real slice of Venetian history and life. *Info:* Dorsoduro #1097, Tel. 338/345-1116.

One of the centers of Venetian art, conserving an extraordinary body of works by Paolo Caliari, better known as **Veronese**, is the church of **San Sebastiano**. The artist's work here can be divided into three periods, the first from 1555 to 1556, and began with the series of old testament paintings in the sacristy. The second phase is from 1558 to 1559 and includes the frescoes on the upper part of the nave, the decoration of the friar choir, and the organ doors and front. The final period of work is from 1565 to 1570 and includes the large altarpiece *Madonna in Glory with St. Sebastian and other Saints*. Fittingly enough, the church is also Veronese's mausoleum, and his tomb can be seen on the wall to the left of the presbytery. *Info:* Campo di S. Sebastiano, Tel. 041/275-0462, www.chorusvenezia.org. Open Monday-Saturday 10am-5pm, Sunday 3pm-5pm. €2.50. Vaporetto-San Basilio.

At one of the outer edges of the great local Campo Santa Margherita is the **Scuola Grande dei Carmini**, a museum that features a magnificent series of paintings by Tiepolo on the ceiling of the upper hall as well as canvasses by A. Zanchi on the walls. The theme that runs through each piece is the mysteries of the rosary and the virtues of the Virgin Mary. In the hall of archives to the left of the altar upstairs are intricately carved inlaid walnut benches and wall closets. In the lower hall are a series of monochrome paintings to reflect the austerity and simplicity of the Carmelite order. *Info:* Campo dei Carmini 2617, Tel. 041/528-9420. From April to October 9am-6pm, Sunday 9am-4pm. From November to March 9am-4pm. €5. Vaporetto-Ca' Rezzonico.

This magnificent palace, **Cà Rezzonico**, houses the **Museum of Eighteenth Century Venice**, and was designed by the greatest Baroque architect of Venice, Baldassare Longhena for the aristocratic Bons family. It is host to a precious collection of 18th century Venetian furnishings and paintings. Of great interest are the palatial rooms containing paintings by G.B. Tiepolo and others. The third floor contains three rooms of an old

Used Books & Internet

The best place to find inexpensive used books (always a necessity when traveling) *and* to access the internet (another important need) is **Logic Internet**. *Info:* Dorsoduro #2799, Tel. 041/09-94-555, open every day 10am-11pm, Map – Dorsoduro.

pharmacy but is also home to the Egidio Martini Gallery and its 300 masterpieces. A veritable treasure trove of paintings and other artistic delights. *Info:* Fondamenta Rezzonico, Tel. 041/522-5492, www.museicivicineneziani.it. April to October 10am-6pm; November to March 10am-5pm, Closed Tuesdays. €6.50. Vaporetto-Ca' Rezzonico or San Toma.

Burano
The brightly colored houses on this island make it a perfect backdrop for some excellent photographs. Located five and a half miles northeast of Venice, **Burano** occupies four tiny islands. It was first settled in the 5th and 6th centuries, after the collapse of the Roman Empire, by refugees from Altinum fleeing Attila's

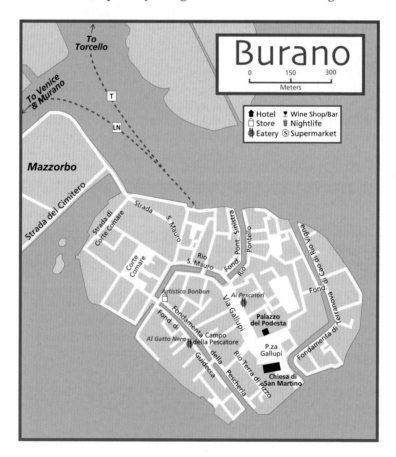

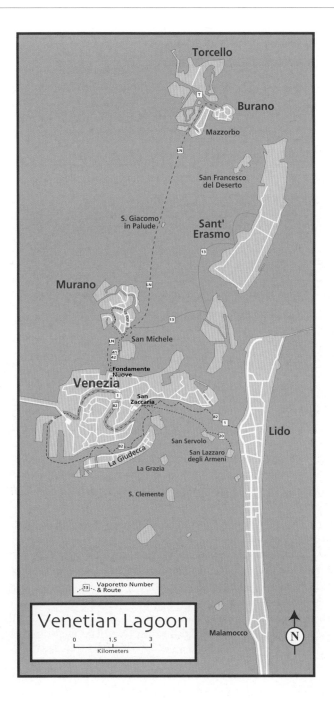

Torcello

Burano

T

Mazzorbo

LN

San Francesco
del Deserto

S. Giacomo
in Palude

Sant'
Erasmo

13

Murano

LN

13

LN

San Michele

41
42

Fondamente
Nuove

Venezia

1

San
Zaccaria

82

82

1

Lido

San Servolo

20

San Lazzaro
degli Armeni

R2

La Giudecca

La Grazia

S. Clemente

13 Vaporetto Number
& Route

Venetian Lagoon

0   1.5   3

Kilometers

N

Malamocco

Burano's Best Eats

• **Ai Pescatori** is an expensive local place that serves tasty fish dishes on the islands main street. *Info:* Via Galuppi 371. Tel. 041/730650. Closed Wednesdays and January. All credit cards accepted. Meal for two €70.

• **Al Gatto Nero** is an exquisite, high-end trattoria with seating on a picturesque canal. *Info:* Via Guidecca 88, Tel. 041/730-120. Closed Mondays. Credit cards accepted. Meal for two €50.

Huns. Mainly known for the traditional art of lace making, which the women of the town have been handing down to their daughters for centuries, Burano is mainly a great place to unwind from the hectic pace of Venice. *Info:* Take Vaporetto LN from Fondamenta Nuove. It takes about 35 minutes.

To start your visit to Burano, take a look at the lace school, **Consorzio dei Merletti**, and satisfy your curiosity about the inner workings of the lace business. *Info:* Palazzo del Podesta in the Piazza B. Galuppi. Tel. 041/730-034. Open Monday–Saturday 9am–6pm, and Sundays 9am–4pm.

Another interesting sight is the **Church of San Martino** in Piazza B. Galuppi, with its leaning tower. This structure has a list of more than 6 feet, not much less than its counterpart in Pisa. Then there is the adorable little shop, **Artistico Bombon** (*Info:* Tel. 041/735-551) that serves up the best candies, all made of glass. Everything here is hand made with exquisite care and tantalizingly detail. Truly whimsical works of art.

Murano

Today the main reason to come to **Murano** is to witness glassware being made the way it has been for centuries, and to wander the streets of an island chain lost in the mists of time, reminding us of a simpler age. Located three quarters of a mile northeast of Venice, and only a five-minute vaporetto ride away, Murano is a tranquil lagoon town spread among five little islands, roughly divided in half by a large canal spanned by the Ponte Longo. During summers local kids like to jump from here into the water.

With only two hotels in the island group, Murano remains predominantly local, what Venice was like before mass tourism overwhelmed it. *Info:* Take Vaporetto **41, 42, 13**, or **LN** from Fondamente Nuove.

Towers dot the skyline, but unlike their ecclesiastical counterparts on Venice which were used as campaniles to ring the faithful to worship, these towers were lookouts for fires from the glass factories. This island chain is world-renowned for its **glass blowing** industry, which dates back to 1291 when the furnaces

Murano's Best Eats

• **Dalla Mora** is on a characteristic canal, in an elegant space, and serves great food. *Info:* Fondamenta Manin 75, Tel. 041/736-344. www.ristorantedallamora.com. Open every day. Meal for two €35.

• **Da Tanduo** is on the same canal as dalla Mora and is a little more local and down to earth. *Info:* Fondamenta Manin 67-68, Tel. 041/739-310. www.datanduo.it. Closed Tuesdays. Meal for two €30.

were banned from Venice as a precaution against fire and industrial espionage. At its height in the 16th century, Murano had 37 glass factories and a population of 30,000. Today the population is a little under 8,000.

What used to be the closely guarded industrial secret of glass manufacture is today common knowledge, but Murano glass is still in demand all over the world because of the skilled artisans that prepare these fine works of art. Check out the **glass factories** on *Fondamenta dei Vetrai*, three of which offer glass blowing exhibitions. If you don't want to take the time to get to these places, **Civam** is convenient to the Vaporetto. (*Info:* Viale Garibaldi 24, Tel. 041/739-323.) Another recommended sight is the **Museo dell'Arte Vetraria**, the glass museum (*Info:* Fondamenta Giustiniano and Fondamenta Manin. Tel. 041/739-586. Open Mondays, Tuesdays, Thursdays and Saturdays 10am–4pm, Sundays 9am–12:30pm. Closed Wednesdays.) Finally, for simplicity and serenty a visit to **Santi Maria e Donato** is in order. (*Info:* Campo San Donato. Open 8am - noon, 4pm - 7pm.)

San Giorgio Maggiore

Besides **the church**, the reason to come here are the **views from the campanile**, which was erected in 1791 to replace an older one that collapsed in 1773. There seems to be a history of collapsing towers in Venice!

The façade of the Basilica is distinctly Palladian, with its three sections divided by four Corinthian columns. In two niches between the columns are statues of *Sts. George* and *Stephen*, and on either side are busts of *Doges Tribuno Mommo* and *P Zini* all by Giulio Moro. The interior is simple yet stunning. It has a single aisle and is shaped like an inverted Latin cross. Three works to admire are: *Crucifix* by Michelozzo in the

second altar on the right, and *Last Supper* and *Shower of Mana* by Tintoretto at the main altar. *Info:* Vaporetto 82 from San Zaccaria or Le Zattere.Tel. 041/522-7827. Open May - September 9.30am-12.30am, 2.30pm-6.30pm, and October - April 9:30-12:30am, 2-5pm. Bell tower €3. Enter from inside church to the far left.

La Guidecca

This island is technically a part of Dorsoduro, but as it is so removed from the main part of Venice, I decided to put here with the other islands. It is home to many locals, a huge Hilton hotel complex, one of Elton John's many homes, and the amazing church of Santissimo Redentore. Out here, though it is only a brief vaporetto ride away (#82 from San Zaccaria or Le Zattere) there will be very few tourists, and a much more relaxing atmosphere.

The main sight to see on this island is **Santissimo Redentore**, one of the most famous and venerated churches in Venice, and the centrepiece of one of the city's most deeply felt public celebrations. During the Feast of the Redentore, on the third Sunday in July, a bridge of boats is built from Dorsoduro all the way to the Redentore. The church itself was constructed between 1577 and 1592 by Andrea Palladio and Antonio Da Ponte, as part of thanks giving for the end of another of the many plagues that struck Venice.

The whitewashed interior has all the grandiose simplicity of a classical temple. The ground plan is not an actual Latin-cross but rather an ingenious series of interconnected spaces (nave, presbytery, choir) forming a ceremonial progression from entrance to high altar. Inside you'll find a magnificent Baroque altar adorned with bronzes by Campagna. In the first chapel on the left is *Christ's Ascension* by Tintoretto, in the third chapel on the right is another work by Tintoretto, and in the third chapel on the left is the *Transport of Christ* by Palma il Giovane. *Info:* Campo del SS. Redentore, Tel. 041/275-0462. www.chorusvenezia.org. Open Monday-Saturday 10am-5pm, Sunday 1pm-5pm. €2.50.

Other than this church, take the time to walk along the waterway facing the Zattere. This is where the community life of the island percolates. There are a couple of places to eat here, but an absolutely fabulous and completely local place to dine, well off the beaten tourist path, yet still easily accessible is **Ristorante Mistra** *(see Best Eats)*.

6. UMBRIA

Umbria – the "Green Heart of Italy" – is a picturesque slice of mother nature's paradise, filled with stunningly beautiful fairy-tale medieval towns.

Besides the natural beauty of the rolling hills, lush valleys, and forested mountains, Umbria is filled with stunningly beautiful medieval towns such as the capital, **Perugia**. Spreading majestically over the ridges of a series of hills, Perugia is interlaced with winding cobblestones streets, an aqueduct turned walkway, ancient *palazzi*, Etruscan and Roman arches, and picturesque piazzas. Besides Perugia, the main towns of interest in Umbria include, **Spoleto**, **Todi**, **Gubbio**, **Orvieto** and **Assisi**. For more information, go to www.bellaumbria.net.

We offer no one-day plans here, but instead weekend and one-week plans. We encourage you to get outside the big three Italian cities and try a weekend, or a week, in a place like Umbria!

A FANTASTIC WEEKEND IN UMBRIA

The ambient medieval city of **Perugia** is an Escher print come to life. With winding streets snaking over and through the hills, archways and palazzi traversing the passageways, sometimes it feels as if up is down and down is up. Along with intriguing museums, great restaurants, fine shops, a vibrant community life abounds. After Perugia, then visit **Assisi**, one of the world's main pilgrimage sites.

Friday Evening

After checking into your hotel in **Perugia**, head over to the **Corso Vannucci** where you will find the typically Italian pastime of "La Passeggiatta" being played out. This is an intricate social dance wherein old and young, male and female, laborer and lord, all stroll in each other's company, break off into smaller groups, re-engaging with the wandering crowds, and generally making those connections that make life in Italy so vibrant.

After wandering with the crowds or sitting at a cafe and watching them parade, head down to the best restaurant in Perugia, **La Taverna**. Excellent atmosphere with its vaulted ceilings and arched doorways, simply superb food, and attentive service. Come prepared to have a great meal in authentic medieval surroundings. This is an upper echelon restaurant — make sure you dress for the occasion. *Info:* Via delle Streghe 8. Tel. 075/572-4128. Closed Mondays, January 7-21 and all of July. All credit cards accepted. Meal for two €60.

After dinner, the social dance continues along the Corso Vanucci, so join back in. Or stop in the **Caffé Sandri** (*see sidebar, page 166*) on the Corso Vanucci, Perugia's best café.

Perugia's Best Cafe

This authentically Perugian eatery, **Caffé Sandri**, is the best place to grab a cappuccino or a bite to eat on the Corso Vannucci. The proprietors are from the same Swiss family, the Schucan's, who founded the café over 130 years ago. *Info:* Corso Vannucci 32. Tel. 075/61012. Open 7am - 11pm daily.

Saturday Morning

Start the day by taking an escalator ride through the **Rocca Paolina** fortress. An entire medieval neighborhood, as well as the Baglioni Palazzi, was covered over to create this ostentatious display of papal authority. In 1860 the fortress was destroyed; what remains underground is a unique exhibition space and a conduit for the escalators from the parking lot at the Piazza Partigiani.

After this short visit, head down the Corso Vannucci to the **Prior's Palace**. Home to the **National Gallery of Umbria** on the third floor, the Prior's Palace is also known as the Town Hall and is an outstanding example of medieval architecture. Begun in 1293, it was completed in 1443 after the building was consolidated with other homes and pre-existing towers all under one huge roof. Check out the ornamental entrance with its friezes, twisted columns, sculptures and ornamental foliage. The Atrium inside the entrance off of Corso Vannucci and is a covered courtyard with pillars and vaults.

The entrance on the Piazza IV Novembre is just to the left of the tourist information office, up a flight of stairs and through a pointed portal. Through the portal is the **Sala dei Notari** (Lawyer's Room), an impressive hall that has some exquisite frescoes and grandiose arches. See also the **Sala del Consignio Comunale** (City Council Hall), which contains a fresco by Pinturicchio, and the **Sala Rossa** (Red Hall) containing a mural by Dono Doni.

The National Gallery is the third floor and is a must-see in Perugia. It contains masterly examples of the paintings from the Umbrian school, which date from the 13th century CE to the 19th. Perugia's most famous artist, **Perugino**, is featured in rooms 12-14 with his *Adoration of the Magi* (room 12), *Miracles of San*

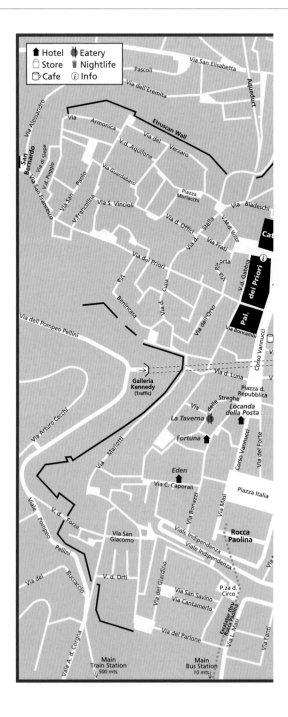

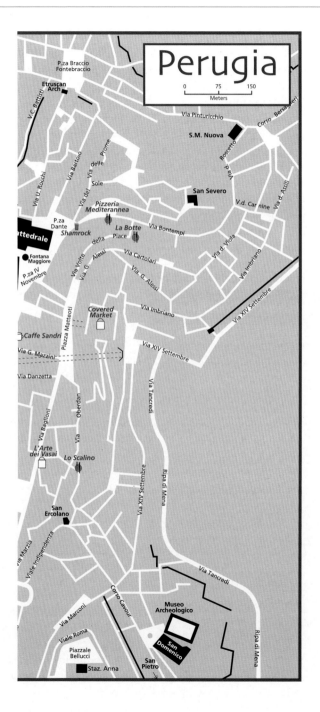

Bernardino (room 13) and *The Dead Christ* (room 14). *Info:* Corso Vannucci, Tel. 075/574-1247. Closed the first Monday of the month. Open 9am-7pm, holidays 9am-1pm.

Saturday Afternoon
Now head out to the Piazza IV Novembre and the **Fontana Maggiore**, the monumental heart of medieval Perugia. Built between 1275 and 1278 with the decorative sculptures created by Nicola and Giovanni Pisano, and topped by a bronze basin, the fountain has an upper stone basin held up by slender columns with a variety of capitals.

Time for a lunch of the best pizza in town at **Pizzeria Mediterannea**, Piazza Piccinino 11/12 (*see Best Eats*).

After refueling, head back down the Corso Vanucci to the Piazza IV Novembre and the **Cattedrale di San Lorenzo**. The steps on the left side of the building facing the Piazza IV Novembre and the Fontana Maggiore is *the* place to hang out, whether it's sunny or not. The building itself is an imposing Gothic church constructed between the 14th and 15th centuries CE leaving an incomplete facade. The main entrance is between Piazza Dante and Piazza IV Novembre and has a coarse stone facade with a massive Baroque portal and a large circular window above that.

Inside, the Chapel of the Holy Ring is enclosed by 15th century wrought iron railings — to the left as you enter — has a silver and gold plated copper tabernacle which contains the

Land of Truffles

Truffles have been described as the ultimate indulgence, and if you have ever tasted a dish flavored with them you will realize that this is an incredible understatement. The aroma of *tartufi*, or as the epicureans say 'perfume', is tantalizingly seductive. When in Umbria during truffle season (Oct-Dec), you simply must order truffles. Compared to US prices, in Umbria they cost very little. So indulge!

onyx wedding ring purported to have been worn by the Virgin Mary. Hmmm? Note also the beautiful stained glass windows and carved choir seats. In the right transept are the tombs of three popes.

From here, let's head to the nearby **Roman Aqueduct** on Via di Aquedotto. What used to be a functioning aqueduct is now a pedestrian street. This may be your only chance to walk along an ancient aqueduct, so take it while you have it. Lining the aqueduct are quaint homes. From this height you can look down onto other streets and passageways, offering an interesting perspective.

From here head over to the **Etruscan Arch** in Piazza Fortebraccio. Also known as the Arch of Augustus, the original structure was built in the 3rd and 2nd century BCE. Later there were Roman-era additions as well as some during the 16th century. This huge and imposing structure is bordered by some of the old walls of Perugia. Comprised of two powerful Etruscan towers, the right one lowered by an invasion, while the one on the left has an enticing private patio on the top and a Roman fountain on the bottom. Above the gate is a sentinel arch, so named because that is where the guards for the city would keep watch.

And now, after seeing the best sights in Perugia, let's head to the nearby small town of **Deruta**, where the world famous pottery of the same name is made. Located 15 kilometers outside of Perugia, this old town is situated on a hill overlooking the valley of the Tiber. *Info:* If you do not have a car, the only way to get here is by bus. Pick up the bus schedule at the information office in Perugia.

Saturday Evening
After returning to Perugia, head over to **La Botte**, a small, simple, down-to-earth trattoria that serves scrumptious food (*see Best Eats*).

Sunday Morning
Today we head over to **Assisi**, one of Italy's most frequented pilgrimage sites. Dramatically situated on a verdant hill highlighted by olive groves and cypress trees reaching right up to the city walls, the beautiful medieval home to St. Francis and St. Clare stretches majestically along the slopes of Mount Subasio. This stunningly beautiful little Umbrian hill town is a center for art and culture, and a major religious pilgrimage site. As a result, be prepared for crowded streets.

Sadly, some of the town's charm was instantaneously leveled when an earthquake struck in 1997, causing severe damage to the city's structures, especially the Basilica of St. Francis. Many of Giotto's fine frescoes were destroyed in this natural catastrophe. An extensive renovation of the church was completed a few years ago. Assisi is a wonderful destination, but you may still find scaffolding and supports in place to secure certain structures of historic significance.

The place to start any tour of Assisi is at the **Basilica of St Francis**. Majestic and picturesque, the basilica and its accompanying cloistered convent have graced this rural landscape for many centuries. The **Lower Church** is entered through an intricate double portal surmounted with three rose windows. Even in the dim light the star-spangled blue vaults between the arches is stunningly beautiful. The **remains of St. Francis** are located in a stone urn in the crypt, which is down a staircase located in the middle part of the nave. A number of side chapels have significant frescoes, including some by Cimabue and Giotto.

The façade of the **Upper Church** faces the town and looks over the wide lawn of the Piazza Superiore di San Francesco; it consists of one nave with a transept and a polygonal arch, with stunningly colorful frescoes by Cimabue.

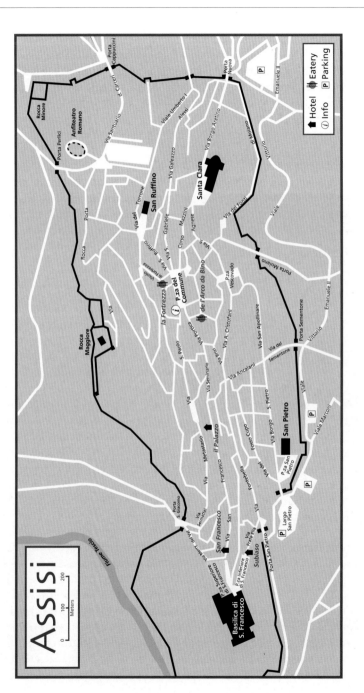

Assisi

0   100   200
Meters

Hotel
(i) Info
Eatery
P Parking

Next up is the **Church of San Pietro** located just inside the city walls, this Romanesque-Gothic 13th century church has a simple yet beautiful rectangular façade. The upper level has three rose windows, and the lower has three portals. The interior contains one nave and two aisles, and has some 14th century frescoes and the ruins of some tombs of the same century. For simple beauty and peaceful serenity this is a fine church to visit.

Sunday Afternoon
For lunch, let's wander up to the **Piazza del Commune** at the

center of the town. All around are places to eat, but the two best are **La Fortrezza** and **Taverna de L'Arco da Bino** (*see Best Eats*).

Next up is the **Basilica of Santa Clara**. Classically Gothic, this 13th century church dominates the piazza of the same name. Attached to the left side of the building are three large flying buttresses with a slender bell tower rising up from the apse. The facade is decorated with two closed horizontal bands, is divided into three levels, and has a wonderful rose window and a plain portal flanked by two lions. The interior is in the form of a Latin cross with a single nave. The crypt, reached by a flight of steps, contains some of the remains of St. Clare in a glass coffin; the rest are in SM Sopra Minerva in Rome.

From here, head over to the **Cathedral of San Ruffino**. Commonly known as the **Duomo**, the beautiful Romanesque facade is divided into three sections. To the side of the Duomo is the massive bell tower adorned with small arches at the top and an offset clock on the same level as the top layer of the church. Inside, the baptismal font in the right aisle was used to baptize St. Francis, St. Clare, St. Agnes, and St. Gabriel. And don't miss the crypt, underneath the cathedral: you can find a Roman sarcophagus that once contained the remains of San Ruffino.

Just down the road from here past Piazza Matteoti is a **Roman amphitheater** worthy of a short visit. After that … your weekend in Umbria is over.

A WONDERFUL WEEK IN UMBRIA

A week in Umbria will offer you a wonderful introduction to Etruscan, Roman, Romanesque and Renaissance works of art and architecture. **Perugia** has the imposing and historically significant Etruscan Arch and Roman aqueduct turned walkway. In **Gubbio** there are excellent examples of an ancient Roman temple, mausoleum, and theater just outside of an incredibly beautifully, well-preserved and scenic medieval hill town. **Orvieto** has its extensive Etruscan Necropolises and an awe-inspiring cathedral. **Todi** a wonderful respite from the hectic pace of modern life. **Spoleto** is the jewel of the region, an ambient hill town home to some of the best restaurants in Italy, a direct result of the fact that this town hosts the world-renowned **Spoleto Festival** every summer. **Assisi** is a colorful hill town made famous by being the birthplace of two saints, St. Francis and St. Clare, and has long been a major pilgrimage site. *Info:* www.bellaumbria.net.

RECOMMENDED PLAN: The towns to visit are listed in order of preference (Perugia, Gubbio, Orvieto, Todi, Spoleto, and finally Assisi). And within each town, sights for that town are listed in order of preference as well. Spend two days in Perugia, then spend a day each in the other towns. Getting to Gubbio and Todi you will definitely need a car.

Perugia
Note: see map on pages 166-167.

With winding medieval streets snaking over and through the hills, archways and palazzi traversing the passageways, **Perugia** offers intriguing museums, great restaurants, fine shops, and a vibrant community life. *Info:* turismo.comune.perugia.it.

The best place to start any visit to Perugia is on the **Corso Vanucci**, the city's main street. Here at all times of the day you will find the populace wandering in a free form community stroll, known in Italy as a *Passeggiatta*. Come here before and after dinner, and on Saturdays to really see what true community life is like. The Corso starts at the Piazza Italia where you can find the Rocca Paolina, and ends at the Piazza IV Novembre where you can find the Fontana Maggiore.

At one end of the Corso Vanucci is the **Rocca Paolina**, a fortress built by Sangallo the Younger for Pius III to emphasize the Papal States dominance over the city of Perugia. An entire medieval neighborhood, as well as the Baglioni Palazzi, were razed over to create this ostentatious display of papal authority. In 1860 upon the liberation of Italy the fortress was destroyed by the populace, and what remains underground is now used as a unique exhibition space, and as a conduit for the escalators from Piazza Partigiani.

Located on the other end of the Corso Vanucci in the Piazza IV Novembre is the **Fontana Maggiore**, the monumental heart of medieval Perugia. Built between 1275 and 1278 with the decorative sculptures created by Nicola and Giovanni Pisano. Topped by a bronze basin, the fountain has an upper stone basin held up by slender columns with a variety of capitals.

Just down the hill from the Fontana Maggiore are the remains of a once-functioning **Roman Aqueduct** that is now a pedestrian street. This may be your only chance to walk along an ancient aqueduct. From this height you get to look down onto other streets and passageways, offering an interesting perspective of this Umbrian hill town.

Back up on the Corso Vanucci is the **Prior's Palace**, home to the **National Gallery of Umbria** on the third floor, the Prior's Palace is an outstanding example of medieval architecture. The entrance on Corso Vannucci is through a round portal, almost underneath an imposing tower and guarded by two Griffins – the symbols of the city – sinking their claws into two calves. Before entering, take some time to check out the ornamental entrance with its friezes, twisted columns, sculptures and ornamental foliage.

The National Gallery contains masterly examples of the paintings from the Umbrian school, which date from the 13th century CE to the 19th. Perugia's most famous artist, Perugino, is featured in rooms 12-14 with his *Adoration of the Magi* (room 12), *Miracles of San Bernardino* (room 13) and *The Dead Christ* (room 14). Also accessible off of the Corso Vanucci is the Collegio del Cambio. To the left of the facade of the Palazzo dei Priori, beyond the archway to the Via dei Priori are three portals, through which you can enter the fresco-laden room containing major works by the cities most famous artist, **Perugino**. *Info:* Corso Vannucci. Tel. 075/574-1247. Closed the first Monday of the month. Open 9am-7pm, holidays 9am-1pm.

Located in the Piazza IV Novembre, the **Cathedral of San Lorenzo** is an imposing Gothic church constructed between the 14th and 15th centuries CE and has a coarse stone facade with a massive Baroque portal and a large circular window above that. The left side of the building facing Piazza IV Novembre is decorated with ornamental masks by Scalza flanking the plain portal with its ancient wooden doors. Above the portal is the votive Crucifix placed here in 1539. To the right side of the portal is the 15th century pulpit of San Bernardino. To the left of the portal is the *Statue of Pope Julius III*, an intricate bronze by Danti from the 16th century.

Perugia's Market

The **covered market** of Perugia is located off of the Piazza Matteoti and through the Palazzo Capitano del Popolo, offering dry goods, leather products and other crafts in the upstairs section, and fruits, vegetables and other foods downstairs. *Info:* Open 7:00am-1pm Monday-Saturday.

The interior is divided by octagonal columns into one nave and two aisles. The Chapel of San Bernardino — to the right as you enter — which is enclosed by beautiful wrought iron railings, contains a stunning fresco by Federico Barocci. In the **Chapel of the Holy Ring**, enclosed by 15th century wrought iron railings — to the left as you enter — is a silver and gold plated copper tabernacle which contains the onyx wedding ring purported to have been worn by the Virgin Mary.

Also note the 16th century multi-colored stained glass windows by Arrigo Fiammingo and the 16th century carved choir seats. In the right transept are the tombs of Pope Martino IV, Pope Urbano IV and Pope Innocenzo III as well as the marble sculpture of Pope Leo XIII.

Dedicated to the patron saint of Perugia, the **Church of San Ercolano** stands on the exact spot where he was martyred when the Goths seized the city in 547 CE. The interior is accessed through a beautiful double staircase built in 1607. At the high altar is a noteworthy sarcophagus that contain the remains of San Ercolano. Around the dome are some exquisite frescoes dating to the 16th century which depict a number of scenes from the Bible. Every inch of these walls are covered with frescoes and bas-relief work. *Info:* Via Marzia. Open 7am-noon & 4-7pm.

Built in the 10th century on the site of an even older cathedral, the **Basilica of Saint Peter** is dominated by a beautiful 15th century campanile. You enter the church through a run-down but at the same time elegant porticoed courtyard. The dark interior contains a single nave with two aisles divided by 18 Roman columns. This church is elaborate in its decoration — very much like San Ercolano — and has a wealth of art, including some works by

Caravaggio and Perugino. Behind the altar, through the intricately carved 17th century choir, is a small terrace at the back of the church overlooking an incredible panoramic view of the surrounding countryside. *Info:* Borgo XX Giugno. Open 7am-noon & 4-7pm.

The date that the **Oratory of San Bernadino** was completed

(1461) can be seen on the facade in roman numerals (MCCCCLXI). Masterly crafted, the facade is a wonderful series of sculptures of saints in the Perugia-Renaissance style. The 15th century Gothic interior contains the Tomb of Beato Egidio and an ancient 4th century CE Roman-era Christian sarcophagus. *Info:* Piazza San Francesco. Open 7am-noon & 4-7pm.

The **Etruscan Arch** is located in Piazza Fortebraccio and is also known as the Arch of Augustus; the original structure was built in the 3rd and 2nd century BCE. Later there were Roman-era additions as well as some during the 16th century. This huge and imposing structure is bordered by some of the old walls of Perugia, clearly indicating the lengths attackers would have to go through to sack the city. Comprised of two powerful Etruscan towers, above the gate is a sentinel arch, so named because that is where the guards for the city would keep watch.

Deruta
Located 15 kilometers from Perugia, Deruta is where the world famous pottery of the same name is made. This old town is situated on a hill overlooking the valley of the Tiber and is filled

with the largest selection of fine ceramic pottery anywhere. *Info:* If you do not have a car, the only way to get here is by bus. Bus schedules are available at the information office in Perugia.

Gubbio

Gubbio is an ancient settlement that spreads languidly out along the wind-swept ridges of **Mount Ingino** with the **Torrente Camignano** river flowing through the center. This incredibly beautiful hill town was founded by the ancient Umbrian people and eventually taken over by the Etruscans, as chronicled to in the **Eugubine Tablets** — the Rosetta Stone for ancient central Italian languages, culture, and history — which are located here in Gubbio. These seven bronze tablets give illuminating insight into how the city was run between the 3rd century and 1st century BCE, and are partially written in the Umbrian language — which is a derivation of Etruscan — and simultaneously in a rudimentary form of Latin. *Info:* www.comune.gubbio.pg.it/territorio/turismo.htm.

The layout of the town is Roman with its structured grid pattern and it is also quite medieval with its ancient buildings, city walls, and winding streets and steps flowing up and down the mountain. Also added onto this atmosphere are plenty of more 'modern' Renaissance towers and palazzi mingling with Gothic churches, making Gubbio one of the most beautiful places to visit in Umbria.

Looking out over the town is the imposing structure of the

Palazzo dei Consoli. Located at the east end of the Piazza Grande this is the architectural and monumental core of the city. Ringed with Renaissance *palazzi,* one of which is the **Palazzo Pretorio**, from this piazza you can get some stunning panoramic views.

The Palazzo dei Consoli is really two 14th century buildings, architecturally associated but clearly distinct. Simple and elegant, the palace is graced with a magnificent Gothic portal, in which are a set of steps that face out onto the piazza. The facade is divided by vertical pilaster strips, topped with turrets over which looks a small bell tower.

Also known as the Palazzo dei Popolo, the building now houses the **Picture Gallery** which has some paintings from Gubbio dating from the 14th and 16th centuries; and the **Archaeological Museum**, which houses the seven historically significant **Eugubine Tablets**, the Rosetta Stone for Central Italy. These tablets have a corresponding Umbrian language text, which evolved alongside the Etruscan, and a rudimentary form of Latin. There are also some interesting ancient archaeological finds like stone ceramics and coins. Not organized and catalogued too precisely, but interesting and educational nonetheless.

A simple austere brick **Duomo** built in the 12th century is located up the hill from the older Roman town. Simple and plain inside, except for the paintings and frescoes of the 16th century Umbrian artists along the walls, the church also has an incredibly detailed altar space, organ and choir. This cathedral is a wonderful example of austere medieval beauty.

Located directly across from the Duomo, the **Palazzo Ducale** is a prime example of Renaissance architecture. Built in 1470 on the site of an older Lombard palace, this building contains a splendid internal courtyard surrounded by porticos. In the basement there is an archaeological excavation of the alterations made atop the building during the Renaissance. The palace's foundation can be seen as can segments of the original plumbing. Fragments of medieval ceramics found during the excavations are also on display.

A cable car ride away is the **Basilica of San Ubaldo,** at the summit of Mount Ingino, the terminus for the traditional **Corsa dei Ceri festival**, a celebration where an ancient tower is carted up the hill. The three wooden towers used in the Corso dei Ceri festival are on display here year round. On the hillside above the church are the remains of the 12th century Rocca.

On the other side of town, in the valley just outside the old city

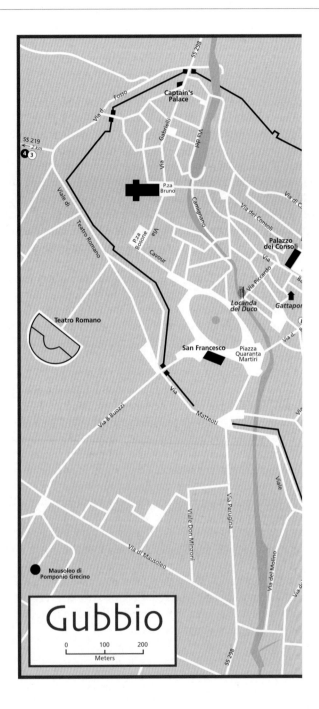

SS 298

Via d. Fosso

Captain's Palace

Via Gabrielli

Via del

SS 219
2 km
4 3

Viale di

Via di Teatro Romano

P.za Bruno

Camignano

P.za Bosone

Via

Via Cavour

Via dei Consoli

Via di Co

Palazzo dei Consoli

Via

Via Riccardo

B

Locanda del Duco

Gattapo

i

Teatro Romano

San Francesco

Piazza Quaranta Martiri

Via d.

Via

Matteoti

Vi

Via B Buozzi

Viale Don Minzoni

Via Perugina

Viale

Via del Molino

Via di

Via di Mausoleo

● Mausoleo di Pomponio Grecino

Gubbio

0   100   200
Meters

SS 298

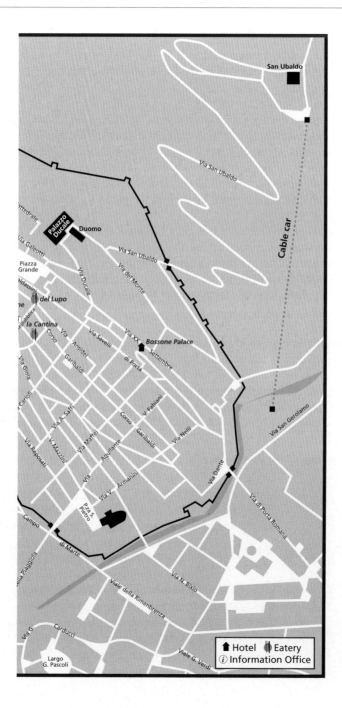

San Ubaldo

Via San Ubaldo

Cable car

Cattedrale

Palazzo Ducale

Duomo

Via Galeotti

Piazza Grande

Via San Ubaldo

Via del Monte

Via Ducale

aldassini

del Lupo

epubblica

la Cantina

Via Savelli

Via Ansidei

Via XX Settembre

di Porta

Bossone Palace

Corso Garibaldi

Via Gioia

Carioli

Via A. Saffi

Corso Garibaldi

V. Fabiani

Via Nelli

Via San Gerolamo

V. Mazzini

Via Marei

Via Aquilante

Via V. Armanini

Via Dante

Via di Porta Romana

Via Reposati

Via

P.za S. Pietro

Campo

di Marte

elia Piaggiola

Viale della Rimenbrenza

Via N. Bixio

Via G. Carducci

Viale G. Verdi

Largo G. Pascoli

🛏 Hotel 🍴 Eatery
ⓘ Information Office

walls, is the ancient **Roman Theater** (*Teatro Romano*), one of the largest and best preserved in Italy. Now converted to a verdant park, the old theater is home to live productions through July and mid-August.

Nearby, on the large Piazza Quaranta Martiri, is the **Church of St. Francis**, built in the 13th century with a bare facade, a Gothic portal and a small rose window. When the sun streams in through the large pointed windows along the sides and the colored windows in the apse, this church simply glows. The attached cloisters should be visited if open.

In another part of town is a gory but educational display. In the 13th century **Captain of the People's Palace** you will find the **Museum of Torture Instruments**. The displays are enlightening, a refreshing reality check concerning the relative safety of modern life. *Info:* Via del Capitano del Popolo #6.

Orvieto
Orvieto is one of Umbria's most scenic towns, resting picturesquely on the top of a hill bordered by protective cliffs. Orvieto has a rich array of winding medieval streets and stunning architecture, not the least of which is the magnificent Duomo. The town is also famous for the savory Orvieto wine and its tasty olive oil. The town also is a ceramic center and local artisans create intricate wood carvings as well as delicate lace. *Info:* www.orvietoonline.it.

The heart of this Umbrian hill town is its absolutely stunning **Duomo**. Located in the Piazza del Duomo, its facade is covered with bas-reliefs, colorful mosaics, and radiating frescoes. The pointed portals literally jump out at you, and the rose window — flanked by figures of the Prophets and Apostles — is a treasure to behold. Bring binoculars to admire all the intricate detail, since the facade is an entire museum in and of itself.

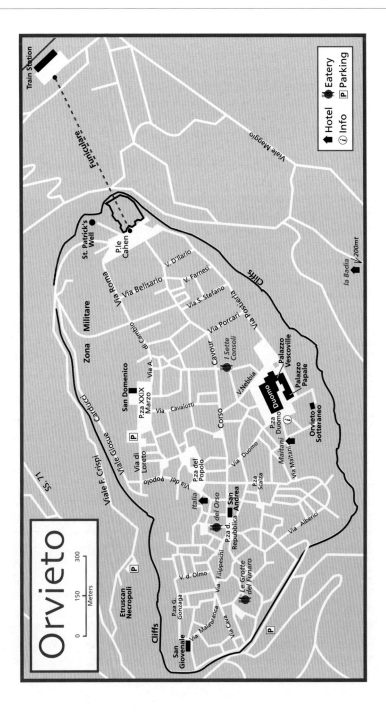

Orvieto

0 150 300
Meters

Train Station

Funiculare

Viale Maggio

Hotel ● Eatery
ⓘ Info Ⓟ Parking

la Badia

↗ 200mt

St. Patrick's Well

P.le Cahen

V. D'Ilario

V. Farnesi

Via Belisario

Via Roma

Zona Militare

Via S. Stefano

Via Porcari

Via A.. di Curpio

Cliffs

Via le postierla

Cavour

I. Sette Consoli

Palazzo Vescoville

San Domenico

Pza XXIX Marzo

Via Cavalotti

V.Nebbia

Palazzo Papale

Corso

Duomo

Pza Duomo

ⓘ

Orvieto Sotteraneo

Maitani

Via Maitani

Via Capucci

Viale Giosue

Ⓟ

Via di Loreto

Via Duomo

Pza del Popolo

Viale F. Crispi

S.S. 71

Via del Popolo

Pza Scalza

Italia

del Orso

Pza d.

San Andrea

Pza d. Repubblica

Via Alberici

Ⓟ

Etruscan Necropoli

V. d. Olmo

Via Filippeschi

Le Grotte del Funaro

Pza G. Gonzaga

Via Malabranca

Via Cava

San Giovenale

Cliffs

Ⓟ

The exterior walls are alternating horizontal layers of black basalt and pale limestone in the distinctive Pisan style. This same style is translated into the interior, covering both the walls, and the columns that divide the church into a nave and two aisles. The christening font is stunning in its intricacies. The apse is lit by 14th century stained glass windows by Bonino and contains frescoes by Ugolino di Prete Ilario.

In the right transept behind an artistic 16th century wrought iron railing is the beautiful *Capella Nuova*, which contains Luca Signorelli's superlative *Last Judgment*. It is purported to be the inspiration for Michelangelo's Last Judgment in the Sistine Chapel. A must see, since it is considered one of the greatest frescoes in Italian art. The chapel also contains frescoed medallions depicting poets and philosophers ranging from Homer to Dante.

Recently excavated and opened for tourists, the tours of **Orvieto Sotteraneo** under the city take you on a journey through history, including Etruscan wells, a 17th century oil mill, a medieval quarry, ancient pigeon coops and much more, all thoroughly narrated by well-trained guides. *Info:* Guided tours every day starting at 11am and go until 6pm. €5. Tours in English at 12:15pm and 5:15pm.

Located near where the cable car brings you up from the train station, **St. Patrick's Well** was built for Pope Clement VII and served as a reservoir for the nearby fortress if the city was ever put under siege. Hence it is also known as the Fortress Well. Its ingenious cylindrical cavity design was completed in the beginning of the 16th century. Going to a depth of 62 meters, there are two parallel concentric staircases, each with 248 steps ... go on and count them if you want. The water carriers with their donkeys used one spiral staircase for going up and the other for going down. Each staircase has a separate entrance and is ringed by large arched windows. In the public gardens above the well are the overgrown remains of an Etruscan temple. *Info:* Open daily from 9am to 6pm.

Located to the right and at the rear of the Duomo, the **Palazzo Vescoville** houses the **Archaeological Museum**, which has a collection of material excavated from the Etruscan Necropoli that are located nearby the city. *Info:* Open 9am – 7pm, Holidays 9am-1pm; admission €2.

Located to the right of the Duomo, the **Palazzo Papale** was once the residence of a long line of popes when they came to visit the city. On the first floor is the **Cathedral Museum**, which displays miscellaneous works of art, mostly from the Duomo or about the Duomo. *Info:* Open 10:30am-1pm and 2-6pm in winter and 3-7pm in summer.

On the edge of the Piazza della Repubblica, the plain church of **San Andrea** is best known for its dodecagonal campanile, a twelve-sided bell-tower. Inside, the wooden altar by Scalza is worthy of note, as is the pulpit.

This part of town is the ideal location to take relaxing walks, filled with stunning panoramic vistas. So take out your walking shoes and hike around the outside of this town soaking up the glorious vistas.

Todi
An ancient and attractive city surrounded by medieval walls and filled with quaint winding streets, **Todi** rises up among green hills above where the Naia flows into the Tiber. Todi stands apart from the advance of time, and the residents of the city still far outnumber the tourists, a situation you will find true all over Umbria, but especially so in Todi. *Info:* www.comune.todi.pg.it.

Todi is a place to undertake casual meandering around the hilly cobblestone streets lined with medieval homes – some set into old Roman and Etruscan walls.

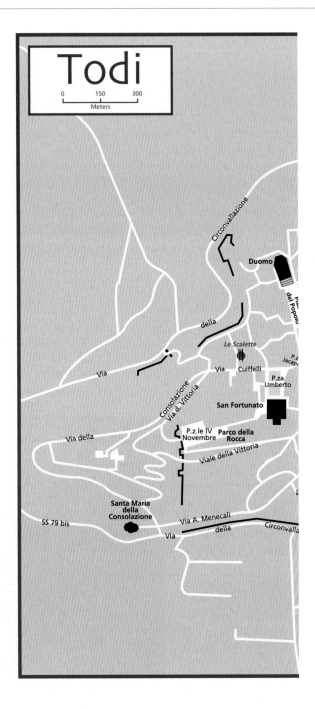

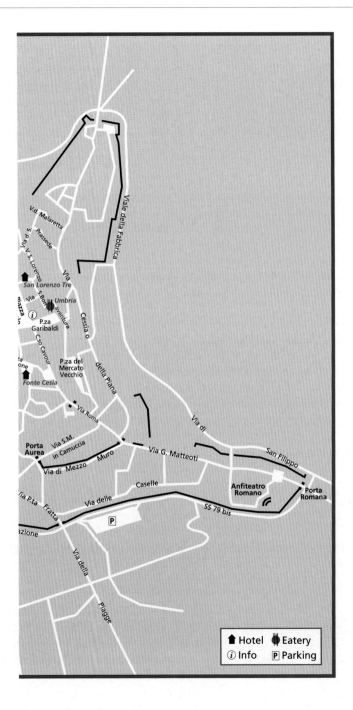

V.d. Malaretta

Prassede

Via di S. Lorenzo

Via S. Lorenzo

Via

Viale della Fabbrica

San Lorenzo Tre

Via S. Bon...

Umbria

S. Bonaventura

(i)

P.za Garibaldi

Cessia o

Piazza

C.so Cavour

della Piana

P.za del Mercato Vecchio

ta one

Fonte Cesia

Via Roma

Via di

Via G. Matteoti

San Filippo

Porta Aurea

Via S.M. in Camuccia

Muro

Via di Mezzo

Caselle

Anfiteatro Romano

Porta Romana

Via P.ta Fratta

Via delle

SS 79 bis

P

...azione

Via della

Piagge

| ↑ Hotel | ♨ Eatery |
| (i) Info | P Parking |

The **Piazza Vittorio Emanuele II**, also known as the **Piazza del Popolo**, is the heart of Todi. Located on the site of an ancient Roman Forum, it is one the most beautiful medieval squares in all of Europe. Dominated by the Duomo, the piazza is surrounded by numerous monumental palaces. Across from the Duomo is the turreted **Palazzo dei Priori**, built in the 14th century then joined together with some pre-existing buildings. The bronze eagle — the symbol of Todi — which stands out above the second order of windows, was cast in 1339.

Also in the piazza is the **Palazzo del Capitano**, from the 13th century, and how houses the **Roman-Etruscan Museum and Civic Picture Gallery**, where you will find Roman and Etruscan artifacts and some fine paintings by Umbrian and Tuscan artists, as well as gold and ceramic work.

The **Duomo** dominates the Piazza Vittorio Emanuele II with its rectangular facade of three Rosetta windows and the same number of Gothic portals. Flanking this facade is the robust bell tower that was once used as a military watchtower. The interior is divided into three sections. In the left aisle is an interesting bronze of San Martino by Fiorenzo Bacci. The counter facade has a 16th century fresco of the *Last Judgment* by Faenzone. Unfortunately it has not been well preserved but is still powerful. Also take note of the wooden choir behind the altar, as well as the two paintings portraying *St. Peter* and *St. Paul*, to the left and right of the altar, done by Spagna. For €7.50 you can get a ticket to see the crypt which is a rather non-descript underground area but interesting for medieval history buffs.

Rising up above the town the Gothic church of **San Fortunato** was built between the 13th and 15th centuries. The half-completed facade overlooks the top of a scenic but fatiguing series of steps and their accompanying green space. There are three portals, the middle one richly decorated with a variety of colonnades, and is flanked by two statues of *Gabriel* and *Virgin Mary*. *Info:* Open winter 9:30am-12:30pm & 3-5pm; summer 8:30am-12:30pm & 3-7pm.

Near San Fortunato is the **Parco della Rocca** where you have nice panoramic views, peace and quiet — a place to picnic or cuddle — with a rose garden to stimulate your nose.

Located a little ways outside of the city walls, **Santa Maria della Consolazione** is a delightful example of Renaissance architecture. Begun in 1508 and finished almost a century later, this lovely church, like San Fortunato, stands out from the diminutive skyline of the town. In the shape of a Greek Cross with a large central dome there are four apses each crowned with its own half dome.

Spoleto

Spoleto is a great destination because of the combination of medieval charm, natural setting, excellent restaurants, refined shops and galleries, few tourists, and incredibly friendly and accommodating locals. The ancient medieval town itself, with its winding streets and old buildings, is like something out of a storybook. *Info:* www.comune.spoleto.pg.it.

Even though this is one of the better-preserved medieval towns in all of Italy, Spoleto is still only lightly touristed. That is except during the world-famous **Spoleto Festival** held in June every year, when tens of thousands of tourists descend here to savor a two-week extravaganza of performing arts.

Because of this festival Spoleto has some of the best restaurants in all of Italy, superb artisans' shops, and small galleries and studios filled with locally produced painting and sculpture that is of top quality. But that's not all. The main distinguishing feature about Spoleto is that it offers instant access to inspiring natural settings.

Around the **Rocca** fortress is where the locals do their evening Passegiatta. The structure itself dominates the cityscape of Spoleto. Finished in the second half of the 14th century, from here you can get wonderful panoramic photos of the town and valley. Once a residence of the popes and other aristocracy, it has now been restored to its former splendor and today you can go on brief guided tours. The Rocca is being prepared to house a museum relating to the medieval duchy of Spoleto. *Info:* €5, open 3-6pm Monday-Friday, 10am-noon & 3-6pm Saturday and Sunday.

Past the Rocca is a medieval aqueduct, the **Ponte delle Torre**, spanning a gorge and leading to a pristine, verdant hill covered

with hiking trails. This 13th century span connects two hillsides and is 230 meters long and 76 meters high and has towering piers and narrow arcades, which cast incredible shadows over the valley in the late afternoon light. It no longer carries water but serves as a footbridge over the valley.

Rising up from the picturesque main square is the Romanesque **Duomo**. Built in the 12th century, it has an imposing facade of Rosetta windows and a mosaic created by Solsterno in 1207. The bell tower was constructed with material removed from ancient Roman ruins. The interior is simple with a nave and two aisles. You will find a variety of religious art including some magnificent works by Pinturicchio in the Chapel of Bishop Eroli. *Info:* Open November-February 8am-1pm & 3-5:30pm; March-October 8am-1pm & 3-6:30pm.

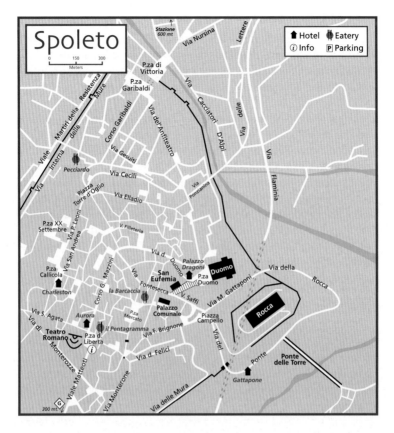

Located near the Duomo, **San Eufemia** is one of the finest examples of simple Umbrian-Romanesque architecture. Constructed in the first half of the 12th century, the facade is basic but inspiring, with a portal window and a sweep of arches on the crown. The interior is white, austere and stark and is divided into three parts – one of which being the women's section above the main floor where women had to sit so as not to distract the men during services. Devoid of much finery, this church is a wonderful example of the piety and beauty of simplicity.

A well-preserved first century CE construction, the **Teatro Romano** is located just off of the Piazza della Liberta and surrounded on one side by the stables of the 17th century Palazzo Ancaiani. The **church of Santa Agata** occupies what once was the stage area. Also included with the price of entry (€2) is access to the **Museo Archeologico Nazionale** *Info:* Via S. Agata, 9am-7pm; holidays 9am-1pm) which has a few interesting pieces, including artifacts from a warrior's tomb, jewelry, pottery and other material from the Bronze Age through the Middle Ages.

Up the Via del Municipio from the Piazza del Mercato — which used to be a Roman Forum — is the **Palazzo Comunale** with its tall tower, small piazza and large flag out front. Begun in the 13th century and renovated in the 18th, this palazzo is now home to the Pinoteca Comunale which contains a small but captivating local museum. My favorite part is the display of old mint pieces that were used to make coins. As you enter, prior to going up to the museum, take a little time to admire the frescoes in the entranceway. *Info:* Open 10am-1pm & 3-6pm, closed Tuesdays. €2.50.

Assisi
Note: see map on page 171.

Dramatically situated on a verdant hill highlighted by olive groves and cypress trees reaching right up to the city walls, the beautiful medieval home to St. Francis and St. Clare stretches majestically along the slopes of Mount Subasio. Today **Assisi** still bears the mark of a robust little medieval town, is a center for art and culture, and a major religious pilgrimage site. *Info:* www.assisi.com, www.abcassisi.com, www.comune.assisi.pg.it.

Sadly, some of the town's charm was leveled when an earthquake struck in 1997, causing severe damage to the city's monuments,

especially the Basilica of St. Francis. Many of Giotto's fine frescoes were destroyed. You may still find scaffolding and supports in place to secure certain structures of historic significance.

Majestic and picturesque, the **Basilica of St Francis** and its accompanying cloistered convent have graced this rural landscape for many centuries. The **Lower Church** is entered through an intricate double portal surmounted with three rose windows. The remains of St. Francis are located in a stone urn in the crypt, which is down a staircase located in the middle part of the nave. The side chapels are all wonderfully decorated with 13th century stained glass windows as well as frescoes by Giotto and Cimabue. Mnay of which regrettably were damaged in the 1997 earthquake. Restoration work continues.

The **Upper Church** faces the town of Assisi and looks over the wide lawn of the Piazza Superiore di San Francesco and has a pure linear Gothic look. The one embellishment is the large rose window staring out at the town. The interior of this level is bright and airy, in contrast to the lower church. It consists of one nave with a transept and a polygonal arch, with stunningly colorful frescoes by Cimabue decorating the walls of the apse as well as the transept. The upper part of the nave is adorned with 13th century stained glass windows.

Located just inside the city walls near the Basilica of St. Francesco, the Romanesque-Gothic 13th century **Church of San Pietro** has a simple yet beauitful rectangular facade with two orders. The upper level has three rose windows, and the lower has three portals. The interior contains one nave and two aisles, and has some 14th century frescoes and the ruins of some tombs of the same century. For simple beauty and peaceful serenity this is a fine church to visit.

Located in the heart of the old town, built on the site of an old Roman forum and in the midst of some ancient medieval buildings, is the center of Assisi, the **Piazza del Commune**. The 14th century **Prior's Palace** houses the town council offices, the **Municipal Picture Gallery** contains Byzantine, Umbrian and Sienese frescoes, and the turreted 13th century **Palazzo del Capitano del Popolo** has the 14th century **Municipal Tower** rising out from it. Next to that is the **Church of Santa Maria Sopra Minerva**, built in the first half of the 16th century over the ancient Temple of Minerva.

On the other side of the piazza, the classically Gothic 13th century **Basilica of Santa Clara** dominates the piazza of the same name. Attached to the left side of the building are three large flying buttresses with a slender bell tower rising up from the apse. The facade is decorated with two closed horizontal bands, is divided into three levels, and has a wonderful rose window and a plain portal flanked by two lions.

The interior is in the form of a Latin cross with a single nave and is as simple and bare as the outside. A good place to come for soul-enriching serenity. The crypt, reached by a flight of steps, contains the remains of St. Clare in a glass coffin. In the chapel of St. George is the painted cross which supposedly spoke to St. Francis when it was located in the Church of St. Domain.

Up from Santa Clara, commoly known as the **Duomo**, is the beautiful Romanesque facade of the **Cathedral of San Ruffino**. It is divided into three sections, the uppermost is triangular with a pointed Gothic arch; the middle is divided vertically by pilasters and is decorated with three fine rose windows and myriad carvings; and the lower section has three portals, the left of which is used to enter the church. To the side of the Duomo is the massive bell tower adorned with small arches at the top and an off-set clock on the same level as the top layer of the church.

Inside, the apse contains an outstanding 16th century wood choir. The crypt is a must-see. Situated underneath the cathedral, and once part of an earlier church, you can find a Roman sarcophagus that once contained the remains of San Ruffino.

Just down the road from here past Piazza Matteoti is a **Roman amphitheater** worthy of a short visit. Down the Via Rocca Porta is the imposing **Castle of the Rocca Maggiore.** Built after the Lombard occupation, the fortress with its imposing ramparts and towers completely dominates the town below. An ideal medieval fortress for kids of all ages to explore.

7. MILAN & THE LAKE COUNTRY

Though steeped in commerce and flavored with high fashion, Milan also has an important cultural and historic side. Because Milan was virtually razed during World War II from allied bombing, the sights here are few and far between. What is left includes the impressive **Gothic Cathedral**, the nearby **Galleria**, and the most famous opera house in the world, **La Scala**. There is also Leonardo da Vinci's famous (but in my view) unimpressive *Last Supper*, the **Leonardo Da Vinci Museum of Science and Technology**, and that's about it.

In contrast to the hectic pace and sterile feel of Milan, the **lake region** is filled with tranquility and the warm embrace of community life. It has been a preferred spot for vacationers for centuries, the most important of whom was **Julius Caesar**, whose legions left a lasting impression on the landscape with the remains of the forts and cities they built many years ago. Despite their beauty and charm, the medieval lake towns with their terraced gardens and terra-cotta roofed villas, pale in comparison to the natural splendor of the breathtaking scenery. *Info:* www.milanoinfotourist.com/home.htm.

A FANTASTIC WEEKEND IN MILAN & THE LAKE COUNTRY

In Milan, focus on the **Duomo**, the **Galleria**, and Da Vinci's *Last Supper* and the nearby **Da Vinci museum**. Then spend a day seeing **Lake Como** and **Bellagio**.

Friday Evening

Arrive, settle into your hotel and head out to see the **Duomo**. Here you have Gothic at its best. This ornately decorative church crowned by 135 spires and adorned with intricate statues was begun in 1386 and is the work of countless architects, artists, and artisans who labored on it for centuries. At night the spires are lit making for an inspiring scene. One of  the best ways to get a bird's eye view of the square is to ascend to the outside viewing area above the facade of the cathedral.

The interior, like the exterior, is covered in statues, relief work, and many other decorations. The stained glass windows are of particular interest especially on a bright sunny day. *Info:* Piazza del Duomo. Open 7am–7pm. October–May 9am–4:30pm. Access to the top of the cathedral costs €2. By elevator €3.

After the Duomo, head next door to the **Vittorio Emanuele Galleria** *(see photo, previous page)*. This is the model from which American shopping malls emerged. Makes you wonder what the designers of our monstrosities were thinking after seeing this beauty. Started on March 7th, 1865, it was finally finished in 1877 – and so was the architect Mengoni. The day before the opening ceremony the architect plunged to his death from the scaffolding. Built in the form of a cross, inside you'll find shops and restaurants that serve as a central meeting place for business people, artists, opera singers, fashion models and tourists alike. It is really the heart and soul of Milan. Devastated in the bombings during World War II, it has been lovingly re-created to its original form.

Dinner tonight is at the world famous **Il Ristorante (Peck)**. This is the place to come and sample everything that this local gourmet delicatessen chain to offer. Located downstairs from the **Bottega del Vino**, the setting is relaxing even without windows, the service is excellent and, of course, the food is sublime. *Info:* Via

Victor Hugo 4, Tel. 02/876-774. Credit cards accepted. Meal for two €90.

After a light early dinner, let's head off to **Teatro La Scala**, the most famous and prestigious of all opera houses in the world, for a performance. Remember to have made a res-
ervation. Built between
1776 and 1778 on the old
site of the church of
Santa Maria alla Scala,
the facade has a covered
portico and gable with a
relief work depicting
Apollo's Chariot. If you
do not want to watch a

performance here, come later in your visit to their museum which displays many objects that trace the evolution of the theater, and recordings of over 600 different opera singers. *Info:* Via Dei Filodrammatici 2, Tel 02/861-781 or 861-772, Fax 02/861-778. Open Monday–Saturday 9am–noon and 2–6pm. Sundays 9:30am–12:30pm and 2:30pm–6pm. €5.

Saturday Morning
Time for Leonardo's *Last Supper*. To the left of the church of Santa Maria delle Grazie is the refectory of the Dominican convent that houses Leonardo's most famous work. Painted between 1495 and 1497, the humidity in the room hasn't helped to maintain the fresco, and "restoration" work done in 1726 and 1770 actually contributed to the painting's deterioration. Efforts are underway now, using modern techniques, to save the invaluable work. *Info:* Piazza Santa Maria delle Grazie. Tel. 498-7588. Metro-Carioli. Open Tuesday–Sunday 8:30am–1:30pm. €3.

After the viewing head over to the relatively nearby **Da Vinci Museum of Science and Technology** where many of Leonardo's inventions have been brought to life in full scale model. There are also other engaging exhibits all related to science and technology as well as an excellent reproduction of Leonardo's *Last Supper* painted by Giovanni Mauro Dellarovere at the end of the 16th century. So if you don't want to brave the line and see the real one, come here instead. *Info:* Via San Vittore 21, Tel. 4801–0040. Metro - San Ambrogio. Open Tuesday–Sunday 9am–5pm. €5 – Adults; €3 kids under 18.

Saturday Afternoon

Before we head to the train station to go to Lago di Como, time for either a sit down snack at one of the **Peck** stores (*see sidebar*), or pick something up to bring with you on the train. All of these stores are in the same neighborhood, within walking distance of one another and of the Duomo.

Peck Food Shops

Peck stores have been around since 1883 and are the place in Milan to titillate taste buds. *Info:* www.peck.it.
• **Bottega del Maile** offers everything possible created from its namesake, *Il Maiale* (The Pig). *Info:* Via Victor Hugo 3.
• **Bottega del Vino** is a gourmet "fast-food" establishment. *Info:* Via Victor Hugo 4.
• **Casa del Formaggio** is a cheese lover's fantasy with over 300 varieties. *Info:* Via Speronari 3.
• **Gastronomia Peck** is packed with platters of prepared foods, fresh pastas, smoked meats, and vegetables and fruits to go. *Info:* Via Spadari 9.
• **Rosticceria Peck** is a takeout place for spit-roasted chicken pork, beef, and vegetables, as well as prepared pasta dishes. *Info:* Via Cantu 3.

Saturday Evening

Head to **Como**, just north of Milan, for the evening. The train should not take long. Once you arrive, settle in to your hotel and go find a café (*see Best Sleeps & Eats*) by the lake and relax.

Lago di Como has been a top European tourist destination for centuries as a result of its beautiful landscapes and scenery. You can find every imaginable outdoor activity around the lake as well as space for more sedate pursuits. There are parks, exotic gardens, lush villas, picturesque villages, and ancient castles, basilicas, art galleries and museums scattered to enjoy, as well as restaurants and *enoteche* galore. *Info:* www.lakecomo.com.

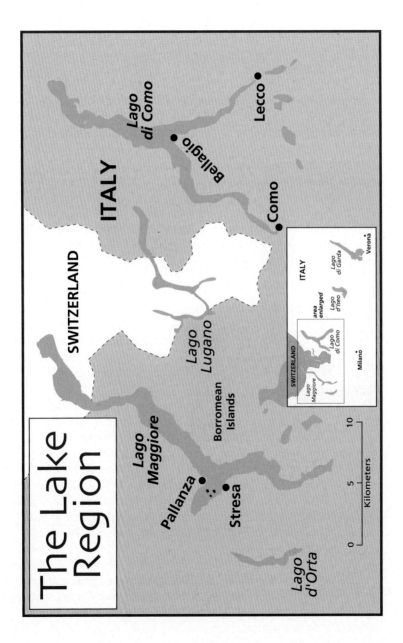

After recharging your batteries, if you feel like it, hop on the *funiculare*, located on the north edge of the city, and go up to the **Brunate** section of Como that is dotted with exquisite mansions and gardens. From here you have some stunning views over the town and the lake.

For dinner tonight back in Como, let's try **Imbarcadero**, located a few meters from the water's edge, this place offers great traditional dishes, simple in preparation but bursting with flavor. In the summer they open up their terrace so you can enjoy a great meal right on the lake. *Info:* Via Cavour 20, Tel. 031/277-341. Closed the first ten days in January. Credit cards accepted. Dinner for €60.

After which it's time for the traditional Italian *passegiatta*. So take a stroll with the other denizens of Como, find a gelateria, grab a café, and ease into the flow of life on the lake.

Sunday
Today we are going to hop on a ferry and take a tour of the lake.

Get off where you wish, or keep on going and simply do a giro of the lake. *Info:* www.navigazionelaghi.it.

I suggest you visit **Bellaggio**. Surrounded by the lake on three sides, here you can enjoy strolls through the winding medieval streets, head to the quiet fishing port of **Pescallo** with its many boats, or visit **Villa Melzi** (*Info:* Lungolario Marconi, open 10:30am-4pm, www.thevillapassalacqua.com/index.php/villa-melzi/) and the **Villa Serbelloni** (*Info:* a five star hotel whose gardens are only open to non-guests from 10:30am to 4pm, closed Mondays, www.villaserbelloni.com).

And that's it for your day on the lake. If it has left you wanting more, you can always come back and spend more time, say a week (see next section), and really begin to savor the peace and tranquility of this region.

A WONDERFUL WEEK IN MILAN & THE LAKE COUNTRY

A week in Milan and the Lake Country offers a combination of **urban chic** and **lakeside peace**. Start in Milan, and get the hectic pace out of the way, then head into the Lake Country to relax, take ferry boat trips, eat good food, and settle into a tranquil vacation. *For Milan, see map on page 197.*

RECOMMENDED PLAN: Spend two days and one night in **Milan**, then head off to **Lago di Como** in the evening of the second day. You can get there by train easily. Spend days three and four on Lago di Como, rent a car, then head over to **Lago Maggiore** where you will spend the rest of your time.

Milan

At the heart of Milano is the ornately decorative **Duomo**, crowned by 135 spires adorned with statues and bas reliefs. Make sure to ascend to the outside viewing area above the facade of the cathedral. The interior, like the exterior, is covered in statues, relief work, and many other decorations. The stained glass windows are of particular interest especially on a bright sunny day. *Info:* Piazza del Duomo. Open 7am–7pm. October–May 9am–4:30pm. Access to the top of the cathedral costs €2. By elevator €3.

Next to the Duomo is the model after which American shopping malls emerged, **Vittorio Emanuele Galleria**. This is the central meeting for locals and visitors alike. Devastated in the bombings during World War II, it has been lovingly re-created to its original form.

Located near the Duomo and Galleria is the most famous and prestigious of all opera houses, **Teatro La Scala**. Built between 1776 and 1778, their museum offers many objects that trace the evolution of the theater, as well as 40,000 books that deal with opera and the theater, and archives of over 600 recorded opera singers. *Info:* Via Dei Filodrammatici 2, Tel 02/861-781 or 861-772, Fax 02/861-778. Open Monday–Saturday 9am–noon and 2–6pm. Sundays 9:30am–12:30pm and 2:30pm–6pm. Admission €5.

A ways from the center of Milan, to the left of the church of Santa Maria delle Grazie is the refectory of the Dominican convent that houses the most famous of Leonardo's work, *The Last Supper*. Painted between 1495 and 1497, the humidity in the room doesn't help maintain the fresco, and – shocking but true – a doorway was built underneath this priceless fresco severing off one of Christ's legs that was visible under the table. On top of all this, "restoration" work that was done in 1726 and 1770 actually contributed to the painting's deterioration. Efforts are underway now, using modern techniques, to save the invaluable work. *Info:* Piazza Santa Maria delle Grazie. Tel. 498-7588. Metro–Carioli. Open Tuesday–Sunday 8:30am–1:30pm. Admission €3.

Somewhat nearby to the Last Supper is **Da Vinci Museum of Science and Technology** where you'll find reproductions of Leonardo's designs and mechanical models of his inventions. There are also copies of pages from the *Gates Codex* on display as well as an excellent reproduction of Leonardo's *Last Supper* painted by Giovanni Mauro Dellarovere at the end of the 16th century. So if you don't want to brave the line and see the real one, come here instead. *Info:* Via San Vittore 21, Tel. 4801-0040. Metro San Ambrogio. Open Tuesday–Sunday 9am–5pm. Admission €5 – Adults; €3 kids under 18.

On the other side of the city, is the magnificent **Castello Sforzesco**. What you see today is only a smaller scale of the original citadel. Despite its reduction in size it is still Italy's largest castle with its immense towers and imposing walls. In the **Ancient Arts Museum**, you'll see works by Michelangelo and Leonardo da Vinci. There is also a hall dedicated to ancient axes, shields, spiked clubs, spears and more. *Info:* Foro Buonaparte. Open Tuesday–Sunday 9:30am–5:30pm. Metro – Carioli.

In 1772 the **Palazzo di Brera** began its current life as an institute of artistic preservation. Today you can find works from the 14th century up to present times. Among the most noteworthy are Moccirolo's *Oratorio*, Raphael's well-known *Sposalizio delle Vergine*, Mantegna's *Cristo Morto* and Bramante's *Cristo alla Colonna*. *Info:* Via Brera 28, Tel. 862–634. Open Tuesday–Saturday 9am–2pm and Sundays 9am–1pm. Admission €4.

Lago di Como
Over the centuries **Lake Como** (Lago di Como) has been a popular vacation destination with European *conescenti* as a result of its intense landscapes and scenery. There are parks, exotic gardens, lush villas, picturesque villages, and ancient castles, basilicas, art galleries and museums scattered around the lake. And plenty of restaurants, *enoteche*, cafes and water sports to enjoy as well. *Info:* www.lakecomo.com.

Como
The town of **Como** is the perfect jumping-off point from which to explore the lake and its many little towns either by ferry, bus or car. You can also hop on the *funiculare*, located on the north edge of the city, and go up to the **Brunate** section of Como that is dotted with exquisite mansions and gardens. A short way outside of town (5 km) is the village of **Cernobbio**, where you can find the princely **Villa d'Este** with its lush gardens and enormous grounds. The villa is now the area's best five star deluxe hotel, and is where Leonardo di Caprio had his wedding reception.

Besides attracting actors, Como produces almost one-fifth of the world's

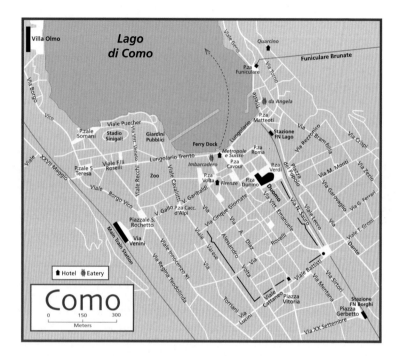

silk supply. Merchants stole the secret of the silk worm from the Chinese many centuries ago, and began production of the seductive cloth along the banks of Lake Como. As a result, you can find many silk products on sale in Como.

If shopping is of little interest, you can visit the neo-classic **Villa Olmo** also on the outskirts of town. It is currently the seat of the local government, but the magnificent gardens are open to the public year round. *Info:* 9am–noon and 1:30pm–6pm.

ALTERNATE PLAN
If you like golf, then head over to the **Golf Club Carimate**. Located 27km from Milan and 15km from Como this is an 18-hole, par 71 course that is 5,982 meters long. It is open year round except on Mondays. They have a driving range, tennis course, and a fine bar and restaurant. *Info:* Via Airldi 2, 22060 Carimate. Tel. 031/790-226, Fax 031/790-226.

Bellaggio

Surrounded by the lake on three sides, the vistas are sublime. While here you can enjoy strolls through the winding medieval streets or engage in any number of water sports. Down on the eastern shore of the peninsula is the quiet port of **Pescallo** with its many boats. The most famous sights here are the Villa Melzi and the Villa Serbelloni. *Info:* www.bellagiolakecomo.com.

The **Villa Melzi** (*Info:* Lungolario Marconi, open 10:30am-4pm) is known for its gardens ornately strewn with monuments and a small little pond covered with lily pads and flowers. The **Villa Serbelloni** is now a five star hotel whose gardens are only open to non-guests from 10:30am to 4pm. A magical place to stay, but very expensive. Come visit the gardens instead. *Info:* Closed Mondays. www.bellagiolakecomo.com.

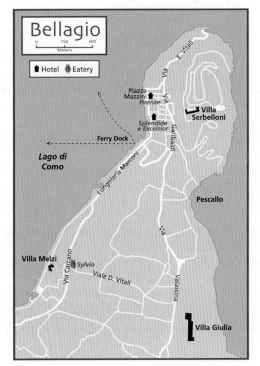

Touring the Lakes

The best way to tour each individual lake is by **ferry**. Though ferries take longer than driving a car around the *lungolago* road, on the water you will be blessed with far superior views of majestic villas and gardens. *Info:* www.navigazionelaghi.it.

Lago Maggiore

Lago Maggiore, also known as **Verbano**, was formed during the Ice Age from glaciers scouring their way down from the Alps. Today, the majority of the lake is in Italy, but a small section extends into Switzerland offering visitors the ability to do some cross border sightseeing. Don't forget your passport.

Lago Maggiore, similar to Como, is a place to relax, to savor a slower pace of life; more a place to "be" rather than to "do." Come to Lago Maggiore for the peace, tranquility, and amazing vistas. *Info:* www.lagomaggiore.net.

Visit the **Villa Taranto**, a house built in 1875 and located on the Castagnola between the towns of Intra and Pallanza. (These two towns are so close together they are commonly known as Verbania.) At the villa you'll find over 20,000 species of plants flourishing on over 20 hectares of land. The botanical gardens are quite splendid. Take a relaxing stroll through terraces, lawns, and fountains that make up the grounds.

If architecture is your pleasure, see the fabulous **Santa Caterina del Sasso**, located between Reno and Cerro on the water. Approach by boat, where you can get the mesmerizing view of the monastery hewn out of the rock walls in the 13th century.

Another building of architectural interest is the fortified palace in **Angera**. Built in 1350 on the ruins of an earlier fortress, this place is worth a visit because of the vaulted ceilings and its medieval charm. I also love the tiny village set at the palace's feet that looks as if it hasn't changed in centuries.

Then there are the remains of the **Vitaliano Castle**, built between 1519 and 1526 that now rests on one of the three islands that are between Canero and Cannobio. The ferry doesn't stop here (it's really just a speck of an island with a fortified castle on it) but does get close enough for pictures to be taken.

Looking for something to bring back home, either for yourself or a friend? Don't miss the **Wednesday Market** at **Luino**, where you can get crafts, food, local clothing, and more. At the same time you can enjoy the sights and sounds of a boisterous local market.

Stresa
For those of you who insist on the best hotels with all the amenities, such as swimming pools, saunas, tennis courts, and more, then you'll want to come to **Stresa**. Called the Pearl of Lago Maggiore, Stresa sits below the green slopes of **Mottarone** (which are accessible via a cable car … a great place for short hikes) and offers a comfortable climate in the summer and mild temperatures in the winter. You also have picturesque beaches, beautiful landscaped gardens, fine restaurants, an abundance of Italian culture and refinement, and much much more. Stresa is an ideal

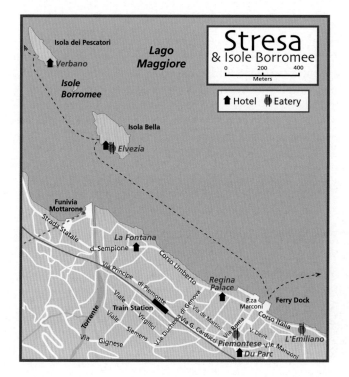

place to stay. And from here you can explore the rest of Lago Maggiore. *Info:* www.stresa.net.

Isole Borromee
Just offshore from Stresa, the three enchanting **Borromean Islands** are peace and tranquility embodied. The **Isola dei Pescatori** has an ancient and picturesque little fishing village. The **Isola Bella** has its imposing **Palazzo Borromeo**, complete with a spectacular terraced garden, and rooms furnished with Venetian chandeliers, mirrors, and more. *Info:* Tel. 30556; open April–November 9am–noon and 1:30pm–5:30pm. Admission €6).

The **Isola Madre** is world-famous for its **villa** and landscaped **gardens** featuring a wide variety of exotic birds. Inside the villa you'll find a collection of dolls and puppets dating from the 16th to the 19th centuries. All the islands are just a short ferry ride away from Stresa. *Info:* open April–November 9am–noon and 1:30pm–5:30pm; Admission €6.

Verbania
Verbania is really the two tiny towns of Pallanza and Intra. The main draw here, as mentioned earlier, is the **Villa Taranto**, a house built in 1875 and located two kilometers north of town, where you'll find over 20,000 species of plants flourishing on over 20 hectares of land. Besides the lovely botanical gardens, there are quaint grounds in which you can take relaxing strolls through terraces, lawns, and fountains. *Info:* Open April–October 8:30am–7:30pm. Admission €6.

8. BAY OF NAPLES & THE AMALFI COAST

The Bay of Naples is the gateway to the scenic island of **Capri** and the ancient Roman towns of **Pompeii** and **Herculaneum**. In **Naples** itself is the best Roman archeological museum in Italy, and some say all of Europe, filled with the artifacts from those ancient Roman towns that were covered in the ash and lava from the eruption of Mt. Vesuvius almost 2,000 years ago.

A little way beyond the bay are the picturesque villages of the **Amalfi Coast** perched scenically on the slope overlooking the pristine blue waters of the Mediterranean, where you will find **Positano**, **Amalfi**, and **Ravello**, among others.

A FANTASTIC WEEKEND IN THE BAY OF NAPLES

There is much to do in and around the **Bay of Naples**. This weekend is packed with scenic vistas, relaxing islands, ancient Roman towns, exemplary museums, and more.

Friday Evening

As you pass through Naples, feel its energy, notice the chaos, smell the exhaust fumes, and be thankful you will be spending your weekend on the pristine island of Capri. Though we will be returning to Naples tomorrow to visit the National Museum and nearby Pompeii, for a peaceful evening there is no better place than the **Isle of Capri**.

People flock to Capri because the scenery is stunning, the pace of life relaxing, the restaurants are excellent, and the hotels world-class. With footpaths crossing the island, hiking on Capri is a common activity. It can be done from cafe to cafe and town to town, all along trails cut into the verdant hillsides. In other words, very sophisticated hiking.

Sunbathing and other water sports are also available. But the favorite pastime on Capri is to relax and soak up the incredible atmosphere. Despite the hordes of tourists that descend in the summer, Capri still maintains a quiet pace and a strong sense of community. *Info:* www.capritourism.com.

But first we have to get here. From the train station in Naples take a taxi to the Stazione Maritima at Molo Angionino where you will catch either the ferry (*traghetto*) or hydrofoil (*aliscafo*) to Capri. Ferries cost half as much but take twice

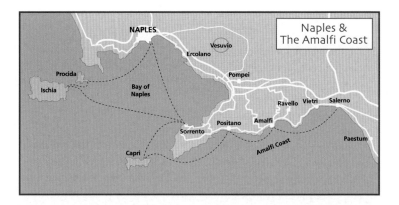

as long. Signs indicate which company goes to which destinations. Pick up a schedule for your return visit tomorrow.

You arrive on Capri at the Marina Grande. From there, take either the funiculare, bus, or taxi up to the town of **Capri**. This is the center of the island. From here you will have to walk to your hotel unless your hotel is out of town.

After settling into your hotel, take the time to wander Capri to get your bearings. Grab a drink at a café and settle into the slow pace of island life. This weekend is less about "doing" and more about "being" relaxed.

For dinner tonight, unless you find a place that catches your fancy, let's try **La Campannina**, a fine family-run, upscale, but rustic establishment. Near Piazza Umberto where the funiculare stops, here you will be able to savor local fare in a great atmosphere. *Info:* Via delle Botteghe 14, Tel. 081/837-0732. www.capannina-capri.com. Closed Wednesdays and November to Easter. All credit cards accepted. Meal for two €70.

Saturday
From our island refuge, we are going to head into **Naples**. To say that this city is chaotic is a gross understatement. Cars ignore red lights, scooters drive on sidewalks, and so on. Couple this with the omnipresent threat of getting your pocket picked, and it is hard to imagine why people come here. But they do.

ALTERNATIVE PLAN
Stay on Capri: visit the Blue Grotto, take the chair lift from Anacapri up to the top of Monte Salaro for a wonderful view of the whole bay, hike down, visit Roman Emperor Tiberius' villa dating from 27 AD, or simply luxuriate in the tranquil ambiance of the island. See later in this chapter for details. Below, the beautiful **Blue Grotto**.

For our purposes this weekend, however, all we need to do is get into Naples, head to the National Museum, then train out to Pompeii for a visit.

On the northwestern outskirts of the *centro storico* just off of Piazza Cavour is the **National Archeological Museum**, which boasts an amazingly rich collection of antiquities culled from Pompeii and Herculaneum. Considered by many to the best archeological museum in Italy, if not Europe. One of its best exhibits is the **Gabinetto Segreto**, the secret closet. Filled with erotic statues, mosaics and other pieces of art of a sexual nature, these pieces definitely give you an insight into daily life back in the Roman era.

Info: Piazza Cavour. Tel. 081/440-166. Information and reservations: 848/800-288. www.marketplace.it/museo.nazionale. Open daily 9am–7pm. Until 8pm on holidays. Closed Tuesdays. €6.5.

After witnessing the treasures culled from the excavations of **Pompeii**, let's head over to that world-famous site. Tens of thousands of people died when **Vesuvius** erupted in 79 CE, submerging Pompeii with volcanic emissions. The lava and ash created an almost perfect time capsule, sealing in an important cross-section of an ancient civilization.

Before Pompeii was buried by lava, it was a major seaport linking it to the rest of the Roman Empire. As such it was an established city with a multicultural population of about 25,000 Greeks, Egyptians, Gauls, Iberians and every other nationality in the Empire. By 80 BCE, it was also a favorite resort for wealthy Romans.

Getting to Pompeii

To get to Pompeii by train from Naples, go one floor below the Central Station to the **Circumvesuviana** station for a local train to **Pompeii Scavi**. The trip takes about 30-40 minutes.

Shaken by an earthquake in 62 CE, Pompeii recovered, brushed itself off and went back to business. 17 years later on August 24, 79 CE, Mt. Vesuvius erupted, spewing ash and pumice pebbles that covered the city, preserving it and some of its unfortunate residents in time. In places there are human forms and family pets forever preserved having died in the embrace of the volcanic flow. You can see where gardens, food shops, apartment buildings, and villas used to be.

After many years of mismanagement, Pompeii is slowly re-emerging to be a true world wonder. The ancient city is now being restored to a semblance of its former glory. Pompeii is unique anywhere in the world, and is a must-see stop when in this part of Italy. *Info:* Open April – October 8:30am-7:30pm. Last entry at 6pm. November to March 8:30am-5pm. Last entry 3:30pm. Admission €10.

A WONDERFUL WEEK IN THE BAY OF NAPLES & THE AMALFI COAST

The history of **Pompeii** and **Herculaneum**, and the sun, sea, and serene living of **Capri** and the **Amalfi Coast** will make this a truly memorable vacation experience. On this trip you can combine urban adventures in one of Italy's most hectic cities, **Naples**, as well as peaceful relaxation along the coast. *Info:* For information about Capri and ferries to the island visit www.capritourism.com. For ferry schedules and everything else associated with the Amalfi Coast, visit www.amalfi.it.

RECOMMENDED PLAN: Stay on **Capri** for the first five days and commute to Naples by ferry, and to Pompeii and Herculaneum by ferry then train. Then for the last two nights pick a town on the Amalfi Coast — I would suggest **Amalfi** itself — to use as your base to explore that area.

Capri
To get to the town of Capri after you've made it to the **Marina Grande**, the main harbor on the island, take the funicular, taxi or bus up the hill. Once you reach the Piazza Umberto I, you can enjoy the memorable view out onto the Bay of Naples. This is the perfect piazza to have a seat on any one of the cafés and watch the world go by.

From here you can walk – granted it's a long way – or take a public bus northeast to the **Palace of Tiberius**, the biggest, best preserved Imperial villa on the island. You won't find elaborate mosaic floors or statues in place here, and at first glance the site might seem disappointing, but what makes this place special is the sheer extent of the ruins located in such a superb setting. Built in the first century, the villa was initially 12 stories high but only partial remains of three remain. But the beehive of passageways

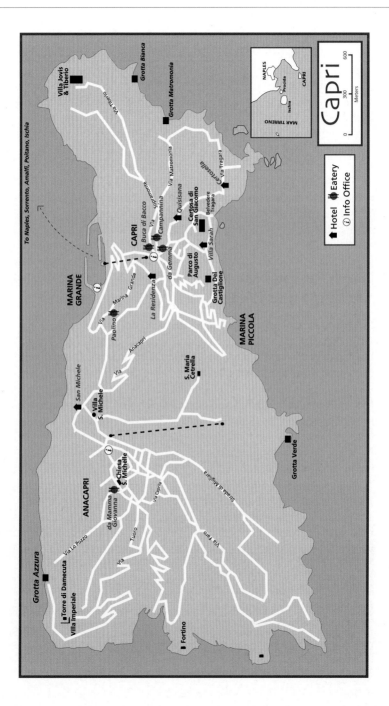

Capri

0 300 600
Meters

Hotel   Eatery
ⓘ Info Office

NAPLES

Procida

Ischia

CAPRI

MAR TIRRENO

Villa Jovis
& Tiberio

Grotta Bianca

Grotta Matromonia

Via Tiberio

Via Matromonia

To Naples, Sorrento, Amalfi, Poitano, Ischia

Buca di Bacco

CAPRI

Via Sopramonte

Campannina

Quisisana

Certosa di
San Giacomo

Via Tragara

Belvedere
Tragara

Carosella

MARINA
GRANDE

ⓘ

ⓘ

Via Marina Grande

Via Paolino

La Residenza

da Gemma

Parco di
Augusto

Villa Sarah

Grotta Del
Castiglione

MARINA
PICCOLA

Via Anacapri

Via San Michele

Villa
S. Michele

S. Maria
Cetrella

ⓘ

Chiesa
S. Michele

ANACAPRI

da Mamma
Giovanna

Via Lo Pozzo

Via Tuoro

Via Caprile

Strada di Migliara

Via Faro

Grotta Verde

Grotta Azzura

Torre di Damecuta
Villa Imperiale

Fortino

leading to many small rooms make it evident that this villa functioned as a mini-city, with baths, store rooms and servants' quarters.

The Palace is perched on an imposing hilltop called **Il Salto** (The Leap) from which the Emperor is said to have thrown his enemies (and if you've read any Roman history this is probably true). *Info:* Open daily 9am until 1 hour before sunset. Admission €3.

On the south edge of town is the **Certosa di San Giacomo**, a 14th century Carthusian monastery that was founded in 1371, destroyed in 1553 and rebuilt soon after. It was used as a prison and a hospice in the 1800s and today houses a secondary school and a library. The cloisters and the dark Gothic church are open to the public. The frescoes in the church are interesting to view but those cloisters can be missed, especially the **Museo Deifenbach** with its dark and crusty oil paintings.

From the monastery walk along the Via di Certosa to the **Parco Augusto**. From the terrace here you will find some fine views to the south of the island over the **Marina Piccola** (small harbor) and the **Faraglioni** rock formations.

My favorite part of the island is **Anacapri**. You get here either by bus, taxi or foot from Capri. Anacapri is more relaxed and down-to-earth as compared to the faster-paced nature of Capri. Perched high up on a rocky plateau, its flat-roofed whitewashed buildings are obviously Moorish in style. Here you can find the 18th century **Church of San Michele** (*Info:* open daily 7am–7pm) with its sober Baroque design and intricate frescoed floors. Also in Anacapri is the **Villa San Michele**, which is known for its beautiful gardens and vast collection of classical sculpture.

 *Info:* open summer 9am–6pm, winter 10am–3pm; admission €6. From these gardens are some of the most spectacular views. If you want to go higher, you can walk or take a chair lift up to **Monte Solaro**, which has amazing views over all of Capri. This is also one

of the world's premier picnic spots, so come prepared. But bring a sweater or jacket even on sunny days since the wind and height tends to cool things down slightly.

Finally, onto the famous **Grotta Azzura** or **Blue Grotto**. You get here from the Marina Grande by motorboat with a number of other people, then transfer to rowboats to enter the grotto. You will have to sit on the floor of the rowboat as the captain (on his back) leads the boat in by pulling hand over hand on a length of fixed chain. The silver-blue light inside sparkles incandescently. An incredible sight. *Info:* Open 24 hours. Boat trips from Marina Grande go from 9am–6pm. Cost €5.

Naples

Naples is chaotic, energetic, passionate, and edgy. Make sure you keep your valuables in safe locations on your body. I have traveled the world, but the only place I ever had my pocket picked was in the Naples. Fear not, however, as a rule no one will harm you for the contents of your wallet. But if you put down your camera and turn your back, or when buying  something set your wallet on the counter ... there's a good chance it will be gone. Still, Naples is also an incredible cultural experience. *Info:* www.comune.napoli.it or www.enit.it.

The place to start your trip is right in the belly of the beast, in the heart of Naples, its **Centro Storico**. Located just north of the harbor, this part of Naples is the best location to walk and get a feel for the city. It has winding streets dotted with small churches and quaint old buildings. A fun place to explore during the day but be careful at night. Even locals advise you not to frequent anywhere between the Duomo and the train station at night.

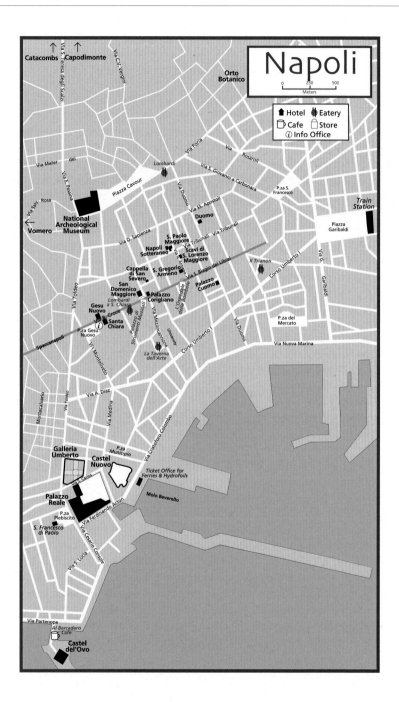

The old main street, called the **Spaccanapoli** ("Naples splitter") is a combination of all the streets from the Via Toledo, through the Via Maddaloni, to the Via Croce, and onto the Via S. Giagio ai Librai. This series of streets, as well as the small alleys that are offshoots from it, are lined with shops of traditional artisans, such as the **Palazzo di Strumenti Musicali** (*Info:* Vico San Domenico Maggiore #9) in front of the San Domenico Maggiore. Up the stairs to the first floor you'll find guitars and other instruments being crafted by hand.

Best Cafe in Naples

Al Barcadero Café is an intimate little cafe in the ritzy part of Naples. Set on the water, you can see fishermen painting their boats with Mt. Vesuvius as a backdrop. *Info:* Banchina S. Lucia 2, Tel. 333/222-7023. Open from 10am to 10pm.

Another unique shop is the **L'Ospedale delle Bambole**, The Doll Hospital (*Info:* Via S Biagio ai Librai). Here you'll find ancient dolls and puppets hanging or strewn haphazardly about. A can't-miss street in the *centro storico* is the **Via San Gregorio Armeno**, which is commonly known as the "Nativity Scene Street" since they sell figurines for crèches year round.

In the *centro storico* is **Napoli Sotteranea**, an amazing underground tour of catacombs, ancient aqueducts, cisterns, and the remains of Roman and Greek buildings that lie below modern Naples. The entrance is to the left of the church of S. Paolo Maggiore. Also featured in this tour are visits inside nearby homes that have been carved out of the ancient Roman amphitheater that used to exist here. You will see old stadium seats incorporated into modern apartments. My favorite part of a trip to Naples. *Info:* Piazza San Gaetano 68. Tel. 081/296-944. napolisotterranea.org. Tours Mon-Fri noon, 2pm, and 4pm. On Thurs at 9am. Sat, Sun and Holidays 10am, noon, 2pm, 4pm, and 6pm. Groups need to book in advance. Admission €8.

Right across the small piazza from Napoli Sotteranea is another excellent archeological excavation deep in the heart of Naples, **Scavi di San Lorenzo Maggiore**. Self-guided, but with a wonderful map, illustrations and descriptions, this is a sight well worth seeing. Located on the Via San Gregorio Aremeno. *Info:* Piazza San Gaetano. Time M-S 9am-5pm, Sun 9:30-1:30. Admission €4.

Finally, a trip to Naples is not complete without a visit to the  **National Archeological Museum**. This museum boasts an amazingly rich collection of antiquities. Considered by many to be the best archeological museum in Italy, if not all of Europe. This is definitely a must-see destination when in Naples. One of its best exhibits is the **Gabinetto Segreto**, the secret closet. Filled with erotic statues, mosaics and other pieces of art of a sexual nature, these works give you an insight into life back in the Roman era. *Info:* Piazza Cavour. Tel. 081/440–166. Information and reservations: 848/800-288. www.marketplace.it/museo.nazionale. Open daily 9am–7pm. Until 8pm on holidays. Closed Tuesdays. Admission €6.5.

After you have done all this, head back to your ferry and return to your island.

Pompeii
This is a city truly trapped in time. One day in 79 CE life stopped for **Pompeii** when Mt. Vesuvius erupted, and was preserved for us to see today. Roads, gardens, shops, bordellos, apartment buildings, villas and more all remain almost as they were from that fateful day.

Some of the best homes to see are the **House of the Faun** and the **House of the Vettii**, both in the residential area north of the **Forum**. Other homes of interest are the **House of the Melander** (located to the east of the Forum), the **Villa of the Mysteries** (located to the west of the main town), and the **House of Pansa** (located to the north of the Forum) that also included rented apartments.

The public **Amphitheater**, in the east of the city, should not be missed because of its scale and level of preservation. A fun activity for you and a companion is to locate the spots on the stage where even if only a whisper is spoken, a person standing at the top-most part of the seating area can hear it clearly.

The ancient town of Pompeii covered 160 acres, and was well supplied with public amenities. Lead water pipes found everywhere show that all but the very humblest of houses were supplied with running water. Most houses either doubled as workshops, or had small workshops in them since the ancient world's slave economy did not foster the development of the factory system. The lives of ancient tradesmen, about which literature tells us almost nothing, becomes more real for us here than anywhere else in the ancient world. Except possibly, for the abandoned port of Rome, Ostia Antica.

Pompeii has also enriched our knowledge of ancient Romans' relations with their gods. Graffiti in Pompeii shows us that the Imperial cult, whereby Emperors were decreed to be deities in and of themselves, was adhered to, though generally only with lip service. One such wall scribbling states "Augustus Caesar's mother was only a woman." Blasphemous!

Also in evidence in Pompeii are symbols of the Greek cult of Dionysis, one of many that flourished in the city. **The Temple of Isis** (to the east of the Forum) testifies to the strong following that the Egyptian goddess had here. The Roman warrior sect of Mithras was also well represented, as were family cults that worshipped dead ancestors. This is evidenced by the fact that

most homes and workshops had private shrines usually housing busts of ancestors. However, the true god of Pompeii was, as with other cities ancient and modern ... money.

Ironically, it was that worship of money that got

many people killed. Going back for their hoards of silver and gold spelled death for many of the residents of Pompeii. Under the hail of pumice stone and ash many were asphyxiated or engulfed. A particularly disturbing cluster of victims, with their children and burdensome possessions, is preserved near the **Nocera Gate**.

An organization called World Monuments Watch has declared Pompeii one of the world's most imperiled cultural sites, but the good news is that they are helping to restore the ancient city to the wonder it once was. *Info:* To get to Pompeii by train from Naples, go one floor below the Central Station to the Circumvesuviana station for a local train to Pompeii Scavi. The trip takes about 30-40 minutes. Open April – October 8:30am-7:30pm. Last entry at 6pm. November to March 8:30am-5pm. Last entry 3:30pm. Admission €10. www.scavidipompei.it.

Herculaneum
Close to Naples, and seventeen miles northeast of Pompeii is the smaller town of **Herculaneum**. At the time of the eruption of Mt Vesuvius in 79 CE Herculaneum had only 5,000 inhabitants, very little commerce, and made most of its living from fishing. The volcanic mud that flowed through every building and street in Herculaneum was a different covering from that which buried Pompeii. This steaming hot lava-like substance settled eventually to a depth of 30-40 feet and became rock-hard, sealing and preserving everything it came in contact with. Dinner was left on tables, wine shops abandoned in mid-purchase, sacrifices left at the moment of offering, funerals never finished, prisoners left in stocks, and watchdogs perished on their chains.

Fortunately for the residents, but not for archeologists, the absence of the hail of hot ash that rained down on Pompeii, which smashed the buildings of that city and trapped many residents of that town, meant that many of the inhabitants of Herculaneum were able to get away in time. Despite the absence of preserved human remains, Herculaneum offers complete houses, with their woodwork, household goods, and furniture.

Although Herculaneum was a relatively unimportant town compared with Pompeii, many of the houses that have been excavated were from the wealthy class. It is speculated that perhaps the town was like a retirement village, populated by prosperous Romans seeking to pass their retirement years in the calm of a small seaside town. This idea is bolstered by the fact that the few craft shops that have been discovered were solely for the manufacture of luxury goods.

Archaeologists surmise that the most desirable residential area was in the southwest part of town, which overlooked the ocean in many different housing terraces. Here you will find the **House of the Stags**, famous for its beautiful frescoes, sculpted stags, and a drunken figure of Hercules. Farther north you can find the marvelously preserved **House of the Wooden Partition**. It is one of the most complete examples of a private residence in either Pompeii or Herculaneum. Near this house to the north are the **Baths**, an elaborate complex incorporating a gymnasium and assorted men and women's baths.

Important to remember as you compare Herculaneum with Pompeii is that this town was only recently excavated, and as a result modern methods and tools were used for the job. This allowed for more advanced preservation efforts. *Info:* To get to Herculaneum by train from Naples, go one floor below the Central Station to the Circumvesuviana station for a local train to Ercolano. The trip takes about 20-30 minutes. Gates to the site open year round 9am to one hour before sunset. Admission €10. www.comune.ercolano.na.it.

Amalfi Coast

The steep slopes and rugged beauty of the **Amalfi Coast** have enchanted visitors for centuries. **Mount Vesuvius** reigns majestically in the distance, dominating the scenery as it once dictated the lives of the area's inhabitants with its eruptions. Dotted with little hillside towns, the serpentine road connecting them usually has bumper to bumper traffic. In the off-season the traffic decreases considerably, but then so does the temperature, and bathing in the sea is one of the attractions of this coastline.

The narrow, two-lane road that joins Vietri (near Salerno) to Positano is dug almost entirely out of the rock, and curves maniacally. Built in the 1800s by the King of Naples, Ferdinando di Borbone, this road follows the lay of the mountains on one side and the stunning curves of the sea on the other. However, every turn offers coastal panoramic views of unparalleled proportions – which means that you will be tempted to take your eyes off the road, an error in judgment that is not advised.

The coastline is filled with high-end hotels, excellent restaurants, nightlife options, ancient medieval streets and passageways, cultural sights and fun-loving locals. Once you come here, the Amalfi Coast is a place you will want to return to time and time again. *Info:* www.amalfi.it.

Positano

Perched up hillsides in a tangle of houses, alleys, stairways and tourist shops, overlooking a series of pristine beaches, the town of **Positano** has been a part of this beautiful landscape for almost a thousand years. When Emperor Tiberius moved to Capri to escape the intrigue of Rome, he had his flour brought in from a mill in Positano, one that is still working today. In the 10th century, as a sea power and active trade competitor with Venice, Pisa

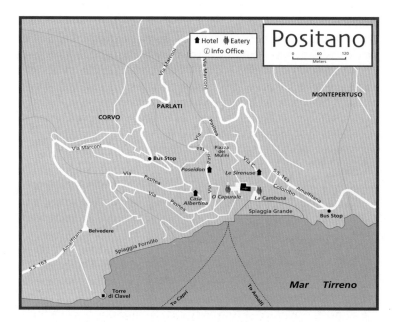

and Genoa, Positano was one of the most important commercial centers on the Italian peninsula. In the 16th and 17th centuries, filled with the wealth from its trading, was when many of the beautiful Baroque homes scattered on the hills of the town were built. *Info:* www.aziendaturismopositano.it

Because of its timeless beauty, Positano has been the playground of the rich and famous for centuries. Writers, musicians, nobles, aristocrats – all have come here to bathe in the azure waters and relax in the lush green hillsides. Today it is no different. Filled with excellent restaurants, world-class hotels, and all manner of water sports, Positano is a perfect holiday destination.

For historic sights, try the **Santa Maria Assunta**, a 12th century church that dominates the Positano hillside. The ancient floor is a Byzantine mosaic and on the main altar is a relief of the Madonna and Child in black marble. Other than that, Positano is a place to relax, read, and connect with the one you love. *Info:* http://positano.starnetwork.it.

Amalfi

What an amazingly beautiful town. Clinging to the rocky coast of the Sorrento peninsula is one of the most picturesque little towns in Italy, **Amalfi**. It is primarily the slow pace, friendly locals and engaging colors of Amalfi that attracts visitors. Set on a backdrop of blue, the pastel colored houses of red and yellow, and the striped fishing boats, fill the canvas of the town. If you want to experience an amazing place, come to Amalfi.

Legend has it that the town was established by Constantine the Great as a respite from the chaos of Rome. By the Middle Ages it had a population of 50,000, but today it is only around 7,000 (when all the tourists leave). As a tourist resort, Amalfi offers everything you could need to make your stay pleasant: fine restaurants, wonderful hotels, nightlife, shopping, water sports and sightseeing.

Some of the sights you can see are the **Duomo of Sant'Andrea** built in the Lombard Romanesque style in 1203. Its fine portico with pointed arches was totally rebuilt in 1865. On the west side is a bronze door that was cast in Constinantinople in 1066. In the crypt you will find the remains of the Apostle, Saint Andrew. How they verify these things I will never know. I guess you have to rely on faith?

High above the town, reachable by a steady hike, is the **Capuccinni Monastery** that offers fine views of the city. Now a hotel, some areas will

Best Pottery

About five kilometers from Salerno (take buses 1, 4 or 9 from the train station and bus 10 from Amalfi), **Vietri** is the ceramic capital of the Amalfi Coast. Nondescript as Amalfi Coast towns go, it has an abundance of **ceramic stores**, all of which contain many designs unique to the region.

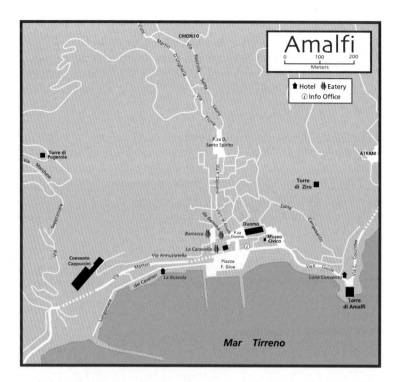

be off limits to visitors who are not guests of the hotel. A 15-minute boat ride away is the **Grotta di Amalfi**, an ancient stalactite cave on the coast. One kilometer away along the coast road is the tiny little village of Atrani, picturesquely sitting along the mouth of a rocky gorge. In the main piazza is the 10th century **church of San Salvatore**, complete with Byzantine bronze doors cast in Constinantinople in 1087.

Ravello

About five kilometers up the hill from Amalfi, **Ravello** is one of the most enchanting spots in the world. Perched on a 350-foot high cliff overlooking the azure sea of the Amalfi Coast, Ravello has preserved its historical monuments through the ages and incorporated them into everyday life. *Info:* www.ravello.it/aziendaturismo.

One of the most important monuments in Ravello is the **Cathedral**, founded in 1086. Here you can admire the Byzantine mosaic work on the pulpit, the bronze doors, and the civic museum located in the crypt. **Villa Rufolo** is another sight to see, especially when the views are complimented with the many music festivals they offer, one of which is the **Ravello Music Festival**, which usually begins in July each year. *Info:* www.ravelloarts.org or www.ravello.info.

The **Villa Cimbrone** also contains lush gardens and is known for its breathtaking views, which have been described by many as the best in the world. Other sights to see while in Ravello are the church of **San Giovanni del Toro** with its mosaic pulpit; the **Villa Episcopio** where King Vittorio Emanuele abdicated the throne; the cloister of the 13th century **convent of St. Francesco** with its amazing library; and the scenic **Piazza Fontana Moresca**.

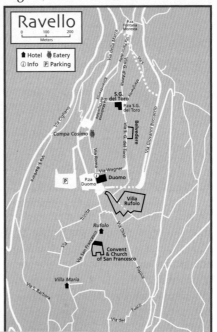

9. CINQUE TERRE & THE GULF OF POETS

The **Cinque Terre** ("the five lands") are the five villages of **Monterosso al Mare, Vernazza, Corniglia, Manarola** and **Riomaggiore**. Each is set precariously on the coastal cliffs and sloping vineyards of Liguria and are connected to each other by narrow winding country paths and an ancient railway line. You will find sublime panoramic vistas and incredibly serene hiking trails, however the life in these towns now revolves almost entirely around tourism. *Info:* www.cinqueterre.it or www.cinqueterreonline.com.

Still on the Ligurean coast, just a little further north are the towns of the **Golfo dei Poeti** ("Gulf of Poets"). Less rustic, more refined, the locations I have selected — **Sestri Levante, Rapallo, Santa Maria Ligure**, and **Portofino** — have been seaside resort towns for centuries. Even so they have lost none of their charm. In fact, I prefer them to the more popular Cinque Terre as they have not been completely taken over by mass tourism. But you be the judge.

A FANTASTIC WEEKEND IN THE CINQUE TERRE & RAPALLO

Already designated a UNESCO world heritage site, in 2002 the Italian government created the **Cinque Terre National Park** (*Info:* www.parconazionale5terre.it) to promote and safeguard the coastal rural territory of the Cinque Terre. The early inhabitants of the Cinque Terre transformed some rather inhospitable areas into a terraced agricultural landscape cultivated almost exclusively with grapevines and held up by nearly 7,000 kilometers of stone walls. With the onslaught of mass tourism in the area, dramatic erosion started to occur, so the National Park was created and an admission established to help recover and protect the landscape and grape production.

By visiting and hiking here, with the purchase of a **Cinque Terre Card** you are now part of the preservation. These one-day, three-day and seven-day cards offer an unlimited number of train journeys along the stretch of La Spezia – Levanto in second-class carriages; the use of electric and/or methane buses working in the centers of the villages of the Cinque Terre; access to all pedestrian walks, botanic paths, and serviced areas, run by the Cinque Terre National Park; and a map of trains and paths.

Friday Evening
First, buy a 3-day Cinque Terre Card from the local information

office of whatever town you choose to stay in. This will be the start of our three days of somewhat strenuous, though not daunting, hiking, interspersed with eating and drinking the delicious local food and wine of this region.

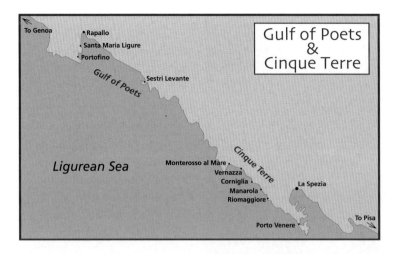

After getting our card, the next step in this weekend of *la dolce far niente*, the sweetness of doing nothing – except for eating, drinking and hiking that is – is to get settled into whatever hotel you have chosen. Try someplace in the middle three villages to be able to completely experience the rustic charm of these lands *(see Best Sleeps & Eats chapter).*

After you get settled in, next find the nearest open cafe or restaurant and begin your training in the fine art of relaxing. To get ready for our assault, of sorts, on this rugged and remote stretch of the Ligurean Coast remember to carb up. Wherever you eat, make sure to try the local pasta dish *al pesto*, made with basil, pine nuts, garlic, and parmesan cheese. As Liguria is the home of this dish, you will find the best in the world here.

Saturday
Just so you know, you can hike the Cinque Terre easily in **under five hours**, one end to the other. But that doesn't account for exploring the villages. All the trails in Cinque Terre are detailed on www.cinqueterre.it. And remember, there is a train that connects each village, so go as far as you can, and train back or forward in your journey if you get tired.

For sake of continuity, let's start our journey in **Monterrosso al Mare**. The church **San Giovanni Battista**, built in 1220, can be

ALTERNATE PLAN
If hiking is not your thing, you can always take the train, but try and visit all the villages of the Cinque Terre. Each has its own charm and character. Or better still you can buy the **Cinque Terre Ferryboat Card** and travel between each village by boat. With this card you get an unlimited number of journeys on the ferryboats in the Cinque Terre Marine Reserve from Riomaggiore to Monterosso al Mare. When buying your card at any of the Cinque Terre Park offices, you can also book guided tours, underwater trips, or a variety of environmental education excursions.

found among the narrow alleyways. The bell tower was initially built in 1400 as a part of a defensive network for the town. The **Cappuccini Convent** dates back to the 17th century and is also worth a look. Finally there is the church of **San Antonio di Mesco** built in 1335. On the new part of the village, known as Fegina, there is the Montale family's liberty style villa. On the promontory that separates Fegina from the historic centre, are the village's system of fortified walls and the Torre Aurora. Resting above the two parts of town are the ruins of a castle and its tower built in the 13th century.

From the town, the steep trail climbs inland via switchback stone steps. You pass tiny farms and gardens set off by stands of willows and overgrown streams. Periodically you will run into other hikers, especially during the high season. Higher up foot traffic decreases, the trail levels off and for the next hour you are in hiking heaven. The magnificent views are of deep blue Ligurian Sea and wave-lashed cliffs climbing the coast. Periodically you'll catch a glimpse of the next town, Vernazza, with its snaggle of red-roofed stone buildings, clinging to a promontory like some sea kingdom from a fairy tale.

Vernazza first appears in historical records in 1080 as a fortified village and maritime base of the Marchesi Obertenghi family. This medieval village filled with multi-hued houses and twisting alleyways is considered one of the most beautiful in Italy. If you make the time, catch the local ferry and arrive at this breathtaking village by sea. The ancient church of **Santa Margherita di**

Antiochia, located just off the small square is a pastiche of eras, with its eastern part is medieval structure, and its western side of renaissance construction. Vernazza also contains the ruins of its fortifications, the **Doria Castle**, the lookout tower from the 11th century, as well as the Tower for the Convent Padri Riformati di San Francesco.

If you do stay for lunch in Vernazza, try **Trattoria del Capitano**, where you'll have a great view of the sea as it crashes on the rocks below. *Info:* Tel. 0187/812-224. Meal for two €60. No credit cards accepted.

From here it is back onto the trail and onto **Corniglia** the only town in the Cinque Terre without access to the sea. To reach the town you ascend a long flight of brick steps. Surrounded on three sides by vineyards and terraces, this ancient Roman village's heritage was recorded by the eruption of Mt. Vesuvius hundreds of miles away in the Bay of Naples. During archeological excavations in Pompei wine amphorae with "Corenelia" written on them were found. To better appreciate that legacy, why not grab a quick glass while here.

You can also visit the eighteenth century square Largo Taragio with its oratory, **Santa Caterina**. Then there is the attractive church of **San Pietro**, built in 1334, which is a good example of the gothic Ligurian style and is one of the most interesting monuments of the entire coast. In the interior, the most interesting piece is the baptismal basin from the 12th century and the statues of the evangelists.

When you get to **Manarola**, maybe it's the exertion, maybe it's the wine, but this town does seem like a sparkling jewel in the crown of Cinque Terre. With its long narrow marina, colorful houses, and surrounding vineyards and olive groves, Manarola is breathtaking. In the low part of town you can admire the old mill and olive press that have been restored by the National Park. In Piazza Papa Innocenzo IV you can visit the **Church of San Lorenzo** built in 1338, the Campanile Bianco attached the church and erected in the 12th century as well. Then there is oratory of **Santissima Annunziata** from the fifteenth century and the historic hospital of San Rocco.

Finally, on to **Riomaggiore**. Nestled between two steep terraced hills that descend in abrupt cliffs to the sea, Riomaggiore is a

striking tableau of uniquely vertical and colorful houses. While strolling the tight network of alleyways, the village's archways and staircases offer an attractive setting. The vertical structures of the town all have two entrances: one on the lower street level, the other at the rear opens onto a higher road that guaranteed an escape route in case of Saracen attack centuries ago.

In the high part of town is 1340 Church of **San Giovanni Battista** and is made up of differently styled columns and with two gothic doors. The oratory of **Santa Maria Assunta**, built in 1500, the oratory of **San Antonio Abbate** and the oratory of **San Rocco** are also worth a visit.

Surrounding many of these breathtaking towns are **steep vineyards**, almost vertical in pitch sweeping as far as the eye can see. Many planted by Roman slaves two thousand years ago, they still turn out a rustic peasant wine, full bodied, and best drunk with a complement of Ligurian pasta. Putting us casual hikers to shame, locals clamber up the hillsides carrying baskets laden with ripe fruit.

Sunday
Wine, pasta, walking, but no rushing … that's the Cinque Terre and Golfo dei Poeti. To get a perspective on the region, and a contretemps to life in the Cinque Terre, catch the train to **Rapallo** for the day. A European holiday resort town for centuries, Rapallo still retains its local charm. It's beaches may be less glamorous and its yachts a little smaller than other nearby towns, but Rapallo has a charm the other two cities can't boast, a charm that has everything to do with its authenticity and simplicity.

On the promenade and the beach are where we will spend our day. An ancient **Castello**, with its square tower, sloping roof of slate, little windows and draw bridge, overlooks the harbor to the north by the little river San Francesco. The central community focus of Rapallo is its **daily market** in the Piazza Venezia, which offers visitors and locals alike a bounty of fresh fruit and vegetables, set against the backdrop of the city's vibrantly painted houses. Near here is **O Bansin** arguably Rapallo's best eatery, where we will have lunch. *Info:* Via Venezia 105, Tel. 0185/231-119, Closed Sundays and Monday nights, Meal for two €33.

A WONDERFUL WEEK IN THE CINQUE TERRE & THE GULF OF POETS

What was true for a weekend, is also true for a week — *la dolce far niente*, the sweetness of doing nothing. But for a week, we can savor more of it, in more places. Beyond the hiking of the **Cinque Terre** described in the weekend section above, and which will encompass the beginning of this week along the coast, there are some more refined towns in what is called the *Golfo dei Poeti*, the **Gulf of Poets**, we are also going to visit. Located north of the celebrated Cinque Terre and frequented for centuries by the European *conoscenti* of seaside living, this pristine gulf on the Ligurian Sea is populated with some amazing fishing villages, scenic towns and a relaxed pace of life that brings visitors back over and over again.

The most famous town in the area is **Portofino**. A movie set backdrop, with tiny cobbled streets, excellent hotels, superb restaurants, and a celebration of life has made this tiny village a place to visit for ages. Other towns to explore in this area, which over time have played host to all manner of celebrities include: **Santa Margherita Ligure**, **Rapallo** and **Sestri Levante**. Try one or sample all. If you are looking for a refined Italian beach resort-style vacation, these are all great places to stay and visit.

RECOMMENDED PLAN: Spend the first couple of days in one of the towns on the **Cinque Terre**. All are very pleasant. Then for the remainder of this relaxing week, make **Rapallo** your base of operations to visit Portofino and Santa Margherita Ligure. Each is accessible easily, inexpensively, and quickly by train, except for Portofino, which you have to take bus #82 to get to from the Santa Margherita Ligure station. Check at your local station or visit www.trenitalia.it for schedules.

Cinque Terre

Refer to the weekend section above and combine that with the sections below for a week in this area. Remember, you can hike the Cinque Terre easily in under five hours, one end to the other. But there are the villages themselves to explore. There is also a train that connects each village, so go as far as you can, and train back or forward in your journey if you get tired. *Info:* www.cinqueterre.it.

Rapallo

Unlike nearby Santa Margherita Ligure and Portofino — which are richer and more sophisticated — **Rapallo** really isn't a tourist town. Though Italian families vacation here in the summer, this is still more of a local place. In the off-season, while the Cinque Terre are still inundated with tourists, Rapallo returns to its languid pace of life. As such, it is definitely my favorite town in the area. Rapallo's beaches may be less glamorous and its yachts a little smaller, but Rapallo has a charm the other two cities can't boast, a charm that has everything to do with its authenticity and simplicity. *Info:* www.comune.rapallo.ge.it.

The central community focus of Rapallo is its daily market in the Piazza Venezia, which offers visitors and locals alike a bounty of fresh fruit and vegetables, set against the backdrop of the city's vibrantly painted houses. An amphitheater of hills protects Rapallo from cold northern winds, and as a result the climate is temperate year round. Rapallo is bisected by two streams that empty into its large bay, along which you will find a tree-lined promenade and tiny shops, restaurants and cafés.

On the promenade you will find the open air gazebo-like structure, the **Rotunda Marconi**, from which concerts are performed in the evenings during the summer months. An ancient **Castello**, with its square tower, sloping roof of slate, little windows and draw-

Take the Ferry

The best way to get around the Cinque Terre and Golfo dei Poeti is by **ferry**. Walking the towns, and visiting by train are a special way to experience this area, but nothing beats the peace, tranquility, and panoramic vistas of going by boat. *Info:* www.navigazionegolfodeipoeti.it.

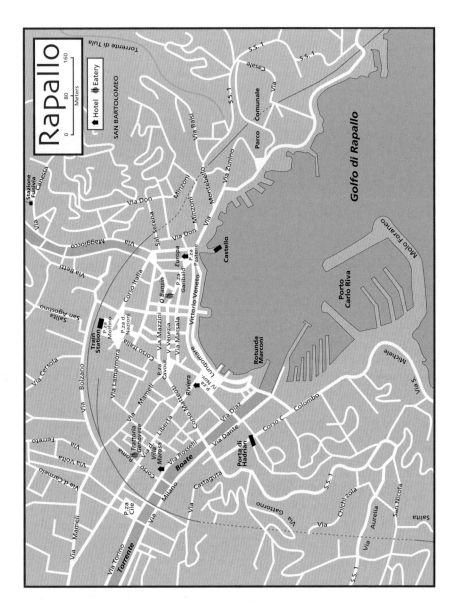

bridge, overlooks the harbor to the north by the little river San Francesco. Further north around the harbor entrance are the extensive gardens of the **Parco Comunale Casale**. By the river Baote across the harbor are some other gardens, the **Giardini Publici**, smaller but equally as relaxing.

Other sights to see in Rapallo are the **Sanctuary of Montallegro** (which you can get to by Funicular a short ways north of the town) and the Gothic ruins of the former convent of **Santa Maria in Christ Valley** up in the hills surrounding the town.

Santa Margherita Ligure

Slightly less frantic and fashionable than Portofino is **Santa Margherita Ligure**. It is still very local, as it too returns to a relaxed pace of life in the off-season. As a result, starting in October (the beginning of the off-season) is the best time to visit. A wide, spacious harbor and promenade take you into the quiet, friendly center, alive with artists, traditional shops, cafes, and time-honored, family run *trattorie* that thrive on the trade of locals and travelers alike. *Info:* www.turismoinliguria.it/turismo_en/santa-margherita-ligure.htm.

The Sunday promenade of families and friends along her shoreline clearly shows this amicable community-oriented approach to life. Stop for a coffee or ice cream along the promenade at the local favorite, **Bar Colombo**, an old apothecary-turned-café which is as elegant as it is engaging. Santa Margherita Ligure is one of the classicly beautiful places in the Golfo dei Poeti, and as such, cannot help but entrance.

The city is guarded by an imposing **castle** built by the Genovese when they controlled this port city. Today it houses the local **Museo Storico**. The central core of the town is referred to as **Pescino**, named for the fishing industry that for centuries was the town's main form of commerce. The harbor is lined with fashionable boutiques, cafes and restaurants, and is filled with a

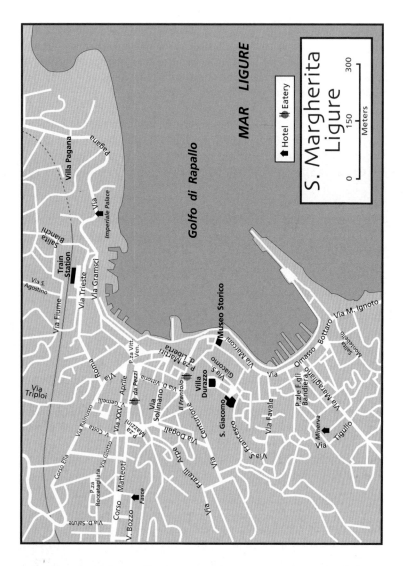

a lively atmosphere of commerce. You can still see the fishing boats returning, where their catch is gobbled up by the buyers for the local restaurants, as well housewives looking for bargains.

Besides wining and dining, you can visit the **Villa Durazzo** and its gardens dating back to 1560. Inside the villa is the **Museo G.**

Rossi, dedicated to the famous local journalist and novelist. You should also check out the church of **San Giacomo di Corte**. Located near Villa Durazzo and located on a panoramic hill overlooking the port, it is adorned with precious marbles and frescoes. Besides the beauty of the church, you can get some great photos of the bay and town from this vantage point.

Portofino

Originally a secluded little fishing village, **Portofino** was first discovered by the artistic set, then the sailing fraternity, and finally the rich and fashionable. Accented by the deep blue of the water and the lush green of the nature preserve hillsides, the colorful buildings of Portofino stand out like a movie set. This beauty has now turned the quiet little village into an extremely hip and stupefyingly expensive place to visit. Attracting many of Europe and Hollywood's *glitterati*, there are now hotels lining the narrow road that links Portofino with Santa Margherita Ligure. *Info:* www.comune.portofino.genova.it.

The center of Portofino is filled with high-end cafes, boutiques, and restaurants. Nonetheless, Portofino will stun you with her beauty despite the summer crowds. To get here take bus #82 from the Santa Margherita Ligure train station.

Leave the *piazzetta* and its pier lined with fishing nets drying in the sun, and you can amble up the hill to the **Chiesa** and **Castello di San Giorgio**. Here you will find the remains of the famous St. George, the dragon slayer. *Info:* open 9am–5pm, admission to the Castle is €3. From this vantage point you can walk through lush gardens and have superb scenic views over the town and the water on both sides of the peninsula. Going in the other direction from town you can hike up to a spot with wonderful views of the area, the **Belvedere**.

Sestri Levante

Located on the extreme southwest end of the *Golfo dei Poeti*, closest to the Cinque Terre, the town of **Sestri Levante** is a wonderful Italian seaside resort town: beautiful, refined, elegant, and relaxing. One of its two inlets, the Gulf of Ponente, was renamed the **Baia delle Favole** (Bay of Fables) by Hans Christian Andersen because of its fairy tale beauty. On the other side of the 'island' is the **Baia del Silenzio**, so named for its peace and quiet.

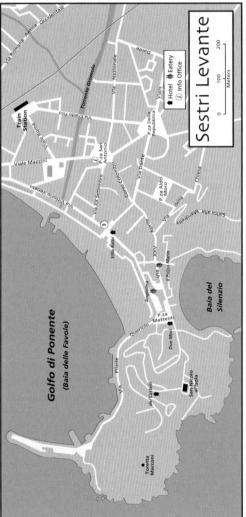

The 'island' really is a peninsula upon which the **Toretta Marconi** (Marconi's Tower) sits watching over the town. Gugliemo Marconi began his experimentation with short wave radio signals here. Also on the peninsula is the rustic little **Church of San Nicolo**, built around 1511, and the superb high end hotel, **Dei Castelli**. So named because the hotel structures are former castles that once guarded the town.

The peninsula on which the tower sits at one time was an actual island, but around the 11th century silt had built up from the Gromolo stream between it and the shore. Today people still refer to it as the 'island' – see, the past is still alive in Italy.

Come to Sestri Levante to sunbathe, swim, go sailing, eat great food, and simply to relax. Whatever you do, wherever you stay, Sestri Levante and the Golfo dei Poeti are a peaceful respite from the world, while also offering easy access to the art and culture of the Italian Peninsula. The best of both worlds. *Info:* www.sestri-online.com.

10. BEST SLEEPS & EATS

Italy has an incredible array of hotels and restaurants, and I've selected the best in each price category for this book. The **hotel star rating system** that the Italian Tourist Board officially uses has little to do with the prices, but more to do with the amenities you will find. The prices for each category will vary according to the locale, so if it's a big city, a four star will be super-expensive; if it's a small town, it will be priced like a three or two star in a big city.

And the **food and wine** – by far the best and most varied in the world. Created with the freshest ingredients and always with a distinctly local flair, the cooking is healthy and nutritious and the variety of flavors and tastes will tantalize and satisfy like no other cuisine. Treat yourself to great wines like Chianti, Ruffino, Frascati and many more.

The hotels and restaurants in this chapter can be found on the maps that go with each destination chapter (see map locator in the Table of Contents).

ROME

BEST SLEEPS
Five stars
Eden is an incredible place to stay … if you have the means. *Info:* Via Ludovisi, 49, Tel. 06/474-3551, Fax 06/482-1584. www.hotel-eden.it. 100 rooms. Single €440-460; Double €650-750, Suites €1,800-3,400. Continental breakfast is €14 extra, buffet breakfast is €20. Rome Map A.

Hassler is the choice for many of the *glitterati* that visit Rome because of its refined elegance and location. *Info:* Piazza Trinita Dei Monti 6, Tel. 06/699-340, Fax 06/678-2651. www.hotelhasslerroma.com. All credit cards accepted. 80 rooms. Single €430-460; Double €520-790. Suites €1,800-3,200. Continental breakfast €23 extra. Buffet breakfast €35 extra. Rome Map A.

Four stars
Barocco *(see photo on page 246)* is an ideally located small boutique hotel that is refined, elegant, and comfortable. *Info:* Piazza Barberini 9 (entrance on Via della Purificazione 4), Tel. 06/487-2001/2/3, 487-2005, Fax 06/485-994. www.hotelbarocco.com. 37 rooms. Single €200-250; Double €250-400. Breakfast included. All credit cards accepted. Rome Map A.

Mecenate Palace is the best four star by the train station. *Info:* Via Carlo Alberto 3, Tel. 06/4470-2024, Fax 06/446-1354. www.mecenatepalace.com. All credit cards accepted. 62 rooms. Single €260-320; Double €370. Breakfast included. Rome Map D.

Three stars
Internazionale is an elegant boutique hotel near the top of the Spanish Steps. Highly recommended. *Info:* Via Sistina 79, Tel. 06/6994-1823, Fax 06/678-4764. www.hotelinternazionale.com. All credit cards accepted. 42 rooms. Single €120-200; Double €180-300; Extra bed €55. Buffet breakfast included. Rome Map A.

Locarno is the tops, the Mona Lisa of three stars in Rome. *Info:* Via della Penna 22, Tel. 06/361-0841, Fax 06/321-5249. www.hotellocarno.com. All credit cards accepted. 38 rooms. Single €150; Double €220-310; Suite €310-510. Breakfast included. Rome Map B.

Modigliani is an artistic hotel near the Spanish Steps and one of my favorite places to stay in Rome. *Info:* Via della Purificazione 42, Tel. 06/4281-5226. www.hotelmodigliani.com. 28 rooms. Single €120-160; Double €160-200. All credit cards accepted. Rome Map A.

Scalinata Di Spagna is located directly at the top of the Spanish Steps. A great place to stay. *Info:* Piazza Trinita Dei Monte 17, Tel. 06/679-3006 and 06/679-0896, Fax 06/684-0598. www.hotelscalinata.com. All credit cards accepted. 16 rooms all with baths. Double €130-370. Breakfast included. Rome Map A.

Columbia is located near the opera, by the train station, has lovely rooms and scenic but small roof garden. *Info:* Via del Viminale 15, Tel. 06/474-4289, Fax 06/474-0209. www.hotelcolumbia.com. 45 rooms. Single €125-230; Double €165-230. Off Rome Map A.

De Petris is a quality three star in an ideal and tranquil location. A good choice in the heart of Rome. *Info:* Via Rasella 142, Tel. 06/481-9626. Fax 06/482-0733. www.hoteldepetris.com. 53 rooms. Single €130-180; Double €130-230. All credit cards accepted. Breakfast €15. Rome Map A.

Richmond is simply fantastic. The rooms are large and incredibly

accommodating, there is a lovely terrace with stupendous views over the Forum and Colosseum. *Info:* Largo Corrado Ricci 36, Tel. 06/6994-1256, Fax 06/6994-4145. www.hotelrichmondroma.com. 13 rooms. Single €135-170; Double €200. Breakfast included. Rome Map D.

Trevi is an elite, upscale three-star in a wonderful location, near the Trevi Fountain. Along with great rooms there is also a wonderful roof garden. There are two other hotels of note in this small hotel group, so if this one is full, check out the other two. *Info:* Vicolo del Babuccio 20/21, Tel. 06/6994-1406, Fax 06/6994-1407. www.gruppotrevi.it. 29 rooms. Single €190-225; Double €270. All credit cards accepted. Breakfast included. Rome Map A.

Rome

Two stars

Merano is well located, has comfortable rooms, good prices, and is one of the top two stars in Rome. *Info:* Via Vittorio Veneto 155, Tel. 06/482-1796, Fax 06/482-1810. www.guestinitaly.com/hotels/rome/r002.htm. All credit cards accepted. 30 rooms 28 with bath. Single without bath €50-60; Single €60-70; Double without bath €70-90; Double €90-120. Rome Map A.

Parlamento is located in the center of the city, near everything, a great place for budget travelers. *Info:* Via delle Convertite 5, Tel. 06/6992-1000, Fax 06/679-2082. www.hotelparlamento.it. All credit cards accepted. 22 rooms, 19 with bath. Single without bath €65. Single €80-130. Double €90-170. Breakfast included. Rome Map A.

Trastevere is situated in my favorite part of town, and in my opinion is the best two star in the city. They also have expansive and inexpensive apartments for rent. *Info:* Via Luciano Manara 24/25, Tel. 06/58-14-713, Fax 06/58-81-016. www.hoteltrastevere.net. 30 rooms. All credit cards accepted. Single €100; Double €140. Breakfast included. Rome Map B.

Golden is an upscale *pensione* just off of the world-famous Via Veneto. All the amenities of a three star, in a great location at the prices of an upscale two star. *Info:* Via Marche 84, Tel. 06/482-1659, www.hotelgoldenrome.com. 12 of the 13 rooms have private baths. All credit cards accepted. Single €60-100; Double €90-150. Rome Map A.

Rome

BEST EATS

Re degli Amici is close to the Spanish Steps and has been serving traditional Roman food for years. Try any of the Roman pasta specialties: *carbonara, amatriciana,* or *arrabiata. Info:* Via della Croce 33b, Tel. 06/679-5380 or 678-2555. Credit cards accepted. Closed Mondays and the last three weeks in June. Meal for two €40. Rome Map A.

Otello alla Concordia is a family-run, small *trattoria* serving traditonal Roman fare. The best place to sit is on their terrace just off of Via della Croce. *Info:* Via Della Croce 81. Tel. 06/679-1178. Credit cards accepted. Closed Sundays. Meal for two €40. Rome Map A.

Dinner with a View

These places are all high-end eateries in top-of-the-line hotels that also offer some **tantalizing views over Rome.** Make reservations and specifically request a table with a view.
• **Eden Hotel Restaurant,** Via Ludovisi, 49, www.hotel-eden.it, Map A.
• **Hassler Hotel Restaurant,** Piazza Trinita dei Monti 6, www.hotelhasslerroma.com, Map A *(photo below).*
• **Risorante Olimpio,** Piazza Barberini 23, www.berninibristol.com, Map A.

Vecchia Roma is in one of Rome's best locations in a great piazza near the Jewish Ghetto. The ambiance is delightful, the service great, and the food fantastico. *Info:* Piazza di Campitelli 18, Tel. 06/656-4604. No credit cards accepted. Closed Wednesdays. Meal for two €43. Rome Map B.

La Cafetteria is an upscale and traditional cafe that serves some of the best quick and tasty food in Rome. *Info:* Piazza di Pietra 65, Tel. 06/679-8147. Closed in August and Sundays in July. Hours 7am-9pm. Meal for two €25. Rome Map A.

La Canonica is situated in a converted chapel just off the Piazza Santa Maria in Trastevere. Combined with that incredible atmosphere are a variety of local Roman dishes. *Info:* Vicolo dei Piede 13, just off of the Piazza Santa Maria in Trastevere. Closed Mondays. Major credit cards accepted. Tel. 06/580-3845. Meal for two €40. Rome Map B.

Sora Lella is located on an island in the Tiber, and has the food to match its incomparable atmosphere. *Info:* Via di Ponte IV Capi 16, Tel. 06/ 686-1601. www.soralella.com. Closed Sundays. Credit cards accepted. Meal for two €60. Rome Map B.

Best High-End Dining

Rome

• **Dal Bolognese** serves up delectable fare in an elegant environment. *Info:* Piazza del Popolo 1-2, Map B.
• **Sabatini I** has been a staple of refined dining in Rome for decades. *Info:* Piazza Santa Maria in Trastevere 13, Map B.
• **Buccone** is a tiny, local wine bar *and* the best place to buy a bottle to bring home with you. *Info:* Via di Ripetta 19, Map B.

Al Piccolo Arancio is a local place hidden down a side street near the Trevi Foutain that serves traditional Roman cuisine. *Info:* Vicolo Scandberg 112, Tel. 06/678-6139. www.ristorantidiroma.com. Closed Mondays. Credit cards accepted. Meal for two €45. Rome Map A.

Le Grotte is a superb *pizzeria/trattoria* in the heart of Il Tridente. It looks like a cave inside, hence the name. *Info:* Via delle Vite 37. Tel. 06/679-5336.. Credit cards accepted. Meal for two €35. Rome Map A.

La Buca di Ripetta is my favorite restaurant in Rome. Rustic and refined and completely local with superb food. You will definitely need to make reservations. *Info:* Via di Ripetta 36, Tel. 06/321-9391. Closed Mondays and the whole month of August. No credit cards accepted. Meal for two €35. Rome Map A.

La Carbonara is a historic restaurant, ideally situated and serves

Rome
Florence

great food in an incredible atmosphere. *Info:* Campo dei Fiori 23, Tel. 06/686-4783. Credit cards accepted. Closed Tuesdays. Meal for two €45. Rome Map B.

Enotecantica is a superb wine bar near the Spanish Steps. *Info:* Via del Croce 76, Tel. 06/679-0896. Closed Sundays. Meal for two €28. All credit cards accepted. Rome Map A & B.

Vini e Buffet is the best wine bar in the city. *Info:* Piazza della Torretta 60, Tel 06/687-1445. Open 12:30pm-2:30pm and 7:30pm to midnight. Closed Sundays. Meal for two €25. Rome Map A, B & C.

Cavour 313 is an authentic *enotecha* near the Colosseum. *Info:* Via Cavour 313, Tel. 06/678-5496. Open 12:30pm-2:30pm and 7:30pm-12:30am. Closed Sundays. Meal for two €25. Rome Map D.

Cul de Sac is a savory wine bar near Piazza Navona. *Info:* Piazza di Pasquino 73, Tel. 06/6880-1094. Open 12:30pm-3:30pm and 7pm-12:30am. Closed Mondays for lunch. Meal for two €25. Rome Map B.

FLORENCE

BEST SLEEPS
Five stars
Villa Cora is a superb hotel set in tranquil environs. People with means stay here. *Info:* Viale Machiavelli 18-20, Tel. 055/229-8451, Fax 055/229-086. www.villacora.it. All credit cards accepted. 47 rooms. Single €200-300; Double €300-550. Suite €500-1,450. Breakfast included.

Westin Excelsior is a very high-end hotel in the heart of the city. *Info:* Piazza Ognissanti 3, Tel. 055/264-201, Fax 055/210-278. Toll free number in America 1-800-221-2340. www.westin.com. All credit cards accepted. 200 rooms. Single €415-460; Double €520-580. Continental breakfast €15. American breakfast €22.

Four Stars

Villa Carlotta is like something out of a dream, with its sunlit tea room used for breakfast, a small garden with fountain, and an elegant dining area. Off the beaten path in a quiet and calm section of town. A truly great place to stay. *Info:* Via Michele di Lando 3, Tel. 055/233-6134, Fax 055/233-6147. www.hotelvillacarlotta.it/. All credit cards accepted. 27 rooms. Five more in a gatehouse building. Single €180-250; Double €250-300. Breakfast included.

Florence

Lungarno is all about location. Right on the Arno River, only a few meters from the Ponte Vecchio, and situated down a quaint, Florentine side street with some great restaurants and food shops. This is one of the great hotels in Florence. *Info:* Borgo S Jacopo 14, Tel. 055/264-211, Fax 055/268-437. www.lungarnohotels.it. All credit cards accepted. 66 rooms. Single €230; Double €330-370; Suite €510.

Astoria is a great four star in the heart of Florence. Ideally located. Be prepared to be pampered. They also have an incredible restaurant. *Info:* Via del Giglio 9, Tel. 055/239-8095, Fax 055/214-632. www.boscolohotels.com. 103 rooms. Single €170-280; Double €220-340. (**Agora Restaurant**, Via del Giglio 11, Tel. 055/219-389, www.sinisgalli.com.) Breakfast €15. Parking €20.

Torre di Bellosguardo is my favorite place to stay in Florence.

Overlooking the city, with the most amazing views of the entire cityscape. Situated in a romantic castle/*palazzo* and surrounded by beautiful manicured grounds and two relaxing pools. *Info:* Via Roti Michelozzi 2, Tel. 055/229-8145, Fax 055/  229-008. www.torrebellosguardo.com. 16 rooms. Single €170; Double €290. All credit cards accepted. Breakfast €20.

Three Stars

Pitti Palace is a wonderful three-star only a few paces from the Ponte Vecchio. The two terraces on the sixth floor offer incomparable panoramic views over the Boboli gardens, Palazzo Pitti, the Duomo and the rest of the city across the river. *Info:* Via Barbadori 2, Tel-Fax 055/239-8711. http://pittipalace.hotelinfirenze.com/ . All credit cards accepted. 73 rooms. Single €200-250; Double €300-450. Breakfast included. Parking €22.

Dante is a bed and breakfast style hotel with ten rooms complete with kitchenette. Near the picturesque piazza of Santa Croce this is a great place to stay. *Info:* Via San Cristofano 2, Tel. 055/241-772, Fax 055/234-5819. http://dante.hotelinfirenze.com. All credit cards accepted. 14 rooms. Single €90-110; Double €120-190. Breakfast €10. Parking €12.

Beacci-Tornabuoni is on Florence's equivalent of 5th Avenue and is a refined three-star. *Info:* Via Tornabuoni 3, Tel. 055/212-645, Fax 055/283-594. www.bthotel.it. All credit cards accepted. 28 rooms. Single €130-160; Double €190-250. Extra bed €30. Buffet breakfast included.

Hermitage is at the foot of the Ponte Vecchio with views over the Arno and bridge. High end three star. *Info:* Vicolo Marzio 1 (Piazza del Pesce), Tel. 055/287-216, Fax 055/212-208. www.hermitagehotel.com. Credit cards accepted. 16 rooms all with private bath and jacuzzi. All rooms €120-240. Breakfast included.

Loggiato dei Serviti is situated in a beautiful piazza just outside of

the *centro storico*. I love this place! *Info:* Piazza SS. Annunziata 3, Tel. 055/289-593/4, Fax 055/289-595. www.loggiatodeiservitihotel.it. All credit cards accepted. 29 rooms. Single €90-140; Double €140-205; Suite €190-380. Breakfast included. €40 for an extra bed.

Two stars
Crocini is located outside of the center. A good choice for those

who want high quality but do not want to spend too much for it. *Info:* Corso Italia 28, Tel. 055/212-905, Fax 055/239-8345. www.hotelcrocini.com. Closed December 18-26. All credit cards accepted. 1 suite, 20 rooms (17 with private bath, 2 with shared bath, 1 with private bath outside of room). Single €100; Double €120. Breakfast €8. Parking €10.

La Scaletta is the best two star in town. Ideally located, comfortable, and with a great roof deck. *Info:* Via Guicciardini 13, Tel. 055/283-028, Fax 055/289-562. www.lascaletta.com. Credit cards accepted. 12 rooms, 11 with private bath. Single €60-100; Double €75-150. Breakfast included.

One star
Firenze is surprisingly comfortable for a one-star and has an ideal location. Stay here if you are traveling on a budget. *Info:* Piazza dei Donati 4 (off of Via del Corso), Tel. 055/268-301, Fax 055/212-370. www.hotelfirenze-fi.it. Credit cards accepted. 60 rooms, 35 with private bath. Single €70-90; Double €75-110. Breakfast included.

No Star
Istituto Gould is an orphanage and educational facility for needy children. The proceeds from your stay help fund the Institutes programs. Located in an old palazzo in the Oltrarno, the rooms and common areas here are spacious and comfortable. A great place to stay for budget travelers. The best price/quality ratio in Florence. *Info:* Via dei Serragli 49, Tel. 055/212-576, Fax 055/280-274. www.istitutogould.it. No credit cards accepted. 25 rooms, 20 with private bath. Single €36-41; Double €30-41 per person.

BEST EATS
Bussola serves superb pizza as well as pasta in a central location in Florence. *Info:* Via Porta Rossa 58, Tel. 055/293-376. Credit cards accepted. Closed Mondays. Meal for two €45.

Latini has a distinct local feel and tasty traditional cuisine. One of my favorites. *Info:* Via Palchetti 6, Tel. 055/210-916. Credit cards accepted. Closed Mondays and Tuesdays for lunch. Dinner for two €40.

Buca Lapi is one of the very best restaurants Florence has to offer. *Info:* Via del Trebbio 1, Tel. 055/213-768. All credit cards accepted. Closed Sundays. Meal for two €35.

Le Belle Donne is an eclectically decorated tiny *trattoria* that is always packed with locals clamoring for the excellent food they prepare. If you are looking for classic Tuscan cooking, with friendly and accommodating wait staff, this is a great place to have a meal. *Info:* Via delle Belle Donne 16r, Tel. 055/2380-2609. Closed Saturdays, Sundays and in August. No credit cards accepted. Meal for two €40.

La Cantinetta di Rignana is located in the heart of the Chianti Classico section of Tuscany, down a series of small roads, through a tiny town, and up a dirt road at the top of a hill. Surrounded by olive groves and vineyards where they make their own oil and wine served with meals. The atmosphere is sublime, the food is tantalizing, the wait staff engaging, and the views from the outside eating area stupendous. *Info:* Loc. Rignana 50022 Greve in Chianti, Tel. 055/852-601 or 335/825-2669. www.lacantinettadirignana.it. Closed Tuesdays. Meal for two €50.

Il Pizzaiuolo is a great little pizzeria well off the beaten tourist path. Remember to make reservations since Il Pizzaiuolo is always packed. Via de' Macci 113r, Tel. 055/241171. Closed Sundays and in August. No credit cards accepted. Meal for two €25.

La Spada is my favorite eatery in all of Florence. Down-to-earth and unpretentious, the menu here is varied, tasty, and the portions are immense. A working man's place, come here for a taste of real Florence. *Info:* Via della Spada 62r, Tel. 055/218-757, www.laspadaitalia.com.

Fuori Porta is the best wine bar in Florence. This lively *enotecha* has lovely atmosphere, with a relaxing terrace, definitely off the beaten path, just outside the old walls of Florence at the foot of the hills of the Piazzalle Michelangelo. *Info:* Via Monte alle Croci 10r, Tel. 055/234-2483. Closed Sundays and August. Credit cards accepted. Meal for two €30.

Florence

Tredici Gobbi serves mainly Florentine cuisine, with a few Hungarian dishes added for flair. Located off the beaten path, this place has great atmosphere and food. *Info:* Via del Porcellana 9R. Tel. 055/284-015. Credit cards accepted. Meal for two €35.

Dal Gallo Nero is located in a basement vault and serves authentic Tuscan specialties. *Info:* Via Santo Spirito 6r, Tel. 055/218-898. Closed Mondays and August. Credit cards accepted. Meal for two €30.

Coco Lezzone has long communal tables that are generally filled with Florentines and tourists alike here to enjoy the authentic Tuscan cuisine and atmosphere. *Info:* Via dei Parioncino 26, Tel. 055/287-178. No credit cards accepted. Closed Saturdays and Sundays in the Summer and Tuesdays for dinner. In the winter closed Sundays and Tuesdays for dinner. Meal for two €45.

Nerbone is a small food stand in the Mercato Centrale that has been serving up great food since 1872. Sample their panini sandwiches and dine like a native. *Info:* Mercato Centrale, Tel. 055/219-949. No credit cards accepted. Closed Sundays. Meal for two €12.

Il Cibreo serves a combination of traditional and nouvelle cuisine. *Info:* Via dei Macci 118r, Tel. 055/234-1100. All credit cards accepted. Closed Sundays, Mondays and August. Meal for two €65.

Trattoria 4 Leoni serves superb local food, in a rustic ambiance, deep in the heart of the artisan district. You will definitely need to make reservations. *Info:* Piazza dell Passera, Tel 055/218-562. Closed Mondays. Credit cards accepted. Meal for two €30.

La Casalinga is an authentic Oltrarno-style *trattoria* serving classic Tuscan that is simple, tasty and filling. *Info:* Via dei Michelozzi 9r, Tel. 055/218-624. Closed Sundays and the first 20 days in August. No credit cards accepted. Meal for two €25.

Mamma Gina has all sorts of dishes to satisfy even the most discerning palate. More tourist than local now, but the food is still good. *Info:* Borgo S Jacopo 37, Tel. 055/239-6009, Fax 055/213-908. www.mammagina.it. All credit cards accepted. Closed Sundays. Meal for two €42.

LUCCA

BEST SLEEPS

La Luna is a professionally run boutique three-star hotel. *Info:* Via Fillungo, Corte Compagni 12, Tel. 0583/493-634, Fax 0583/490-021. www.hotellaluna.com. Credit cards accepted. 30 rooms. Single €82; Double €112.

Puccini is a beautifully appointed stylish three-star hotel that is intimate, comfortable and cozy. *Info:* Via di Poggio 9, Tel. 0583/55421 or 53487, Fax 0583/53487. www.hotelpuccini.com. 14 rooms. Single €80; Double €120. Credit cards accepted.

BEST EATS

Da Leo Fratelli Buralli is rustic and local, a true slice of authentic Lucca. By far the best place to have a meal in Lucca. *Info:* Via Tegrimi 1, Tel. 0583/492-236. Closed Sundays. No credit cards accepted. Meal for two €30.

La Buca di Sant'Antonio is an exceptional restaurant, the most classic and refined of all places in Lucca. The atmosphere in here is 19th century opulence and the cuisine is sublime. You need to make reservations. *Info:* Via della Cervia 1/3, Tel. 0583/55881. Closed Sunday evenings, Mondays, and in July. All credit cards accepted. Dinner for two €50.

PISA

BEST SLEEPS

Ariston is a comfortable three-star with all necessary amenities located right by the Leaning Tower. *Info:* Via Cardinale Maffi 42, Tel. 050/561-834, Fax 050/561-891. www.hotelariston.pisa.it. 35 rooms all with bath. Single €60-80; Double €80-105. Breakfast included. All credit cards accepted.

BEST EATS

Dei Cavalieri is a small local place that has good pasta and meat dishes. *Info:* Via San Frediano 16, Closed Saturdays for lunch and Sundays. Meal for two €32.

La Grotta is an old Pisan restaurant that has the look and feel of a cave, hence the name. As such the atmosphere is unique and complements the rustic Pisan cuisine. *Info:* Via San Francesco 103, Closed Sundays and in August. Meal for two €35.

SIENA

BEST SLEEPS

Grand Hotel Continental, a five-star, is the top of the line. The best hotel in Siena. *Info:* Via Banchi di Sopra 85, Tel. 0577/56011. Fax 0577/560-1555. www.royaldemeure.com. Single €295-360. Double €390-540. Suite €630-1350. Breakfast €26. All credit cards accepted.

Stay on a Farm!

If you want to something different, stay at an *Agriturismo*, many of which are working farms that have converted buildings on their property to three-star equivalent accommodations. Generally you will get a great meal and a comfortable place to stay in serene surroundings. One *agri* near Montepulciano is **Agriturismo Poggio Etrusco**. Owned by an American couple, this villa, grounds and swimming pool are a refreshing change from the urbanity of Italian cities. *Info:* Via del Pelagro 11, Loc. Fontecornino-S. Albino di Montepulciano. Tel/Fax 0578/783-370. In the US 805/963-7289. www.foodartisans.com.

Palazzo Ravizza is situated in a tranquil spot in the *centro storico*

with good views over the city and the surrounding countryside. The best three-star in town. *Info:* Pian dei Mantellini 34, Tel. 0577/280-462, Fax 0577/221-597. www.palazzoravizza.it. 30 rooms. Single €80-130; Double €100-270. Breakfast included. All credit cards accepted.

Villa Liberty, another nice three-star, is a little ways outside the walls of Siena and is more of a bed and breakfast than a hotel. The back garden is a great place to relax in warm weather. *Info:* Viale Vittorio Veneto 11, Tel. 0577/449-666, Fax 0577/44770. www.villaliberty.it. 12 rooms. Single €50-75; Double €90-135. All credit cards accepted. Breakfast included.

Lea is a superb two-star located in a small villa from the 1800s, in a tranquil residential area near the center, surrounded by a small garden set with tables and chairs. *Info:* Viale XXIV Maggio 10, Tel & Fax 0577/283-207. 12 rooms. Single €50; Double €70. All credit cards accepted. Breakfast included.

BEST EATS
Da Divo, behind the Duomo and well off the beaten tourist path, has fabulous ambiance and great food. A high end establishment. Come here and savor a well created and presented Sienese meal. *Info:* Via Franciosa 25, Credit cards accepted. Meal for two €60.

Malborghetto is my favorite place in Siena, behind the campo but with views of nearby fields. Having a meal here is like being in the country, but it is only 100 meters from the center of Siena. Sit on their relaxing terrace and savor their excellent local cuisine *Info:* Via di Porta Giustizia 6. www.malborghetto.it. Closed Tuesdays. Meal for two €50.

Tullio is completely local, boisterously Italian, and serves great local cuisine. The ambiance is charmingly rustic, and is located well off the beaten path, keeping the tourist influx to a minimum. *Info:* Vicolo di Provenzano 1, Closed Wednesdays. Credit cards accepted. Meal for two €50.

Il Biondo has an ambient terrace and great food including *spaghetti alla vongole* and *penne alla puttanesca* (literally translated it means whore's pasta, made with tomatoes, garlic, black olives, olive oil and meat). *Info:* Vicolo del Rustichetto 10, Closed Wednesdays. Meal for two €40.

Siena

San Gimignano

SAN GIMIGNANO

BEST SLEEPS
L'Antico Pozzo is located in a magnificent three-star 15th century

palazzo, and is an elegant and refined boutique hotel. *Info:* Via San Matteo 87, Tel. 0577/942-014, Fax 0577/942-117. www.anticopozzo.com. 18 rooms. Single €90; Double €150. All credit cards accepted. Breakfast included.

La Cisterna is a nice three-star located in the most charming square of this incredibly beautiful town. *Info:* Piazza della Cisterna 24, Tel. 0577/940-328, Fax 0577/942-080. www.sangimignano.com/lacisterna/. 50 rooms. Single €70; Double €120.

BEST EATS
Bel Soggiorno has an elegant and refined ambiance serving traditional Tuscan cuisine. By far the best restaurant in town. Come dressed appropriately. *Info:* Via S. Giovanni 91, Closed Wednesdays and between Jan 6 and March 1. Meal for two €60.

Osteria delle Catene has arched brick ceilings and white walls and serves superb Tuscan cuisine. *Info:* Via Mainardi 18, Closed Wednesdays. Meal for two €50.

CORTONA

BEST SLEEPS

San Michele is a wonderful four-star deep in the heart of town.

Info: Via Guelfa 15, Tel.0575/ 604348, Fax 0575/630147. www.hotelsanmichele.net. 37 rooms. Single €90, Double €140. All credit cards accepted. Breakfast included.

San Luca is a comfortable four-star with commanding views over the surrounding countryside. *Info:* Piazza Garibaldi, Tel. 0575/63-460. www.sanlucacortona.com. 60 rooms. Single €70, Double €100. All credit cards accepted. Breakfast included.

BEST EATS

Dardanno is an authentic and down to earth family *trattoria* with great food. The specialty pasta of the house is ravioli with all sorts of fillings, including *cinghiale* (wild boar) and *anatra* (turkey). *Info:* Via Dardanno 24, Tel. 0575/601944. Closed on Mondays. No credit cards accepted. Dinner for two €30.

Del Teatro is filled with soft classical music echoing off of terra cotta floors, wood beamed ceilings, and walls decoratively arrayed with quality art. Best of all, the food is superb and the prices are reasonable. *Info:* Via Maffei 2, Tel. 0575/630-556. Closed Wednesdays. Meal for two €45.

Pane e Vino has rustic charm, a great wine list, friendly service, and traditional, simple, organic food. *Info:* Piazza Signorelli 27, Tel. 0575/631-010. www.pane-vino.it. Closed Mondays. Only open in the evenings. Meal for two €25.

MONTEPULCIANO

BEST SLEEPS
Il Borghetto is a character-filled three-star hotel in the heart of Montepulciano, situated in a 16th century building. Request one of the rooms with views over the surrounding countryside. *Info:* Via Borgo Buio 7, Tel. 0578/757-535, Fax 0578/757-354. www.ilborghetto.it. 15 rooms, 2 suites. Single €95; Double €105.

Il Marzocco is located inside the old city walls. Situated in a 16th century palazzo, this three-star has been run by the same family for over 100 years, and has been a hotel since 1860 ... and in some places it is a little rough around the edges. *Info:* Piazza Savonarola 18, Tel. 0578/757-262, Fax 0578/757-530. www.cretedisiena.com/albergoilmarzocco. 16 rooms. Single €60; Double €90. All credit cards accepted.

BEST EATS
Trattoria di Cagnano is where the locals eat in Montepulciano. Replete with rustic charm and superb culinary offerings. *Info:* Via del' Oppio ne Corso 30, Tel. 0578/758-757. Closed Mondays. Meal for two €40.

Caffé Poliziano is an upscale cafe and restaurant in Montepulciano. *Info:* Via di Voltaia ne Corso 27, Tel. 0578/758-615.

VENICE

BEST SLEEPS
Four stars
Ca dei Conti is a wonderful little hotel, on probably the most picturesque canal in Venice and is in my favorite area of town. Fondamenta di Remedio 4429, Tel. 041/277-0500, Fax 041/277-0727. www.cadeiconti.com/en/index.htm. Credit cards accepted. 30 rooms. Single €155; Double €200-260. Venice Map – Castello I.

Cipriani is an exquisite hotel occupying three beautiful acres at

Venice

the east end of Guidecca. This hotel is probably as close to heaven on earth as you'll find in Venice. Fondamenta San Giovanni 10, La Guidecca, Tel. 041/520-7744, Fax 041/520-3930. www.cipriani.orient-express.com. Credit cards accepted. 98 rooms. Single €499-755; Double €640-1,350. Venice Map – Giudecca.

Santa Marina is located in a distinctly local square, on three floors of an old palazzo. Here you're in the middle of everything, but just far enough away to be a part of the true life of Venice. Campo Santa Marina 6068, Tel. 041/523-9202, Fax 041/520-0907. www.hotelsantamarina.it. 19 rooms. Single €250; Double €300-350. Venice Map – Castello I.

Bonvecchiati is an elegant and refined hotel in a wonderfully central location. Calle Goldoni, 30124 Tel. 041/528-5017, Fax 041/528-5230. www.hotelbonvecchiati.it. Credit cards accepted. 86 rooms. Single €145-225; Double €130-290. Breakfast included. Vaporetto Stop – San Marco. Venice Map–San Marco.

Three stars
San Cassiano is by far the best three-star in Venice! Located in a 16th century Gothic palazzo on the Grand Canal, ideally located near San Marco but off the beaten path enough to offer a real Venetian experience. Calle della Rosa 2232, Tel. 041/524-1768 Fax 041/721-033. www.sancassiano.it. All credit cards accepted. 35 rooms. Single €80-235; Double €100-335. Breakfast included. Venice Map – Santa Croce & San Polo II.

Belle Arti is a top notch three-star hotel with great rooms, a comfortable and relaxing garden area, superb furnishings, and a character filled ambiance. Dorsoduro 912/A, Tel. 041/522-6230, Fax 041/528-0043. www.hotelbellearti.com. Single €95-150; Double €150-210. All credit cards accepted. Breakfast included. Vaporetto Stop – Accademia. Venice Map–Dorsoduro.

Abbazia was once a part of a monastery and is now a comfortable hotel filled with loads of charm. Calle Priuli 68, Tel. 041/717-333, Fax 041/717-949. www.abbaziahotel.com. Credit cards accepted. 31 rooms. Single €80-235, Double €90-260. Breakfast included. Vaporetto Stop – Ca' d'Oro. Venice Map–Canareggio.

Venice

Locanda Canal is on the most beautiful canal in Venice and near the wonderfully local Campo Santa Maria Formosa. This place is a jewel in the heart of Venice. Fondamenta di Remedio 4422/c, Tel. 041/52-34-538, Fax 041/24-19-138, www.locandacanal.it. 16 rooms. Single w/out bath €80; Single €115; Double w/out bath 120; Double €150. Breakfast included. Venice Map–Castello I.

Pensione Accademia is an amazing place, tucked away just off the beaten path. I cannot recommend this place enough for the ambiance, accommodations and service. Fondamenta Bollani 1058, Tel. 041/ 521-0188, Fax 041/523-9152, www.pensioneaccademia.it. Single €80-130; Double €130-250. Breakfast included. Venice Map – Dorsoduro.

Santo Stefano is a charming hotel located on the colorful local Campo Santa Stefano close to the Accademia and Piazza San Marco. A high quality place to stay in Venice. Campo Santo Stefano 2957, Tel. 041/ 520-0166, Fax 041/522-4460. www.hotelsantostefanovenezia.com. Credit cards accepted. 11 rooms. Single €110-220; Double €150-360. Breakfast included. Venice Map – San Marco I.

Two stars
Messner is off the beaten path, in a relatively secluded part of Venice, and is clean, quiet and comfortable. A good place to stay for budget travelers in one of my favorite parts of town. Madonna della Salute 216/217, Tel. 041/522-7443, Fax 041/522-7266. www.hotelmessner.it. All credit cards accepted. Single €110. Double €155. Breakfast included. Vaporetto Stop – Salute. Venice Map–Dorsoduro.

Venice

Alla Salute is comfortable two star in a great area. Fondamenta Ca' Bala, Tel 0415/235-404, Fax 0415/222-271. www.hotelsalute.com. 40 rooms. Single without bath €85; Single €120; Double without bath €110; Double €150. All credit cards accepted. Breakfast included. Venice Map–Dorsoduro.

Falier is an excellent two-star in a great local neighborhood. Salizzada San Pantalon 130, Tel. 041/710-882, Fax 041/520-6554, www.hotelfalier.com. 15 rooms. Single €80-180; Double €90-210. Breakfast included. Venice Map–Santa Croce & San Polo I.

Seguso is a little rough around the edges but the location is sublime. Zattere dei Gesuati 779, Tel. 041/528-6858, Fax 041/522-2340. www.pensioneseguso.it. Credit cards accepted. 36 rooms, 18 with bath. Single without bath €90-120; Single €100-154; Double with bath €100-175; Double €110-200. Breakfast included. Venice Map–Dorsoduro.

One star
Alex is a budget travelers dream in Italy's most expensive tourist city. Rio Terra 2606, Tel. 041/523-1341. www.hotelalexinvenice.com. Single w/out bath €35-48; Double w/out bath €50-74; Double €70-100. Venice Map– Santa Croce & San Polo II.

Murano
Locanda Conterie is more of a bed a breakfast and is one of only two places on Murano. Don't expect much for your accommodations other than peace and quiet. *Info:* Calle Conterie 21, Tel. 041/527-5003. www.locandaconterie.com. 14 rooms, €75-105 for a double with breakfast. Venice Map – Murano.

Locanda al Soffiador is less out of the way than the Conterie and is also more of a B&B than hotel. What you are really paying for is the chance to stay on the amazing island of Murano.. *Info:* Viale Bressagio 11, Tel. 041/739-430. www.venicehotel.it. 9 rooms, €65-95 for a double with breakfast. Venice Map – Murano.

BEST EATS
Ae do Marie is down an alley off of a colorful local neighborhood main street filled stores, cafes, and wine shops. If you are looking

for an authentic local wine bar experience, come here. *Info:* Calle dell'Ogio 3129, Tel. 041/296-0424, closed Sundays. Meal for two €30. Venice Map–Castello II.

Al Diporto is located almost at the far end of Venice near the soccer stadium, and is an unpretentious *trattoria* that is truly Venetian. *Info:* Calle Cengio 25-27, Sant'Elena, Tel. 041/528-5978. Closed Mondays. Meal for two €30. Venice Map–Castello III.

Al Marca is a distinctly local wine bar near the Rialto bridge. Really just a hole in wall, with a few benches outside, where you can savor a variety of vintages and some tasty snacks. *Info:* Campo bella Vienna 213, Tel. 347/100-2583, open M-Sat 9am-3pm & 6-9:30pm. Venice Map–Santa Croce & San Polo II.

Al Ponte is nestled at the foot of the bridge leading to Santi Giovanni e Paolo, and is the most characteristically local wine bar in Venice. Come here for the vibrant local ambiance, stay for the wine and food. *Info:* Ponte del Cavallo 6378, Tel. 041/528-6157, open M-Sat 8am-9pm. Venice Map –Castello I.

Bandierette is a favorite with the locals, though some tourists are starting to filter in. Wonderful Venetian ambiance. *Info:* Calle Barbaria delle Tole 6671, Tel. 041/522-0619, closed Monday nights and Tuesday. Meal for two €30. Venice Map–Castello I.

Casin dei Nobili is a large place between the Accademia and Campo Santa Margherita known for pizza, but they also serve up all manner of tasty food. *Info:* Calle del Casin dei Nobili 2765, Tel. 041/241-1841, closed Mondays. Meal for two €45. Venice Map–Dorsoduro.

Da Alberto is stupendous. Come here for the *spaghetti con seppia nera* (with squid ink), a Venetian specialty, and plenty of other tasty local dishes. *Info:* Calle Larga G. Gallina 5401, Tel. 041/523-8153, open M-Sat 10am-3pm & 4pm-11pm. Meal for two €40. Reservations needed. Venice Map–Castello I.

Dalla Marisa is about as local as you can get. Momma Marisa serves up her tantalizing dishes in this simple neighborhood place. Highly recommended. *Info:* Fondamenta di San Giobbe 652, Tel. 041/720-211, closed Mon & Tues nights. Meal for two €30. Venice Map–Cannaregio.

Do Mori is deep in the heart of the tourist shopping area surrounding the Rialto bridge, though it is well hidden escape from all the schmaltz. Locals abound here sampling the simple fare and savoring the vintages. *Info:* Calle 2 Mori, Tel. 041/522-5401. Open 8:30am-10:30pm. Closed Sundays. Venice Map–Santa Croce & San Polo II.

Mistra is hidden in a boatyard on the top floor of a warehouse overlooking the lagoon. This should be one of your destinations for lunch or dinner while in Venice. *Info:* Tel.041/522-0743, Giudecca 212a, closed Monday Evenings and Tuesdays. Meal for two €35. Venice Map–Giudecca.

La Profeta is an absolutely amazing local pizza place, hidden away down a side street off the beaten tourist path. *Info:* Calle Lunga San Barnaba 2669, Tel. 041/523-7466. Meal for two €30. Venice Map–Dorsoduro.

San Toma is a small restaurant with seating in the *campo* of the same name. Good food and ambiance. *Info:* Campo San Toma, Tel. 041/523-8819. Closed Tuesdays. Meal for two €40. Venice Map–Santa Croce & San Polo I.

San Trovaso is a local place serving laborers and academics alike, as well as the odd tourist who wanders in who is not intimidated by the boisterous atmosphere. *Info:* Fondamenta Priuli 1016, Tel. 041/523-08-35, closed Mondays. Meal for two €35. Venice Map–Dorsoduro.

La Zucca has great food and wonderful atmosphere. Set on a small canal, this is an intimate place that serves superb local food made with a creative flair. Reservations suggested. *Info:* Calle del Megio 1762, Tel. 041/524-1570. Credit cards accepted. Closed Sundays. Meal for two €40. Venice Map–Santa Croce & San Polo I.

Murano

Dalla Mora has wonderful atmosphere and great food. *Info:* Fondamenta Manin 75, Tel. 041/736-344. Open every day. Meal for two €35. Venice Map – Murano.

Da Tanduo is a local hangout with great food. *Info:* Fondamenta Manin 67-68, Tel. 041/739-310. www.datanduo.it. Closed Tuesdays. Meal for two €30. Venice Map – Murano.

Burano

Ai Pescatori is located in the center of the island on the main street that is known for its seafood. *Info:* Via Galuppi 371. Tel. 041/730650. Closed Wednesdays and January. All credit cards accepted. Meal for two €70. Venice Map – Burano.

Al Gatto Nero is an exquisite, high-end *trattoria* with seating on a picturesque canal. *Info:* Via Guidecca 88, Tel. 041/730-120. Closed Mondays. Credit cards accepted. Meal for two €50. Venice Map – Burano.

PERUGIA

BEST SLEEPS
Eden is a wonderful little two-star just off the Piazza Italia with spacious, clean, and comfortable rooms. A great budget hotel in a superb location with excellent prices. *Info:* Via Cesare Caporali 9, Tel. 075/572-8102, Fax 075/572-0342. 50 rooms. Single €60. Double €80. All credit cards accepted. Breakfast included.

Fortuna is a wonderful little three-star in an ideal location. *Info:* Via Bonazzi 19, Tel 075/572-2845, Fax 075/573-5040. www.perugiaonline.com/hotelfortuna. All credit cards accepted. Single €70-100; Double €115-135.

Locanda della Posta is the best hotel on the best street in Perugia, Corso Vannucci, the main promenade where all of Perugia comes out at night to stroll. The four-star hotel is a 17th century *palazzo* that once was the old post office. *Info:* Corso Vannucci 97f, Tel. 075/572-8925, Fax 075/572-2413. www.umbriatravel.com/locandadellaposta. 40 rooms. All credit cards accepted. Breakfast included. Single €90-110; Double €140-170.

BEST EATS
La Taverna has excellent atmosphere with its vaulted ceilings and arched doorways, superb food, and attentive service. This is the best restaurant in town. *Info:* Via delle Streghe 8. Tel. 075/572-4128. Closed Mondays, January 7-21 and all of July. All credit cards accepted. Meal for two €60.

La Botte is a small, simple, down-to-earth *trattoria*, off the beaten path, down in the basement of a medieval building off a small side street, which serves a vast array of tasty pasta and meat dishes at incredibly good prices. *Info:* Via Volte Della Pace 33, Tel. 075/572-2679. Open 12:30-2:30pm and 7:30-10pm. Credit cards accepted. Meal for two €25.

Pizzeria Lo Scalino is a tiny, hole in the wall, frequented by locals not only for the great pizza, but the warm and accommodating atmosphere. *Info:* Via S. Ercolano 8, Tel. 075/5722-5372. Open 12-3pm and 7-10pm. Closed Friday afternoons. Meal for two €20.

Pizzeria Mediterannea only serves pizza and it is so good and the atmosphere so electric that people line up to get it. *Info:* Piazza Piccinino 11/12, Tel 075/572-1322. Closed Tuesdays. Open 12:30-2:30pm and 7:30pm - midnight. Meal for two €25.

GUBBIO

BEST SLEEPS
Gattapone is an ancient building in the center of Gubbio. It is an old and respected hotel, now a three-star and deservedly so. A good place to stay in Gubbio. *Info:* Via Ansidei 6. Tel. 075/927-2489, Fax 075/927-1269, www.mencarelligroup.com. Closed January. 28 rooms, all with bath. Single €70-85; Double €85-105. All credit cards accepted. Breakfast included.

Bosone Palace is a three-star located in a 16th century building, and maintains old world charm and ambiance while offering all modern amenities. An elegant hotel right in the middle of the old city. *Info:* Via XX Settembre 22. Tel. 075/922-0688, Fax 075/

Gubbio

Orvieto

922-0552, www.mencarelligroup.com. 35 rooms. Single €70-85; Double €85-105. All credit cards accepted. Breakfast included.

BEST EATS

Il Taverna del Lupo has beyond a doubt the best food and most welcoming atmosphere in Gubbio. The ambiance is charming, romantic, and upscale. *Info:* Via G. Ansidei 6. Tel. 075/927-4368. Closed Mondays. All credit cards accepted. Meal for two €70.

La Cantina has great atmosphere and wonderful food. The place to be is inside in their expansive and rustic dining hall. A down-to-earth, local place to eat. *Info:* Via Piccotti 3. Tel. 075/922-0583. All credit cards accepted. Dinner for two €35.

Locanda del Duca is a friendly and irreverent restaurant in a quiet neighborhood. They serve tasty pastas and meats, but are really known for their exquisite pizzas. *Info:* Via Picardi 1. Tel. 075/927-7753. All credit cards accepted. Meal for two €25.

ORVIETO

BEST SLEEPS

Maitani is a four-star, a wonderful place to stay while in Orvieto in an ideal setting. *Info:* Via Lorenzo Maitani. Tel 0763/42011, Fax 0763/660-209. www.hotelmaitani.com. Closed January 6-26. 40 rooms. Single €100; Double €160-200. All credit cards accepted. Breakfast €10.

La Badia is an unbelievably beautiful 12th century abbey at the foot of Orvieto. The rooms in this four-star are immense, the accommodations exemplary, the service impeccable, and the atmosphere stupendous. For a fairy tale vacation, stay here. *Info:* Tel 0763/301-959 or 305-455, Fax 0763/305-396. www.labadiahotel.it. All credit cards accepted. Single €125; Double €300.

Italia is a three-star in an 18th century palazzo in the *centro storico* of Orvieto that offers a pleasant stay. *Info:* Via di Piazza del Popolo. Tel/Fax 0763/42065, www.grandhotelitalia.it. 42 rooms. Single €80; Double €130-165. Credit cards accepted. Breakfast included.

BEST EATS
I Sette Consoli is one of the best places in town with a comfortable local atmosphere, and a beautiful garden for dining during good weather. *Info:* Piazza San Angelo 1/a. Tel. 0763/343-911. Closed Wednesdays and February and March. All credit cards accepted. Meal for two €40.

Trattoria del Orso is located deep in the heart of Orvieto, nestled down a small side street, where you can find genuine and simple Umbrian cuisine. *Info:* Via della Misericordia. Tel. 0763/341-642. Closed Monday nights, Tuesdays and February. Visa accepted. Meal for two €40.

Le Grotte del Funaro is literally situated in a series of *grotte* (caves) carved into the tufa layer upon which Orvieto sits. This place offers you a unique dining experience to go along with their delicious food. *Info:* Via Ripa Serancia 41. Tel. 0763/343-276. Closed Mondays. Meal for two €40.

TODI

BEST SLEEPS
Fonte Cesia is an excellent small town four-star hotel. Their sundeck is a great place to relax as are the downstairs common areas. A good place to stay in Todi. *Info:* Via Lorenzo Leony 3, Tel. 075/894-3737, Fax 075/894-4677. www.fontecesia.it. 37 rooms. Single €112-116; Double €140-164. All credit cards accepted. Breakfast included.

Residenza San Lorenzo Tre is a B&B located on the upper floor of a quaint palazzo just off of the Piazza del Popolo. *Info:* Via San Lorenzo 3, Six rooms, four with bath. Tel. & Fax 075/894-4555, www.todi.net/lorenzo. Holiday Jan. 15 – Feb 28. Single without bath €70; Single €75; Double without bath €75; Double €110. Breakfast included. No credit cards accepted.

BEST EATS
Umbria is an excellent choice for great food and high-end atmosphere while in Todi. *Info:* Via San Bonaventura 13. Tel. 075/894-2390. Closed Tuesdays and at the end of December. All credit cards accepted. Meal for two €55.

Le Scalette has authentic local atmosphere, excellent regional cooking, and attentive service, which all translate into a wonderful meal. *Info:* Via delle Scalette 1, Tel. 075/894-4422. Closed Mondays. Open 12-2:30pm & 7pm-1am. Meal for two €35.

SPOLETO

BEST SLEEPS
Palazzo Dragoni is a four-star historic inn just steps from the Duomo. If you want to feel like you've stepped back into medieval times, this is the place to stay. *Info:* Via del Duomo 13, Tel. 0743/222-220, Fax 0743/222-225. www.initaly.com/hisres/palazzo/palazzo.htm. 15 rooms, 9 suites. Double €130-

270. All credit cards accepted. Breakfast included.

Gattapone is another four-star, set in a magical location overlooking the green valley and the medieval aqueduct that traverses it. All the bedrooms overlook this picturesque scene and is the main reason to stay here. *Info:* Via del Ponte 6, Tel. 0743/223-447, Fax 0743/223-448. 14 rooms. Standard Single €95-115; Superior Single €115-125; Standard Double €120-165; Superior Double €165-200. Breakfast €12.

Charleston is a 17th century palazzo that represents a classic blending of the old and new. A great three-star in Spoleto. And if you are wondering about the name of the hotel, Charleston, it is because that South Carolina city hosts a Spoleto festival every year. *Info:* Piazza Collicola 10. Tel. 0743/223-235, Fax 0743/222-010. www.hotelcharleston.it. 18 rooms. Per person €95-125. All credit cards accepted.

Aurora is a great two-star right next to the Teatro Romana and just down from the Piazza del Mercato, the heart of the *centro storico*. This hotel is bucking for three-star status and as such they are a superb two-star, with clean and comfortable rooms and excellent service in an ideal location. *Info:* Via Appolinare 3, Tel 0743/220-315, Fax 0743/221-885. www.hotelauroraspoleto.it. 40 rooms. Single €50-70; Double €60-90.

BEST EATS
Pecciarda has exquisite food, attentive service, great local atmosphere in a completely out of the way location, and all at prices that are easy on the pocketbook. A real taste of Spoleto. *Info:* Vicolo San Giovanni 1. Tel. 0743/221-009. Closed Thursdays. No credit cards accepted. Meal for two €35.

Il Pentagramma a fantastic place, with great local food and a serene musical atmosphere, all at good prices. *Info:* Via T. Martani 4/6/8. Tel. 0743/223-141. Closed Mondays and January 15-31. All credit cards accepted except American Express. Meal for two €40.

La Barcaccia is located just off of the Piazza del Mercato, the heart of the *centro storico*, in an isolated piazza of its own, offering typical local dishes at good prices. *Info:* Piazza F.lli Bardier 3. Tel. 0743/221-171. Closed Tuesdays. Credit cards accepted. Meal for two €35.

ASSISI

BEST SLEEPS
Subiaso is the place to stay in Assisi. Almost right at the foot of the Basilica di San Francesco, this four-star has some breathtak-

ingly panoramic views over the valley from the balconies of some of the rooms, as well as the sun terrace and garden terrace areas. *Info:* Via Frate Elia 2, 075/812-206, Fax 075/816-691. Toll free in Italy 167/015070. 61 rooms. Single €150; Double €250. All credit cards accepted. Breakfast included.

San Francesco is a good small town three-star, a little on the rustic side, with an intimate terrace overlooking the cathedral, a quaint bar area, and a well respected restaurant. *Info:* Via San Francesco 48. Tel-Fax 075/812-281. www.hotelsanfrancescoassisi.it. 44 rooms. Single €120; Double €160. All credit cards accepted. Breakfast included.

Il Palazzo is without a doubt the best two-star in town, and is pressing hard for three star status. *Info:* Via San Francesco 8, 06081 Assisi. Tel. 075/816-841. www.perugiaonline.com/ilpalazzo. 40 rooms. All credit cards accepted. Single €60-100; Double €90-135.

BEST EATS
La Fortrezza is a superb local restaurant attached to a two-star hotel of the same name, in an ideal location right up a small side street from the main piazza. *Info:* Piazza del Comune. Tel. 075/812-418. Closed Thursdays and in February. All credit cards accepted. Meal for two €40.

Taverna de L'Arco da Bino is a pleasant, upscale, local place with great atmosphere — vaulted brick ceilings and woodsy wrought iron decor — as well as scrumptious food. *Info:* Via San Gregorio 8. Tel 075/812-383. Closed Tuesdays, January 8-31, and July 5-15. All credit cards accepted. Meal for two €55.

CAPRI

BEST SLEEPS
Quisisana is an ultra-luxurious five-star with an indoor and outdoor swimming pool, health club, tennis courts, sauna, a great restaurant, and excellent views of the whole island. If you have the means, this is the place to stay. *Info:* Via Camerelle 2, Tel. 081/837-0788, Fax 081/837-6080. www.quisi.com. 150 rooms, 15 suites.

All credit cards accepted. Double €310-650; Suite €640-900. Closed November 1 to March 31.

La Residenza is a four-star with all you could want for your stay  on Capri: a good restaurant with a great view, a pool with scenic views and relaxing garden setting, a hotel bar, location on the sea, clean and comfortable rooms, transport around the island, and more. *Info:* Via F Serena 22, Tel. 081/837-0833, Fax 081/837-7564. www.hotellaresidenza.com. 114 rooms. All credit cards accepted. Single €140-160; Double €260-610; Suites €600-800.

Certosella offers pleasant and comfortable accommodations and includes a swimming pool. A great little three-star hotel. *Info:* Via Tragara 13, Tel. 081/837-0713, Fax 081/837-6113. www.certosella.com. Closed November and Easter. 12 rooms. Double €160-260. All credit cards accepted. Breakfast included.

San Michele is located in Anacapri on the edge of a cliff overlooking the water. Almost all the rooms in this three-star have the most spectacular view you could find anywhere. *Info:* Via G Orlandi 3, Tel. 081/837-1427, Fax 081/837-1420. www.sanmichele-capri.com. 100 rooms. Double €82-420; Breakfast extra. All credit cards accepted.

Villa Sarah is a villa with a garden located in a tranquil setting along the road that takes you to the Villa Tiberio. A great three-star in Capri. *Info:* Via Tiberio 3, Tel. 081/837-0689, Fax 081/837-7215. www.villasarah.it. Closed from the end of October until Easter. 20 rooms. Single €80-125; Double €125-195. Credit cards accepted. Breakfast included.

BEST EATS
Buca di Bacco da Serafina is a small *trattoria* with an extensive menu and great atmosphere. Highly recommended. *Info:* Via Longano 35, Tel. 081/837-0723. Closed Wednesdays and November. All credit cards accepted. Meal for two €40.

La Campannina is a fine family-run place that is upscale but rustic. Here you will get peasant fare in a local down-to-earth ambiance. *Info:* Via delle Botteghe 14, Tel. 081/837-0732. www.capannina-capri.com. Closed Wednesdays and November to Easter. All credit cards accepted. Meal for two €70.

Da Gemma is famous for their *spaghetti alle vongole* (with clam sauce) and the *fritto alla Gemma* (fried mozzarella and zucchini and other vegetables). *Info:* Via Madre Serafina 6, Tel. 081/837-0461. www.dagemma.com. Closed Mondays and November. All credit cards accepted. Meal for two €25.

Da Mamma Giovanna is a small, local *trattoria* that makes great pizzas as well as grilled or oven cooked meats and fish. Located in the heart of Anacapri. *Info:* (Anacapri) Via Boffe 3/5, Tel. 081/837-2057. Closed Mondays and the ten days after Christmas. All credit cards accepted. Meal for two €40.

Paolino has old stoves and other cooking devices supporting the tables, which lends the place a nice down to earth touch that goes well with their expensive prices. *Info:* Via Palazzo a Mare 11, Tel. 081/837-6102. Closed Mondays and January 15 to Easter. All credit cards accepted. Meal for two €60.

POSITANO

BEST SLEEPS
Le Sirenuse, a five-star, is definitely the place to stay in Positano. There is a pool at your disposal, a sauna, and a small boat to ferry you along the coast. Their restaurant, **La Sponda**, is one of the best, if not the best, in the city. Expensive, yes, but when the excellent Neapolitan cuisine is combined with the great views from the terrace, the price is irrelevant. *Info:* Via Cristoforo Colombo 30. Tel. 089/875-066, Fax 089/811-798.

www.sirenuse.it. 60 rooms. Single €280-760. Double €320-800. Credit cards accepted. Breakfast included.

Poseidon is a fine four-star hotel located in the heart of Positano. *Info:* Via Pasitea 148. Tel. 089/811-111, Fax 089/875-833. www.starnet.it/poseidon. 48 rooms. Double €198-298; Suite €284-550. Credit cards accepted. Breakfast included.

Casa Albertina is an excellent family-run three-star located in a tranquil area. They also have a superb restaurant. *Info:* Via della Tavolozza 3. Tel. 089/875-143, Fax 089/811-540. www.casalbertina.it. 20 rooms. Single €120-160; Double €90-230. Credit cards accepted. Breakfast included.

BEST EATS
La Cambusa are known for their great seafood. A little expensive, but the food and ambiance are worth the price. *Info:* Piazza A. Vespucci 4, Tel. 089/875-432. Closed November 11 to December 20. Credit cards accepted. Meal for two €70.

'O Capurale has been in the family for over one hundred years and is part of the life of Positano. People come here for the friendly local atmosphere as well as the fine food. *Info:* Via Regina Giovanna 12, Tel. 089/811-188. Closed Tuesdays (not in summer) and January. Credit cards accepted. Meal for two €35.

NAPLES

Note: as we suggested in Chapter 8, don't stay in Naples, but instead book a hotel in nearby Capri, Positano, or anywhere else on the Amalfi Coast. There are some great things about Naples, and even some great hotels, but overall you are much better off elsewhere. But we do list our favorite restaurants, below, for your (brief!) visit here.

BEST EATS
La Taverna dell'Arte is my favorite place in Naples. A small local trattoria situated in the heart of the *centro storico*. *Info:* Rampa S.

Giovanni Maggiore 1a, Tel. 081/552-7558. Closed Sundays and August. No credit cards accepted. Dinner for two €40.

Lombardi is located near the Museo Archeologico Nazionale and has some of best Pizza Napoletana in town. *Info:* Via Foria 12, Tel. 081/456-220. Closed Mondays. All credit cards accepted. Meal for two €28.

Lombardi a Santa Chiara is the sister pizzeria to Lombardi's. This one is in the heart of the *centro storico* right next to the Chiesa di Santa Chiara and their beautiful cloisters. *Info:* Via B Croce 59, Tel. 081/522-0780. Closed Sundays and three weeks in August. Credit cards accepted. Meal for two €33.

Il Trianon claims to have the best pizza in Naples. Even if it is not, it is definitely in the top ten. As is its vibrant local atmosphere. *Info:* Via P Colletta 46, Tel. 081/553-9426. www.napolibox.it/trianon. Closed Sundays and for lunch, New Years Eve and Christmas. No credit cards accepted. Meal for two €25.

Al Barcadero Café is an intimate little cafe in the ritzy part of Naples. Set down on the water and away from the frenetic pace of the city, this is a great place to come if you have to wait for a ferry. *Info:* Banchina S. Lucia 2, Tel. 333/222-7023. Open from 10am to 10pm.

AMALFI

BEST SLEEPS
Luna Convento is a four-star situated in a convent founded by St. Francis of Assisi in 1222,. This place is awash with charm. A wonderful place to stay in Amalfi. *Info:* Via Comite 33. Tel. 089/871-002, Fax 089/871-333. www.lunahotel.it. 45 rooms. Double €210-290; Suites €310-600. Credit cards accepted. Breakfast included.

La Bussola is a superb three-star hotel strategically placed directly on the walkway along the sea in an old mill and pasta factory. A great place to stay in Amalfi. *Info:* Lungomare dei Cavalieri 16. Tel. 089/871-533, Fax 089/871-369. www.labussolahotel.it. 63 rooms. Single €65-75; Double €100-160. Credit cards accepted. Breakfast included.

BEST EATS
Barracca serves classic seafood cooking prepared with attention and served perfectly. *Info:* Piazza dei Doggi, Tel. 089/871-285. Closed Wednesdays (not from June 15 to September 15) and January 15 to February 15. Credit cards accepted. Meal for two €45.

La Caravella is a little pricey but worth the expense. *Info:* Via Matteo Camera 12, Tel. 089/871-029. www.ristorantelacaravella.it. Closed Wednesdays (not in the summer) and November. Credit cards accepted. Meal for two €75.

Da Gemma represents the best of the local, traditional cuisine in Amalfi. Their terrace is a wonderful place to enjoy your meal. *Info:* Via Fra' Gerardo Sasso 10, Tel. 089/871-345. Closed Wednesdays (not in the summer) and Jan 15 to Feb 15. Credit cards accepted. Meal for two €55.

RAVELLO

BEST SLEEPS
Villa Maria is a great four-star. Highly recommended. *Info:* Via Santa Chiara 2. Tel. 089/857-255, Fax 089/857-071. www.villamaria.it. 18 rooms. Single €150-180; Double €180-220. Credit cards accepted. Breakfast included.

Rufolo is a wonderful four-star with every imaginable amenity. An ideal choice for an unforgettable stay in Ravello. *Info:* Via S. Francesco 1, Tel. 089/857-133. Fax 089/857935. www.hotelrufolo.it. Single €190-240; Double €235-325.

BEST EATS

Cumpa Cosimo is a great little *trattoria*. It comes close to being my favorite in all of Italy. *Info:* Via Roma 44, Tel. 089/857-156. Closed Mondays (not in Spring and Summer). Credit cards accepted. Meal for two €40.

MILAN

BEST SLEEPS

Grand Hotel Duomo is situated right next to the cathedral and the Galleria. A four-star, this is my recommendation for anyone who is staying in Milan and has the means. *Info:* Via San Raffaele 1, Tel. 02/8833, Fax 02/8646-2027. www.grandhotelduomo.com. 162 rooms. Single €250-320; Double €360-420; Suite €500-1000. Breakfast included. All credit cards accepted.

Ariston is a wonderful three-star that is also environmentally friendly. *Info:* Largo Carrobbio 2, Tel. 02/7200-0556, Fax 02/7200-0914. http://brerahotels.com/ariston. Closed in August. 48 rooms. Single €160-180; Double €230. All credit cards accepted. Breakfast included.

Vecchia Milano is a good two-star, the place to stay in Milan for budget travelers. *Info:* Via Borromei 4, Tel. 02/875-042 and 02/875-971, Fax 02/8645-4292. www.hotelvecchiamilano.it. 27 rooms. Single €70; Double €95. Extra person €30. American Express and Visa Accepted. Breakfast Included.

BEST EATS

Bagutta is one of Milan's famous artsy restaurants where you can sample dishes from all over Italy. *Info:* Via Bagutta 14-16, Tel. 02/7600-2767. Credit cards accepted. Closed Sundays. Meal for two €45.

Il Ristorante (Peck) is the place to come and sample everything that the Peck food stores have to offer. Located beneath another Peck place, the **Bottega del Vino**. *Info:* Via Victor Hugo 4, Tel. 02/876-774. Credit cards accepted. Meal for two €90.

Latteria Unione is really a *latteria*, or dairy store, but its alter ego is an extremely popular vegetarian restaurant. *Info:* Via dell Unione 6, Tel. 02/874-401. No credit cards accepted. Open for lunch only. Closed Sundays. Lunch for two €30.

COMO

BEST SLEEPS

Metropole e Suisse is a four-star, one of the oldest and most prestigious hotels in Como. *Info:* Piazza Cavour 19, Tel. 031/269-4444, Fax 031/300-808. www.hotelmetropolesuisse.com. Closed December 20-January 10. 71 rooms. Single €150-180; Double €180-300. All credit cards accepted. Breakfast included.

Firenze is a three-star, located centrally, five minutes from the Duomo, Piazza Cavour or the lake. *Info:* Piazza Volta 16, Tel. 031-300-333, Fax 031/300-101. www.albergofirenze.it. 40 rooms. Single €82-95; Double €110-130. All credit cards accepted. Breakfast included.

Quarcino is located near the funiculare up to Brunate about 10 minutes from the center of Como in a tranquil and lush setting. A two-star and a favorite of budget travelers. *Info:* Salita Quarcino 4, Tel. 031/303-944, Fax 031/304-678. www.hotelquarcino.it. 13 rooms only 3 with bath. Single €55; Double €85. Mastercard and Visa accepted. Breakfast included.

BEST EATS

Da Angela serves scrumptious local food at luxury prices. *Info:* Via Foscolo 16, Tel. 031/304-656. Closed Sundays and August. All credit cards accepted. Meal for two €75.

Imbarcadero is located a few meters from the water's edge, and offers great traditional dishes, simple in preparation but bursting with flavor. *Info:* Via Cavour 20, Tel. 031/277-341. Closed the first ten days in January. Credit cards accepted. Dinner for €60.

BELLAGIO

Bellagio

BEST SLEEPS

Splendide Excelsior is a three-star on the lakeside road and situated in a romantic old palazzo built in 1912. There is a heated indoor swimming pool, a garden area for relaxing, and a good restaurant with a scenic view over the lake as well as a piano bar for entertainment at night. *Info:* Lungolario Marconi 26, Tel. 031/950-225, Fax 031/951-224. www.hsplendide.com. Closed September 20 & March 15. 47 rooms, 13 with bath, 34 with shower. Double €115-130. Credit cards accepted. Breakfast included.

Firenze is a three-star located in the center of town and occupies two romantic old buildings, one built  in 1720, the other from the past century. The entry hall is like something out of the middle ages, the garden area is beautiful, and the restaurant rather good. *Info:* Piazza Mazzini 46, Tel. 031/950-342, Fax 031/951-722. www.bellagio.co.nz/florence/index.html. Closed November and March. 34 rooms, all but one single with bath. Single €110-130; Double €160-180. Credit cards accepted. Breakfast included.

BEST EATS

Silvio is a family-run place near the Villa Melzi. All you'll find here is whatever they caught on the lake in the morning or during the day. They fry, grill, or bake the fish to perfection and also mix it with *risotto* (rice) or ladle it over pasta. *Info:* Via Carcano 12, Tel. 031/950-322. Closed January and February. Master card and Visa accepted. Meal for two €40.

STRESA

BEST SLEEPS

Regina Palace is a superb four-star situated in an historic and

romantic building overlooking the lake. They have a private beach, a pretty garden area for relaxing, outdoor swimming pool, tennis and squash courts, gymnasium, sun room, sauna, snorkeling equipment, day care, discounts on golf at local courses, and more. *Info:* Corso Umberto I, Tel. 0323/933-777, Fax 0323/933-776. www.stresa.net/hotel/regina. 166 rooms. Double €200-250; Suite €350. Breakfast included. All credit cards accepted.

Du Parc, a charming three-star nestled in a verdant setting, set a short distance back from the main street and the shoreline in the upper part of Stresa. *Info:* Via Gignous 1, Tel. 0323/30335, Fax 0323/33596. www.stresa.net/hotel/duparc. Closed October 15 to March 15. 22 rooms. Single €70-100; Double €90-130. Breakfast included. All credit cards accepted.

La Fontana is a tranquil little three-star that has a beautiful internal garden with a fountain. *Info:* Via Sempione Nord 1, Tel. 0323/32707, Fax 0323/32708. www.lafontanahotel.com. Closed in November. 19 rooms. Single €85; Double €100. Credit cards accepted. Breakfast included.

BEST EATS

L'Emiliano is an absolutely fabulous place to eat, 'nuff said. *Info:* Corso Italia 50, Tel. 0323/31396. Closed Tuesdays, Wednesdays for lunch, and January and February. All credit cards accepted. Meal for two €80.

Piemontese specializes in seafood and fish from the lake. *Info:* Via Mazzini 25, Tel. 0323/30235. Closed Mondays and holidays. Credit cards accepted. Meal for two €60.

ISOLE BORROMEE

Is. Borromee

Verbania

BEST SLEEPS

Verbano is a truly magical place to stay. Located in a romantic old building, this three-star has its own private beach and location, location, location ... and a good restaurant. *Info:* Via Ugo Ara 2, Isola dei Pescatori. Tel. 0323/30408, Fax 0323/33129. www.hotelverbano.it. 12 rooms, 8 with bath, 4 with shower. Single €90-120. Double €150-180. Breakfast Included. All credit cards accepted.

Elvezia is a rustic one-star, but pleasant if you are not seeking many amenities. Their restaurant is the best place to eat on the island (*see below*). *Info:* Lungolago Vittorio Emanuele 18, Isola Bella. Tel. 0323/30043. www.elveziahotel.com. 9 rooms, none with bath. Three bathrooms in the hallway. Single €35-45; Double €65-75. Credit cards accepted.

BEST EATS

Elvezia has been in the Rossi family for generations and the food and ambiance are superb. *Info:* Lungolago Vittorio Emanuele 18, Isola Bella, Tel. 0323/30043. Open in the evenings by reservation only. Closed Mondays, November and March. All credit cards accepted. Meal for two €45.

VERBANIA

BEST SLEEPS

Grand Hotel Majestic is a four-star located directly on the lake shore and situated in a romantic old building complete with private beach, indoor swimming pool, private gardens, tennis courts, health club, piano bar, sunbathing terrace, and two restaurants with scenic views over the water. *Info:* Via Vittorio Veneto 32, Pallanza Tel.

0323/504-305, Fax 0323/556-379. www.grandhotelmajestic.it. 119 rooms 56 with bath, 63 with shower. Double €190-330; Suite €400-500. Breakfast included.

Il Chiostro is a beautiful, romantic three-star set in a 17th century monastery with a style similar to colonial Spanish architecture. Good restaurant, room service, lobby bar, tennis courts and more. *Info:* Via del Ceretti 11, Intra Tel. 0323/53151, Fax 0323/401-231. www.chiostrovb.it. 49 rooms, only 40 with shower. Single €45-62; Double €70-90. Credit cards accepted. Breakfast included.

Castagnola is an amazing two-star! Located on the mountain overlooking the water and the sister cities of Pallanza and Intra, here you'll find yourself in a tranquil, romantic environment complete with tennis courts, ample park lands for bocce or calcio, a gymnasium, an excellent restaurant and more. *Info:* Via al Collegio 18, Pallanza Tel. 0323/503-414, Fax 0323/556-341. www.hotelcastagnola.it. 107 rooms, 3 with bath, 104 with shower. Single €45-55; Double €75-85. Visa and Diners Club accepted.

BEST EATS
Milano is the best place to eat in Verbania, especially on their lakeside terrace with the view of the water and the little island of San Giovanni. *Info:* Corso Zanitello 2, Tel. 0323/556-816. Closed Tuesdays, January 10-February 10 and the first 10 days of August. All credit cards accepted. Meal for two €50.

La Cave is located on the lakeshore, serves tasty food in a comfortable and relaxing atmosphere. *Info:* Viale delle Magnolie 16, Tel. 0323/503-346. Closed Wednesdays and the first two weeks of November. All credit cards accepted. Meal for two €45.

CINQUE TERRE

BEST SLEEPS MONTEROSSO
Porto Roca is a four-star built into a cliff above the village. *Info:* Via Corone 1, in Corone, 19016 Monterosso al Mare. Tel. 0187/ 817-502, Fax 010/817-692. www.portoroca.it. 43 rooms. Credit cards accepted. Single €150-220; Double €175-300.

BEST SLEEPS VERNAZZA

Villa L'Eremo Sul Mare is a B&B with only three double bedrooms (two of them air-conditioned) all with shared bathrooms, but if you can get past that little wrinkle, the two large living rooms with fire place, and a large panoramic terrace make for a great place to stay. Located above the town of Vernazza. *Info:* Tel. 339/268-5617, www.eremosulmare.com. Double €90. Breakfast included. No credit cards accepted.

BEST EATS VERNAZZA

Trattoria del Capitano serves tasty local cuisine all with a great view of the sea as it crashes on the rocks below. *Info:* Tel. 0187/812-224. Meal for two €60. No credit cards accepted.

BEST SLEEPS MANAROLA

Ca' d'Andrean is a three-star located outside of the village of Riomaggiore near Manarola. Think rustic charm. *Info:* Via Discovolo 25, Manarola 19010. Tel. 0187/920-040, Fax 0187/920-452. www.cadandrean.it. 10 rooms. Single €60-70; Double €80-95. Breakfast €5. No credit cards accepted.

Marina Piccola is a three-star, with clean and comfortable rooms and a very tasty restaurant. *Info:* Via Discovolo 192, Riomaggiore 19010. Tel. 0187/920-103, www.hotelmarinapiccola.com. All credit cards accepted. 7 rooms. Single €85; Double €110. Breakfast included.

PORTOFINO

BEST SLEEPS

Nazionale is a four-star in a perfect location a few paces away from the seaside piazza, in a romantic old building, with great views. *Info:* Via Roma 8, Tel. 0185/269-575, Fax 0185/269-578. www.nazionaleportofino.com. 13 rooms. Single €125-200; Double €140-350. Credit Cards accepted.

Domina Inn Piccolo has its own private beach, serene garden, excellent restaurant, day care services, relaxing bar and all the other amenities of a quality four-star hotel. *Info:* Via Duca degli

Cinque
Terre
Portofino

Abruzzi 31, Tel. 0185/269-015, Fax 0185/269621. www.dominapiccolo.it/hotels/piccolo/eng/home.aspx. 22 rooms. Single €100-205; Double €140-350. Credit cards accepted.

Splendido is a truly splendid four-star ... and expensive. A great

choice if you have the means. *Info:* Viale Baratta 13, Tel. 0185/ 269-551, Fax 0185/269-614. www.hotelsplendido.com. 86 rooms. Credit cards accepted. Single €535-625; Double €950-1450; Suite €1500-5000. Credit cards accepted.

Eden is a three-star in the center of the little fishing village of Portofino. Only eight rooms, so reserve well in advance. *Info:* Vico Dritto 18, Tel. 0185/269-091, Fax 0185/269-047.www.hoteledenportofino.com. 8 rooms. Single €80-150; Double €140-270. Credit cards accepted.

BEST EATS
Il Pitosforo has a magnificent view of the harbor and tasty, basic, traditional – though expensive – local dishes. *Info:* Via Molo Umberto I 8. Tel. 0185/269-020. Closed Tuesdays and November. All credit cards accepted. Meal for two €120.

Puny is the most famous restaurant in Portofino, located directly in the main port square with a wonderful terrace overlooking the piazza and the port. *Info:* Piazza Martiri Olivetta 5. Tel. 0185/269-037. Closed Thursdays and January 15 to March 15. No credit cards accepted. Meal for two €85.

SANTA MARGHERITA LIGURE

BEST SLEEPS
Imperiale Palace was built in 1889. A five-star, everything about this hotel is wonderful, including the private beach, swimming pool, tranquil garden and fine restaurant. *Info:* Via Pagana 19, Tel.

0185/288-991, Fax 0185/284-223. www.hotelimperiale.com. 102 rooms. Closed from Dec. 1 to March 1. Single €205-220; Double €295-400. Credit cards accepted. Breakfast included.

Minerva is located in a tranquil setting, has a peaceful garden area, as well as a terrace with a nice view of the harbor. A three-star, rooms are all modern and comfortable. *Info:* Via Maragliano 34/C, Tel. 0185/286-073, Fax 0185/281-697. www.hminerva.it/hotel_minerva_en.htm. 28 rooms. Single €70-90; Double €105-160. Credit cards accepted. Breakfast included.

Fasce is located above the center of town a short walk to the Lungomare, and operated by Jane, the ever-present British proprietress and her Italian husband. They have free bicycles for your use, a roof deck and garden area. A quality inexpensive two-star. *Info:* Via L. Bozzo 3, Tel. 0185/286-435, Fax 0185/283-580. www.hotelfasce.it. 12 rooms, 10 with bath. Credit cards accepted. Single €100; Double €110. Breakfast included.

BEST EATS
Il Frantoio is a wonderful high-end restaurant in a great location that serves tasty local cuisine. *Info:* Via del Giunchetto 23/a. Tel. 0185/286-667. Credit cards accepted. Parking available. Closed Tuesdays (except from July 1 to August 31) and November 7-30. Meal for two €45.

Da Pezzi has a simple, basic atmosphere that caters to a varied and loyal clientele that comes here for the great traditional local dishes prepared to perfection. *Info:* Via Cavour 21. Tel. 0185/285-303. No credit cards accepted. Air conditioned. Closed Saturdays and Dec. 20 to Jan. 20. Meal for two €25.

RAPALLO

BEST SLEEPS
Europa is a good four-star in the center of everything. *Info:* Via Milite Ignoto 2. Tel. 0185/64692. Fax 0185/669-847. www.hoteleuropa-rapallo.com. 62 rooms. Credit cards accepted. Single €95-145; Double €140-190. Breakfast included.

Rapallo
Sestri
Levante

Riviera is an ideally situated three-star in the heart of the Lungomare. This is the place to stay in Rapallo. *Info:* Piazza IV

Novembre 2. Tel. 0185/50248, Fax 0185/65668. www.hotel-riviera.it. American Express and Visa accepted. 20 rooms. Single €80-110; Double €100-165. Breakfast included. Closed Oct. 30 to Dec. 23.

Villa Marosa is a small two-star located along the river, a short stroll from the Lungomare. If you are in Rapallo on a budget, this is good place to stay. *Info:* Via Rosselli 10. Tel. 0185/50668/9. www.villamarosa.it/intro_it.htm. No credit cards accepted. 12 rooms. Single €50-70; Double €70-90. Breakfast included.

BEST EATS
O Bansin is right in the heart of the town, near the piazza where the daily market is held, and serves up fine Ligurean dishes fresh and tasty. *Info:* Via Venezia 49. Tel. 0185/55913. No credit cards accepted. Parking available. Closed Sunday and Monday nights. Meal for two €33.

Trattoria Genovese is another down to earth place that serves incredible traditional Ligurian cuisine. Not in a very scenic area, but this place is always packed. *Info:* Via Roma 19, Tel. 0185/61-111. Closed Tuesdays, Meal for two €25.

SESTRI LEVANTE

BEST SLEEPS
Grand Hotel Dei Castelli is immersed in a park like setting on the peninsula at Sestri Levante, and is housed in a castle dating back to the 1100s. A wonderful four-star with all possible amenities. *Info:* Via Penisola 26. Tel. 0185/487-220, Fax 0185/44767. www.hoteldeicastelli.com. 30 rooms. Credit cards accepted. Single €180; Double €220-280. Breakfast included.

Villa Balbi is a four-star in an old historical building constructed in the 1600s. They have a wonderful terrace garden, an outdoor pool and private beach. *Info:* Viale Rimembranze 1. Tel. 0185/ 42941, Fax 0185/482-459. www.villabalbi.it. 96 rooms. Credit cards accepted. Double €200-250. Breakfast included.

Due Mari, a three-star, was built in the 1600s, has some relaxing garden areas, a swimming pool and is overall a great place to stay. *Info:* Vico del Caro 18. Tel. 0185/42695, Fax 0185/42698. www.duemarihotel.it. 26 rooms. Credit cards accepted. Double €115-160; Breakfast included.

BEST EATS
Angiolina is a fine restaurant that serves many traditional dishes. The portions are extremely generous, the service quick and hospitable, and the atmosphere good, especially in the terrace area, which all makes for a fine meal. *Info:* Viale Rimembranze 49. Tel. 0185/41198. Closed Tuesdays and from November through December. Credit cards accepted. Meal for two €70.

Il Polpo Mario is a legendary restaurant in Sestri specializing in seafood. *Info:* Via XXV Aprile 163. Tel. 0185/48-203. Closed Mondays. Credit cards accepted. Meal for two €80.

11. BEST ACTIVITIES

This chapter covers the best activities available in Italy: **shopping, nightlife,** and **sports and recreation**. You'll find that the big three – Rome, Florence, and Venice – offer the biggest array of choices, especially nightlife, but there is always something to do wherever your travels take you in Italy. Read on to find the best out there!

ROME

BEST SHOPPING

The main shopping area is **Il Tridente**, a network of streets bounded by the trident of Via di Ripetta, Via del Corso and Via del Babuino that extends from the Piazza del Popolo and features Via della Croce, Via Frattina, Piazza di Spagna, Via Condotti and more. This area has quaint shops selling everything from shirts to gloves. Department stores are the exception rather than the rule, though some of the best within Il Tridente includes **La Rinascente**, **STANDA**, **UPIM**, and **Coin**. Both STANDA and UPIM are designed for the Italian on a budget, while Rinascente and Coin are a little more upscale.

Some good antique shops in Rome can be found in the **Via del Babuino** and the **Via Margutta**. Other such shops can be found on the **Via dei Coronari**, and the **Via Giulia**. The best area to visit to find antiques and artisan's stores is from **Piazza Navona** and **Campo dei Fiori** to the tip of the peninsula that points towards St. Peter's.

There is nothing like an **outdoor market** to get into the flow of local life where ever you are. The best of which is **Mercato di Campo dei Fiori**, Rome's oldest and definitely best market held in the cobblestone square in the center of Rome's old medieval city.

Fantastico Shopping Streets!

- **Top of the Line Shopping** – Via Condotti, Via Borgognona, Via Bocca di Leone, Via del Corso
- **Mid-Range Fashion** – Via Nazionale, Via Cola di Rienzo, Via del Tritone, Via Giubbonari
- **Antiques** – Via del Babuino, Via Giulia, Via dei Coronari, around Piazza Navona
- **Leather Goods & Apparel** – Via due Macelli, Via Francesco Crispi
- **Straw & Wicker Products** – Via dei Deiari, Via del Teatro Valle

Info: Piazza Campo dei Fiori. Open Tues-Sun 8am-1pm. Then there is Rome's flea market at **Porta Portese**, which stretches along the Tiber from Ponte Sublico (where the Porta Portese is) in the north to the Ponte Testaccio in the south. *Info:* Ponte Sublico. Open 6:30am–2:30pm, Sundays only.

Rome is also filled with all sorts of **unique little shops** and exotic **clothing boutiques**, all brimming with unique products One of my favorites is **L'Impronta** – it has amazing, intricate and colorful prints of the piazzas, monuments, and buildings of Rome, in all shapes and sizes, framed or unframed. Tucked away on a tiny side street between the Pantheon and Piazza Navona. *Info:* Via del Teatro Valle 53, Tel. 06/686-7821. Map A.

For something more personal, try **Ai Monestari**. Located just outside the Piazza Navona, this tiny shop is filled with soaps, jams, patés, olive oils, wines, all made by men of the cloth, hence the name. *Info:* Corso Rinascimento 72, Tel 06/6880-2783. Closed Thursday afternoons. In the summer closed Saturday afternoons. Map B.

If you enjoy rummaging through second-hand stores and the like, come to **Chimera**. This consignment shop/antique store specializes in elegant objects such as paintings, drawings, porcelain, silver, jewelry, art, coins, and much more. A short walk from the Pantheon, located in the basement of a 16th century palazzo, this is where Rome's well-heeled pawn their family heirlooms so they can continue living the life of luxury. *Info:* Via del Seminario 121, Tel. 06/679-2126; open Mon. 3:15pm-7:30pm, Tuesday-Thursday 10:30am-7pm; Friday 10:30am-5:30pm; Mondays and Saturdays 1-7pm; closed Sundays. Map B.

Finally, if you are looking for something for your kitchen, many Romans choose **Gusto**. And if you get hungry, this place is also an *enoteca* and restaurant. *Info:* Piazza Augusto Imperatore 9, Tel. 06/322-6273. Map A.

BEST NIGHTLIFE
Rome starts hopping late and stays up until the wee hours. There

are plenty of places to go out for a drink or clubbing. For dancing and a wild wild wild night try **Alibi** (*Info:* Via di Monte Testaccio 40/44, Tel. 06/574-3448. Free admission Wed, Thur, and Sun. Fri & Sat €8-13. Open after 11pm); **Radio Londra** (*Info:* Via di Monte Testaccio, 65B. Tel. 06/575-0044. Open Monday-Friday 10pm to 3am, and Saturdays until 4am); and **Bush** (Via Galvani 46) all in the Testaccio section of town (*see map below*), known for its nightlife. Get off at the Piramide metro stop and walk to both of these places.

Believe it or not, Italy is known as a jazz and blues haven. If Jazz is what you are looking for, **Alexander Platz** is the place for you. *Info:* Via Ostia 9, Tel. 06/3974-2171. Membership entry €6. Map C. If the Blues is more your style, **Big Mama** serves up the best in Rome. *Info:* Via San Francesco a Ripa 18, Tel. 06/581-2551. www.bigmama.it. Membership entry €5. Map B.

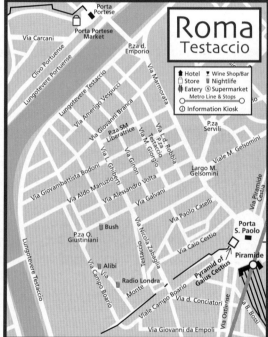

Rome has some very popular Irish pubs! Try **Black Duke**, an Irish-style pub near the Pantheon (*Info:* Via della Maddelena 29, Tel. 06/6830-0381, open for lunch in the summers, until 2am all year long, every day; Map A & B); **Shamrock** located near the Forum (*Info:* Via del Colosseo 1/c, Tel. 06/679-1729, open noon to 2am; the place to play darts in Rome; Map D); and **Trinity College**, which is a more upscale affair located just off the

Via del Corso (*Info:* Via del Collegio Romano 6, Tel. 06/678-64-72, www.trinity-rome.com, open 7:30am to 3pm and 8pm to 2am; Map A).

Finally, party central for the younger set is Campo dei Fiori at night, and within that melee is the **Drunken Ship**, the best American-style bar in the best party piazza in Rome. *Info:* Campo dei Fiori 20/21, Tel. 06/683-00-535. www.drunkenship.com. Open 1pm-2am. Map B.

BEST SPORTS & RECREATION
There are many different sporting activities in and around Rome, since the city is only 15 miles from the beach and 65 miles from great skiing country.

Reckless Roman drivers can make **bicycling** on the city streets  dangerous if you're not careful. But if you are interested in riding a bicycle you can rent them at many different locations and take them for a trip through the **Borghese Gardens** or along the city streets. One of these rental places is **Bici e Baci**, an extensive selection of bicycles, scooters, and cars. They also organize guided bike tours or scooter tours in English. *Info:* Via del Viminale 5, Tel. 06/482-8443. www.romeguide.it/bicibaci/bicibaci.html. Open 8am-7pm. All credit cards accepted. Another is **Bici Pincio** that has rental locations in the Borghese Gardens and one near the Piazza del Popolo. *Info:* Viale di Villa Medici & Viale della Pineta, Tel. 06/678-4374.

Now there is another way to get around Rome, **by boat**. Five river boats now ply the Tiber from the Isola Tiberina to the Olympic Stadium, a distance of eight kilometers, all for only €1 per person. *Info:* Landing areas are near these bridges: Garibaldi, Sisto, S. Angelo, Cavour, Risorgimento, Duca d'Aosta. The regular service sets off daily from Ponte Garibaldi at 8:50am.

Cruises with tourist commentary leave daily at 10am, 11:30am, 3:30pm, and 5pm. Tickets cost €10. Dinner cruises leave Ponte S. Angelo at 10pm. Tickets cost €43 per person. *Info:* Tel. 06/678-9361. www.battellidiroma.it.

Want to get a bird's eye view of the city? Try the **Balloon Rides Over Rome**. *Info:* www.culturalitaly.com/balloonriderome.htm. Every 15 minutes from 9:30 am till sunset. €14 per person.

Rome also has two good **bowling** alleys (*bocciodromi*). However, unless you have a car these places are far outside of the old walls of the city and thus difficult to get to except by taxi. **Bowling Brunswick** is by far the most frequented. *Info:* Lungotevere Aqua Acetosa, Tel. 396-6696. Another choice is **Bowling Roma**. This one is closer in than the other, as it is just outside the city walls. *Info:* Viale Regina Margherita 181, Tel. 861-184.

God forbid, if you get bored with all the amazing art, architecture and history in the Eternal City and want to escape for a while, there are two nearby **golf** courses. The one furthest away, though with more history, is **Golf Club Castel Gandolpho**. This 18 hole par 72 course near the Pope's summer residence is 5,855 meters long and is open all year except on Mondays. *Info:* Via Santo Spirito 13, 00040 Castel Gandolpho. Tel. 06/931-2301, Fax 06/931-2244. **Olgiata** is out the Via Cassia in a rather North American style housing development. It has an 18 hole par 72 course that is 6,396 meters long; and a 9 hole par 34 course that is 2,968 meters long. The course is open all year except on Mondays. *Info:* Largo Olgiata 15, Roma 00123, Tel. 06/378-9141. Fax 06/378-9968.

Finally, if the heat of the Roman summer is getting to be too much, and every fountain you pass is tempting you to jump in, maybe it's time to find a **swimming pool**. Contact the ones listed below, most of which are in local hotels:

- **Hotel Parco dei Principi** - *Info:* Via G. Frescobaldi 5, Tel. 06/854-421. Open 10am-6pm M-F. €25.
- **Shangri La** - *Info:* Viale Algeria 141, Tel. 06/591-6441. Open 9am -6:30pm M-Sat. €6 half day; €10 full day. Sun €10 half day; €15 full day.

- **Cavalieri Hiton** - *Info:* Via Cadlolo 101, Tel. 06/35-101. Open 9am - 7pm M-F €40, Sat and Sun €50. Under 12 half price.
- **Villa Pamphili** - *Info:* Via della Nocetta 107, Tel. 06/6615-8555. Open 9am - 9pm. €12. Under 12 half price.

FLORENCE

BEST SHOPPING

Florence is made for shopping, and the best place to start your hunt for keepsakes or gifts is the **San Lorenzo market**. Here you will find all the products for which Florence is famous: gloves, jackets, shoes, scarves, ceramics, clothes, and much more. Also, nearby, between the Duomo and the Piazza Signoria is a maze of small streets all filled unique little shops.

In that same location are two of Florence's best streets: **Via Calzaiuoli** and the **Via del Corso**, perpendicular to one another forming a lopsided cross. Parallel to the Via Calzaiuoli, but on the other side of the Piazza della Repubblica is the **Via Tournabuoni**, Florence's equivalent to 5th Avenue in New York. If you have the money to spend, this is where the high-end stores are.

If department stores are more your style, the best is in the Piazza della Repubblica, **Rinascente**, which is filled with clothes, shoes, housewares and more. Don't miss the café on their roof, the best in Florence, with superb views over the Duomo and the city. Nearby, on the Via Calzaiuoli, is another department store, **Coin**.

Who can come to Florence with going antiquing? Many of the better known **antique stores** have been located in the **Via dei Fossi** and **Via Maggio** for years, but there are some interesting little shops in the **Borgo San Jacopo** and the **Via San Spirito**, all located in the **Oltrarno** section of Florence across the river.

Then there are the multitude of **artisans** that make Florence their home. If you want to see some artisans at work, you need venture no further than across the river to the Oltrarno section. In these narrow streets you'll find small workshops alive with the sounds of hammers and saws, intermingled with the odors of wood, tanning leather, and glue.

Florence

Some of the best known shops are located around the small **Piazza della Passera**, very near the Ponte Vecchio. When at the Piazza della Passera and in need of some sustenance, try the **Caffe Artigiani**, a funky little coffee shop. *Info:* Via dell Sprone 16r, Tel. 055/291-882. Many shops are on the **Via Toscanella** that radiates out from the piazza, but you can find other artisan studios on the **Via Santo Spirito**, **Via Vellutini**, and **Via Maggio** and in the Piazza Santo Spirito itself.

Florence is also filled with **unique boutiques** and tiny little stores. One of my favorite places to find a wide variety of stationery products and unique pens is **L'Indice Scrive**. Most of the items are hand-made, including the diaries, ledgers, guest books, desk sets. etc. *Info:* Via della Vigna Nuova 82r. Tel. 055/215-165. Another is **Il Torchio**, two blocks east of the Ponte Vecchio (as you cross the bridge turn left). Run by two wonderful female artisans who craft their stationary with exquisite care. Highly recommended. *Info:* Via de Bardi 17, Tel. 055/234-2862.

Florence's Best Markets

• **Cascine Market** – Cascine Park – Tuesdays 7am-2pm – Everything (best market in Florence)
• **San Lorenzo Market** – streets surrounding San Lorenzo – Mon-Sat 9am-7pm – Variety
• **Mercato Centrale** – Piazza del Mercato Centrale – Daily 7am-2pm – Food
• **Sant'Ambrogio** – Via dell Agnolo – Mon-Sat 7am-2pm – Food & Variety
• **Mercato delle Pulci** – Piazza dei Ciompi – Daily 9am-7pm – Variety

For ceramics try **Le Mie Ceramiche**. Located near Piazza Santa Croce, for three generations this store has been creating amazing artisan ceramics based on designs from the 18th and 19th centuries. *Info:* Via Verdi 8r, Tel. 055/246-6007. Nearby is **Sbigoli Terrecotte** where they also make, bake and hand paint their own ceramics on site. They also import some fine pieces from the famous ceramics town in Umbria, Deruta. *Info:* Via S. Egidio 4r, Tel/Fax 055/247-9713.

If housewares and kitchen products are what you seek, look no further than **Dino Bartolini**. Ideally located near the Duomo, knives, plates, glasses, and all sorts of different kitchen products with unique Italian designs can be found here. *Info:* Via dei Servi 30r, Tel. 055/211-895. www.dinobartolini.it.

Tucked away up a small side street near the Ponte Vecchio is a great place to buy some amazing photographs of Florence, **Flavio Galleria.** Instead of hoping that the photos you are taking come out, come here and find the perfect image to place on your walls at home. *Info:* Costa S. Giordio 63 Tel. 055/245-351.

How about some perfume? **Officina Profumo-Farmaceutica** is a centuries-old establishment with the most refined soaps, shampoos, creams, bath and other personal hygiene products. A sight in and off itself. Come here to admire the furnishings, leave with a sensory memory to take home with you. *Info:* Via della Scala 16, Tel. 055/230-2883, www.smnovella.it.

Finally, the place to get all sorts of Italian law enforcement and military-related products, such as badges, hats, flags, shirts, key chains and much more is **Tricolore**. A great place for uniquely Italian gifts for kids of all ages. *Info:* Via della Scala 25/r, Tel. 055/210-166, iltricolore.it.

BEST NIGHTLIFE
Florence is not known for its nightlife. Instead most Florentines generally engage in some form of late night socializing at a restaurant or wine bar that stays open late. However, there are some places, including late night *enoteche*, where you can sample the Florentine night, such as **Space Electronic**, the largest and

loudest discotheque in the city. *Info:* Via Palazzuolo 37, Tel. 055/ 292-082, Fax 055/293-457. For an authentic Irish pub experience look no further than the **The Fiddler's Elbow**. Located in Piazza Santa Maria Novella, this is a popular nightlife spot for expats and locals alike. *Info:* Piazza Santa Maria Novella 7R, Tel. 055/ 215-056. Open 3pm–1:15pm everyday.

Florence

For a more traditionally Florentine nightlife experience, start your evening at **I Fratellini**. Set in the heart of the *centro storico* this place is no bigger than six feet wide by four feet deep, but it is the axis of Florentine nightlife. People come here for a glass before they go out, and a glass and a snack to end their evening's revelry. *Info:* Via dei Cimatori 38/r, Tel. 055/239-6096. Open noon-midnight.

On the other side of the Arno, you can stop at **Caffe Artigiani**, a funky coffee shop, that serves drinks as well, in the artisan district of the Oltrarno. *Info:* Via dell Sprone 16r, Tel. 055/291-882. You may even be enticed to stay, but if not, head out to **Fuori Porta**, the best wine bar in the city. Lovely atmosphere, with an expansive terrace, definitely off the beaten path, just outside the old walls of Florence at the foot of the hills of the Piazzalle Michelangelo. *Info:* Via Monte alle Croci 10r, Tel. 055/234-2483. www.fuoriporta.it. Open 12:30pm to 3:30pm and 7 pm to 12:30am everyday. Closed two weeks in August. Credit cards accepted. Meal for two €30.

You could spend the evening and night at Fuori Porta or segue to the nearby **Il Rifrullo**. This is a charming and relaxing place where you can enjoy a drink in the garden in the summer, in front of the fireplace in the winter, or up at the bar whenever you please. A very popular nightlife spot for Italians. *Info:* Via San Niccolo 55, Tel. 055/213-631. Open from 8am to midnight.

If both these places don't give you the energy you seek, **Zoe's**, which is nearby, will. A café during the day and a hipster techno spot when the sun goes down. In the Oltrarno, near Rifrullo and Fuori Porta, this is a local nightspot with a heavy bass line and deep back beat. *Info:* Via dei Renai 13/c, Tel. 055/243-111. Open 7am-midnight everyday.

BEST SPORTS & RECREATION

Okay, so maybe the art is getting to be too much. If so, let's play some **golf** at **Circolo Golf dell'Ugolino**. Located 9 km from Florence this is a par 72, 18 hole course that is 5,728 meters long. Open all year round except on Mondays. They have tennis courts, a swimming pool, a pro shop, a nice bar and a good restaurant. *Info:* Via Chiantigiano 3, 51005 Grassina, Tel. 055/320-1009, Fax 055/230-1141. A little further afield is the **Poggio de Medici Golf**

& Country Club, located 30 km from Florence this is a 9 hole, par 36 course, that is 3,430 meters long, and is open all year round except for Tuesdays. They have a driving range, putting green and a clubhouse with snacks and drinks. *Info:* Via San Gavino 27, 50038 Scarperia, Tel. 055/83-0436/7/8, Fax 055/843-0439.

If you need a break from touring and want to lounge around a **swimming pool** for the day, below is a list of places that have pools that you can pay to use. Note that some of them are hotels and are conveniently located near the center of town. These places are **generally only open in the summer months**:

- **Costoli** - *Info:* Viale Paoli, Tel. 055/678-012
- **Bellariva** - *Info:* Lungarno Colombo, 6, Tel. 055/677-521
- **Le Pavoniere** - *Info:* Viale degli Olmi, Tel.055/367-506
- **Hotel Villa Medici** - I*Info:* Via Il Prato, 42, Tel. 055/238-1331
- **Hotel Villa Cora** - *Info:* Viale Macchiavelli, 18, Tel. 055/229-8451
- **Hotel Minerva** - *Info:* Piazza S.Maria Novella, 16, Tel. 055/284-555
- **Hotel Kraft** - *Info:* Via Solferino, 2, Tel. 055/284-273

If you have a hankering to serve and volley, here are two tennis clubs in Florence where you can rent a court. **Circolo Tennis alle Cascine** is located in the Cascine Park. *Info:* Viale Visarno, 1, Tel. 055/354-326. And **Tennis Michelangelo** is just down from the Piazzale Michelangelo. *Info:* Viale Michelangelo, 61, Tel. 055/681-1880.

VENICE

BEST SHOPPING

If you want to have an authentic Venetian shopping experience, stay away from the heavily touristed areas, generally around the Rialto, Piazza San Marco and between those two places. I am featuring those artisan workshops that make all the traditional Venetian products including lace, glass, paper products, masks and more. It's easy to find kitsch in Venice. If you are seeking something authentic, try these places, listed below by *siestieri*. **Note**: the stores below are featured on the maps in the Venice chapter with a shopping bag icon.

Cannaregio

In this lightly touristed *siestieri*, you'll find **Il Mercante del Cammello**, a wonderful antique shop. *Info:* Calle Larga 2217, Tel. 041/721-811, open M-F 8:30am-12:30pm & 2:30-6:30pm. Map-Cannaregio. Also located here is a tiny antique and unique home furnishing store **Rossi**, set on a peaceful local canal. *Info:* Fondamenta della Misericordia 2543, Tel. 041/71735, open M-F 5-8:30pm and Sat & Sun 3-8:30pm. Map-Cannaregio. If artisan workshops are to your taste, sample **Valese Foundry**, a metal-working studio extraordinaire. But appointments are necessary. *Info:* Fondamenta Gasparo Contarini 3535, Tel 041/720-234. Map-Cannaregio.

Santa Croce & San Polo

This district is absolutely packed with great shops and wonderful little artisan studios, including **Amadi**, a master glass blower's workshop. Here you can find exquisitely delicate tiny glass animals and insects. *Info:* Calle Saoneri 2747, Tel. 041/523-8089, Open 9:30am-1pm & 2-6:30pm. Map-Santa Croce and San Polo. Nearby is **Punto Arte**, a wonderful etching workshop that turns out many of the prints you see in the shops 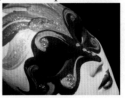 all over Venice. *Info:* Calle Saoneri 2721, www.etchingvenice.com, open 9am-1pm & 2-6pm. Map-Santa Croce and San Polo. Nearby is **Tragicomica**, Venice's best mask store. *Info:* Calle di Nomboli 2800, Tel. 041/

721-102, www.tragicomica.it. Open 10am-7pm. Map-Santa Croce and San Polo.

Just across the bridge near Tragicomica is Venice's best leather accessory workshop, **Mazzon**. Get bags, belts, wallets and more here, all carefully crafted from high end fashion designs, at very reasonable prices. *Info:* Campiello San Toma 2807,Tel. 041/520-3421, open M-Sat 9am-12:30pm & 3:30-7:30pm. Map-Santa Croce and San Polo. Just around the corner is Venice's best artisan chocolate maker **Vizio Virtu**. Come here anytime to sample their wares. Yummy! *Info:* Calle Campaniel 2898a, Tel. 041/275-0149, www.viziovirtu.com. Map-Santa Croce and San Polo.

Also hidden in the labyrinth near San Polo is the high-end jewelers **Labarintho**. Here you can find some unique and beautiful pieces, all hand crafted before your eyes. *Info:* Calle della Chiesa 2236, Tel. 041/710017, open Tues-Sat 9:30am-1pm & 2:30-7pm. Map-Santa Croce and San Polo. Almost next door is **Daniele** where you can buy Venetian hats, capes and other articles of clothing. *Info:* Calle della Chiesa 2235, Tel. 041/524-6242, open M-Sat 10am-12:30pm, 3-6:30pm & 9:30-midnight. Map-Santa Croce and San Polo.

Just around the corner and over a bridge is **Ervas**, the best iron workers in Venice, where you can find large and cumbersone, or intricate and delicate pieces to bring home. *Info:* Calle della Chiesa 2137-2156, Tel. 041/520-0490, open Tues & Wed 10am-1pm & 2-5pm; Thurs-Sat 10am-1pm & 2-7pm. Map-Santa Croce and San Polo.

The same is true for **Franzato**, a blown glass jeweler and stained glass window maker. *Info:* Calle della Chiesa 2155, Tel. 041/524-0770, open 10am-1pm & 3pm-7pm. Map-Santa Croce and San Polo. Down the road from these two is **Carta Venezia**, where you can find artisan made notebooks, diaries, postcards and more. *Info:* Calle della Chiesa 2125, Tel. 041/524-1283, open M-S 10am-1pm & 3-6pm. Map-Santa Croce and San Polo.

San Marco
Segueing across the Grand Canal to the *siestieri* of **San Marco** we

find the **Valese Shop**, the store that sells the wares from the Valese Foundry in Canarregio. *Info:* Calle Fiubera 793, Tel. 041/ 522-7282. Open Mon-Sat 10:30am-7:30pm. Map-San Marco.

On the other side of the *siestieri*, near the Campo Santo Stefano, are the following three places: **Quel Che Manca** is filled with antique furnishings and collectibles. *Info:* Campo San Beneto 3965, Tel. 041/522-2681, open Tues-Sat 11am-7pm. Map-San Marco. **Art Studio** is set in the nook of a bridge and sells an eclectic collection of antiques. *Info:* Ponte dei Frati 3821, Tel. 347/ 980-1466. Open Mon-Sat 10am-7pm. Map-San Marco. Finally there is **De Marchi**, a celebrated woodworkers shop filled with magnificent carvings. *Info:* Piscina San Samuele, Tel. 041/528-5694, open Mon-Fri 9am-12:30pm & 1:30-6pm. Map-San Marco.

Castello
Near the **Campo SS Giovanni e Paolo** is **Constantini**, a glass blower extraordinaire who creates delicate animals and insects. *Info:* Calle del Fumo 5311, Tel. 041/522-2265, Open M-Sat 9:15am-1pm & 2:15-6pm). Map – Castello I. Just up from him is a world famous and unparalleled artisan printmaker **Gianni Basso**. *Info:* Calle del Fumo 5306, Tel. 041/523-4681, open 8:30am-12:30pm and 2:30-6:30pm M-F. Sat open in the mornings only). Map-Castello I.

Just down from both of these shops is the **Olbi Workshop** that creates the high quality artisan stationery (*Info:* Calle Varisco 5421a, Tel. 041/522-4057, Open M-F 9am-12:30pm & 3-6:30pm. Map-Castello I.) for the **Olbi Store**. *Info:* Campo Santa Maria Nova 6061, Tel. 041/523-7655, open M-Sat 10am-12:30pm & 3:30-7:30pm. Map-Castello I.

On the opposite side of Campo SS Giovanni e Paolo is **Ballarin**, an incredible antique store and junke shop. *Info:* Campiello S. Giustina detto di Barbaria 4557, Tel. 347/963-5115, open M-Sat 4-8pm. Map-Castello II; and **Gervasutti**, an eclectic collection of a knick-knacks and antiques. *Info:* Campo Bandiera e Moro 3725, Tel. 348/402-2950. Open M-Sat 10am-3pm as well as visits by appointment. Map-Castello II.

Dorsoduro
Near the Guggenheim Collection is the **Bottega d'Arte S. Vio**, the store of a surrealistic artist with beautiful canvases and prints of scenes of Venice. *Info:* Fondamenta Venier 720b, Tel. 041/528-7934. Open 10am-4pm. **Map**-Dorsoduro.

On the opposite side of the Accademia and near the Campo Santa Margherita are these three stores. First, **Ca' Macana** is an incredible mask store. Maybe not the best, but a close second to Tragicomica mentioned earlier. *Info:* Calle Botteghe 3172, Tel. 041/277-6142, www.camacana.com, open every day 10am-6:30pm. Map-Dorsoduro. On the same street is **il Graffio** a bookbinder and pottery worker's workshop. *Info:* Calle Botteghe 3186, Tel. 041/241-3493, www.ilgraffio.net, open M-Sat 10:30am-12:30pm & 2:30-7:30pm. Map-Dorsoduro.

And still a little further down is **Rosettin** a third generation metalworkers shop where you can find all manner of metal knick-knacks to bring home. *Info:* Calle Cappeller 3220, Tel. 041/522-4195, open M-Sat 9am-1pm & 2:30-7pm. Map-Dorsoduro.

BEST NIGHTLIFE
Venice is definitely not known for its nightlife. The city shuts down real early. But if you are a late night person there are places

dotted throughout the city that stay open for drinks and socializing. The best place to find Venetian nightlife is in and around the **Campo Santa Margherita**, a piazza filled with cafes, bars, Irish pubs, and restaurants. Another prime spot is on the San Polo side of the **Rialto Bridge**. Though fewer in number, there are still bars and dotting around the area. Finally there is **Piazza San Marco**, which is touristy but if this is your first time in Venice, come here to savor the dueling small musical ensembles that the cafes hire to lure in tourist dollars.

BEST SPORTS & RECREATION

Most people do not realize it, but there is a **beach resort** only 30 minutes away from Venice by vaporetto called **Lido**. The beaches of Lido generally come complete with all services April through September. Most of the beaches on Lido are private so you will have to pay to enter. During spring and fall, Lido can be quite enjoyable if you are looking to get away from it all for a while, as it is almost completely deserted of tourists. *Info:* To get to Lido from Venice take Vaporetto 1 or 82.

Venice

Bicycling on Venice would be impossible, but on Lido it is the norm. This rental place is located just off the piazza where vaporetto 1 or 82 drops you from Venice. *Info:* Gran Viale 21b, Tel. 041/526-8019, www.lidoonbike.it.

On Lido, located on the grounds of an old castle guarding the lagoon, you will find an 18 hole, par 72, 6199 meters long **golf course**. It's open year round except on Mondays. They have a driving range, pro shop, bar and restaurant. If you have the golf itch, this will satisfy it. Club rentals are available. To get here from where the vaporetto (1 or 82) drops you off from Venice, take bus A or B going towards Alberoni. Bus stop is to the right as you exit the vaporetto. Take it to the end of the line (Alberoni), walk a little further down Strada Marina, take a right onto Strada della Droma which turns into Stradon Zaffi da Barca as you bear left around the water, then your first left into the golf course. *Info:* Alberoni Golf Course, Strada Vecchia 1, Tel. 041/73-13-33, www.circologolfvenezia.it.

Tour the entire Venetian lagoon in traditional *bragozzi* boats with **Ekos Club Lagoon Tours**. Highly recommended. The website is in Italian, but send an email requesting information for the dates you will be there. Write the message in English, then use the online translator **World Lingo** to translate the message into Italian (www.worldlingo.com/wl/translate). *Info:* Tel. 041/244-4011, Fax 041/244-4928, www.provincia.venezia.it/ekos.

UMBRIA

Every summer, Umbria hosts one of the best events in Italy: the **Spoleto Festival** held in June, when tens of thousands of tourists descend here to savor a two-week extravaganza of performing arts (www.spoletofestival.it). Spoleto also boasts **unique stores** selling ceramics, fabrics, antiques, handmade notebooks as well as galleries and artists' studios. The best shopping is along the Corso G. Garibaldi, up the Via Salaria Vecchia, and all around the Piazza del Mercato.

Spoleto is also a great place for a hike: just across the Ponte delle Torre, an old medieval aqueduct turned walkway, you are in pristine nature, laced with **hiking trails** that snake around the surrounding mountains and through small local hill towns.

In **Perugia**, your nightlife choices will be found on or just off the Corso Vannucci. Try the **Caffé Sandri**. *Info:* Corso Vannucci 32. Tel. 075/61012. Open 7am-11pm daily. Just off the Corso — mainly the parallel streets of Via Baglioni and Via G. Oberdan — you will find traditional little shops offering a wide variety of native arts and crafts as well as local and international fashions. One gem here is **Il Telaio**. *Info:* Via Bruschi 2B, Tel. 075/572-6603. Closed Monday mornings. All credit cards accepted. Off the beaten path, this place sells local hand-crafted linens, pillow cases, sheets, tablecloths and everything associated with fabrics and textiles. For ceramics, head to **Deruta** *(see pages 169 and 177)*.

There are some great festivals in **Gubbio** as well: the **Corsa dei Ceri-Candle Tower Race** held on May 15th, replete with costumes and contests; and on the last Sunday in May, the **Palio della Balestra** – a colorful crossbow competition. The main handicrafts in Gubbio are ceramics as well as wrought-iron work, carpentry, and copperware.

In general there is great shopping in **Orvieto**, many small artisans' shops, unique boutiques, ceramics re-sellers, all of which add to the rich local flavor that Orvieto cultivates. One store in particular you simply must visit is **Michelangeli**. *Info:* Via

Gualverio Michelangeli 3B, Tel. 0763/342-660, Fax 0763/342-461. All credit cards accepted. Filled with intricately carved wooden sculptures, toys, figurines, and appealing murals.

MILAN & THE LAKE COUNTRY

The best and most expensive **shopping streets in Milan** are the **Via Montenapoleone** and **Via della Spiga**, and all the little alleys surrounding these two parallel streets. You should try and check out the Peck stores *(see pages 198 and 200)* and some of Milan's markets, especially the **Fiera Sinigallia**, in the Porta Ticinese. All day Saturdays you'll find countless peddlers and regular stall holders selling everything from tapes to antiques, books, clothing (new and used) and a variety of curiosities. And next door to the Duomo is the great indoor shopping mall, the **Vittorio Emanuele Galleria** *(see pages 197-198 and 203)*, where you will find a wide variety of things to buy.

A good choice for nighttime entertainment is **dell'Operetta**. *Info:* Corso di Porta Ticinese 70, Tel. 02/837-5120. American Express, Visa and Mastercard accepted. Closed Sundays. Dinner for two €45. This place is a Milanese nightlife favorite with a central bar where patrons can stop for a drink up until 2am, is also a *trattoria*. Weekend evenings you can sometimes find live jazz or blues bands playing.

Como produces almost one-fifth of the world's silk supply. As such, you can find many bargains on silk in Como. Try **Mantero**. *Info:* Via San Abbondio 8, Como, Tel. 031/321510.

In between Milan and Como you can golf or play tennis at **Golf Club Carimate**. *Info:* Via Airldi 2, 22060 Carimate. Tel. 031/790-226, Fax 031/790-226. They have a driving range and a fine bar and restaurant.

BAY OF NAPLES & THE AMALFI COAST

If you are in **Naples** from December to June — the traditional opera season — have some formal attire and have a taste for something out of the ordinary, try the **Teatro San Carlo**. *Info:* Via San Carlo 98f, 80132 Napoli, Tel. 081/797-2331 or 797-2412, Fax 081/797-2306.

If opera is not your thing, try **Riot**. *Info:* Via S Biagio dei Librai 26. No phone. Open from 9pm-3am. This place is made up of some rooms in an old building from the 18th century with tall French windows opening out onto a lush terrace of palm trees, pebble paths, and tables at which to sit and enjoy a drink or a smoke. During the summer they have art exhibits and late night bands, mostly American blues and jazz.

The main shopping streets are the **Corso Umberto**, **Via Toledo**, and **Via Chiaia**. Along these byways you'll find your international style, upscale, expensive stores. In the *centro storico*, a unique shop is the **L'Ospedale delle Bambole** (The Doll Hospital), located on Via S Biagio ai Librai, where you'll find ancient dolls and puppets hanging everywhere or strewn haphazardly about. The **Via San Gregorio Aremeno**, commonly known as the Nativity scene street, sells figurines for crèches.

On **Capri**, two fun things to do are the **Blue Grotto** and the chairlift up **Monte Solaro** *(see pages 214, 218-219)*. Walking is by far the best way of getting about the island, but horse-drawn carriages, buses and taxis link Capri and Anacapri.

In **Amalfi**, visit the **Grotta di Amalfi**, an ancient stalactite cave on the coast (see page 229). The boat ride offers fine vistas, so don't forget your camera. If you're looking for pottery, head to **Vietri** *(see page 228)*.

Nightlife is generally limited on the Amalfi Coast to finding a nice restaurant or cafe and lingering over dinner or coffee. In **Positano**, you can go dancing with the younger crowed in a cave at **Music on the Rocks**. *Info:* Via Grotte dell'incanto, 51, Tel. 089/

875-874, www.musicontherocks.it. If you are visiting in July, the **Ravello Music Festival** is a lot of fun *(see page 230)*.

CINQUE TERRE & THE GULF OF POETS

Your best bet in the Cinque Terre is to find a nice restaurant or cafe, preferably with an ocean view, and hang out for the evening over a great bottle of vino. In **Vernazza**, a good spot for an evening of drink and relaxation is **Bar Baja Saracena** on the harbor. In **Monterosso** on Saturday nights are some fun bars, like **Il Casello**. *Info:* Lungo Ferrovia 70.

Hiking from town to town will be your main form of relaxation; again, you can do the entire Cinque Terre in less than five hours if all you want to do is get some exercise and not shop or wander through each town.

In **Portofino**, after dinner stroll along the *piazzetta* or down by the waterfront and stop in at any bar or cafe that strikes your fancy. In **Sestri Levante**, head to the marina and dance the night away at **Piscina dei Castelli**. Indulge in water sports, sailing, or relaxing on the beach in most of these towns.

As for shopping, you will have no problem whether your taste runs to the high-end (especially in Portofino, where you can shop till you drop along and just off the waterfront at stores like Cartier, Gucci and expensive boutiques) or to souvenir shops and one-of-a-kind artisan stores.

12. PRACTICAL MATTERS

GETTING TO ITALY

Italy's three main international airports are Rome's **Fiumicino** (also known as **Leonardo da Vinci**), Milan's **Malpensa**, and Venice's **Marco Polo**. There are other, smaller regional airports in Bologna, Florence, Pisa and more that accept flights from all over Europe as well as the United Kingdom, but not from North America or Australia.

GETTING FROM ROME'S FIUMICINO TO ROME
Direct Link Train. A train service is available from Fiumicino (also known as Leonardo da Vinci) directly to **Stazione Termini** (Rome's Central Railway Station). The trip costs €11 one way and takes 30 minutes. There are trains every half hour. They start operating from the airport to Termini at 7:38am and end at 10:08pm. Returning to the airport the trains also run every half hour, from track 25-29, but start at 6:52am and end at 9:22pm.

Metropolitan Link Train. There is train service from Fiumicino to **Stazione Tiburtina** stopping at the following stations: Ponte Galleria, Muratella, Magliana, Trastevere, Ostiense, and Tuscolana. Departures are every 20 minutes from 6am to 10pm. Trip takes about 45 minutes.

Night Bus. There is a night bus running between Fiumicino and Tiburtina station, which stops at Termini. From Fiumicino the bus leaves at 1:15am, 2:15am, 3:30am and 5am. From Tiburtina station to the airport the bus runs at 12:30am, 1:15am, 2:30am and 3:45am. The trip takes about half and hour.

Airport Shuttles. There is no faster and easier way to get back and forth between Rome's airports and downtown. Listed below are two of the best:

- **Airport Shuttle**. *Info:* www.airportshuttle.it. €30 for one or two passengers. Pick-up service at Ciampino or Fiumicino add an additional €12. Fluent English spoken.
- **Airport Connection Services**. *Info:* www.airportconnection.it. Must be booked at least a day in advance. For €25 per person will take you from the airport to your hotel and vice versa. They also offer a private Mercedes for €40 per person to perform the same service.

GETTING FROM ROME'S CIAMPINO TO ROME
Along with the Airport Shuttles listed above, if you arrive at Rome's Ciampino (which is really only used for flights from European countries), there are dedicated airport buses that leave for the **Anagnina Metro Station** every half an hour starting at 6am and end at 10:30pm. At Anagnina you can catch the subway to Termini station.

GETTING FROM PISA AIRPORT TO FLORENCE
You can take a train from the Pisa Airport directly into Florence in a little over an hour and a half. Trains leave frequently for other destinations throughout Tuscany and the rest of Italy, for the most part once an hour or more every day for most of the day. *Info:* www.trenitalia.com.

Another option is the **Terravision** bus that costs only €8 each way. *Info:* www.lowcostcoach.com.

GETTING FROM FLORENCE AIRPORT TO FLORENCE
Take a **taxi**, which is not that expensive as you are only 20 minutes from the center, and until the new metro is open, there is the **SITA bus** which leave every 1/2 hour between the airport and the bus station, starting at 5:30am until 11pm. It takes 25 minutes and costs €5. The bus station is located next to the train station in Florence just off of the Piazza della Stazione. *Info:* Via Caterina da Siena 3- Florence, Tel. 055/214-721, Toll-free in Italy 800/373-760, 800/424-500.

GETTING FROM VENICE'S MARCO POLO TO VENICE

By Bus. You can take a taxi, which should not be that expensive as Venice is only 20 minutes away, or you can take a bus, and twenty minutes later be in Venice's Piazzale Roma, where you can take water transport to your hotel. Tickets cost only €3 each way. No reservations. You can buy tickets in the arrivals lounge at the **ATVO stand** from 8am to midnight (Tel. 041/541-5180 or 520-5530). For a bus schedule visit their website: www.atvo.it. Buses leave every 20 minutes. When you catch the bus back to the airport, buy a ticket first at the ATVO ticket office next to the Caribinieri office in Piazza Roma.

By Boat. You can also catch a boat from the airport directly into the heart of Venice from the airport. It takes about half an hour to forty minutes from the airport to arrive at San Marco. The office at the airport is open daily from 8am-midnight (Tel. 041/541-6555). Check out their website for timetables: www.alilaguna.it. Price is €10 each way. Though it takes longer than the bus, it certainly is a unique way to enter Venice.

GETTING FROM MILAN'S AIRPORTS INTO MILAN

From Linate and Malpensa there are well-marked buses to the **Milan Central Train Station** leaving every 30 minutes. Duration is 30 minutes. Once at the train station you have access to Milan's extensive **Metro system**, which takes you virtually everywhere you want to go. If you're in more of a hurry or in need of more comfort, take a taxi from in front of the station.

If you want to take a taxi from the airports, the fare starts at €2 and rises rapidly. Be prepared to pay the cost of a night's hotel room for your ride from the airport.

PASSPORTS

A visa is not required for US, Canadian, British, Australian, or New Zealand citizens who are holding a valid passport, unless that person expects to stay in Italy longer than 90 days for study or to seek employment.

GETTING AROUND ITALY

Italy is connected by an extensive highway system (*Autostrada*), a superb train system, a series of regional airports, and naturally, since Italy is virtually surrounded by water and has a number of islands, a complete maritime service involving ferries and hydrofoils. The mode of transportation you select will depend on how long you're staying in Italy and where you are going.

BY AIR
You can fly between many Italian destinations quite easily. If you are on business, using air travel makes sense to fly from Milan to Rome, but not if you are a tourist. You could enjoy a relaxing three hour train ride in the morning to Florence, spend a day shopping and sightseeing, then get on another three-hour train ride to Rome and get there in time for dinner. And the entire cost would only be around $100, a lot less than if you had flown.

BY BUS
Most long-distance travel is done by train, but the regional bus systems can be beneficial for inter-city trips to smaller towns not serviced by rail lines. Conveniently, most bus stations are next door to or near the train station in most towns and cities.

BY CAR
Driving is a good way to see Italy's smaller towns, villages, seascapes, landscapes and monuments. The Italian drivers may be a little *pazzo* (crazy), but if you drive confidently and carefully and keep your eyes on the car in front of you and not get distracted by the beauty all around you should be fine. Remember, Italian drivers are like nothing you have ever experienced.

Driver's Licenses
US, British, and Canadian automobile driving licenses are valid

in Italy. If you want to rent a motorcycle, you will need a motorcycle license from your country of origin. To rent a scooter up to 150 cc, all you need is a pulse.

Car Rental
In all major cities there are a variety of car rental locations, and even such American stalwarts as Avis and Hertz. Driving through the back roads of Italy can offer you some of the best access to secluded little hill towns, clear mountain lakes, snow capped mountains and more. *Info:* Hertz, Tel. 800/654-3001, www.hertz.it; Avis, Tel. 800/331-1084, www.avisautonoleggio.it.

BY TRAIN
Taking the train is by far the most expedient, most relaxing, and definitely the best way to travel throughout Italy. Trains go

almost every place you'd like to visit, they are comfortable, run on time, and free you from having to drive. The railroad system is more extensive in north and central Italy, but main lines run along both coasts, and other routes cross the peninsula in several places. *Info:* www.trenitalia.com.

BASIC INFORMATION

BANKING & CHANGING MONEY
Banks in Italy are generally open Monday through Friday, 8:30am to 1:30pm and from 2:45pm to 4pm, and are closed all day Saturday and Sunday and on national holidays. Each bank offers a different rate and exchange fee, as do the **Casa di Cambio**, smaller exchange office that are everywhere.

These days the way to get the best rate and lowest exchange fee is by using **ATM Machines**. Called **Bancomat** machines, one drawback is that you can only withdraw around €250 each day.

However, the advantages of using ATMs are that they give you excellent, up-to-date exchange rates that are better than most exchange offices. Also, the transaction fee, a fixed rate of around $2, is usually lower than the fees charged by currency exchange offices. Another advantage is that you are not constrained by bank or business hours. You can access your money anytime.

I still strongly suggest bringing some travelers checks with you, or at least making sure you have Euros with you when you arrive. Why? If there is a bank strike (and that could happen at any time in Italy), the ATMs won't be filled up with cash and you'd be left without money. Which also means make sure you have a credit card handy as well.

CLIMATE & WEATHER
The climate in Italy is as varied as the country itself, but it never seems to get too harsh. In recent years the summers have been rather hot, though winters have been rather mild. Winter is generally the rainy season, when flooding can occur. If you visit Venice in the winter, bring some shin-high galoshes in case of slight flooding. Spring and Fall are both very moderate and are my favorite times to visit. However, bring an umbrella and rain coat just in case.

PUBLIC HOLIDAYS
Offices and shops in Italy are closed on the dates below. Virtually everything is closed, so stock up on picnic snacks, soda, whatever, because in most cities and towns there is no such thing as a 24 hour a day 7-11. Florence's feast day is June 24th; St. John the Baptist is the patron saint.

- **January 1**, New Year's Day
- **January 6**, Epiphany
- **April 25**, Liberation Day (1945)
- **Easter Monday**
- **May 1**, Labor Day
- **August 15**, *Ferragosto* and Assumption of the Blessed Virgin (climax of Italian family holiday season. Hardly anything stays open in the big cities through the month of August)
- **November 1**, All Saints Day

- **December 8**, Immaculate Conception
- **December 25/26**, Christmas

SHOPPING
For many people, coming to Italy also involves a world class shopping experience. In my *Best Activities* chapter, I feature some of the best places to shop in each city, helping you sift through the tourist locations and find the best places where the locals shop.

Italian law entitles all non-European Union residents to a **VAT** (IVA) tax refund with a minimum purchase exceeding €150. Ask for an invoice (*fattura* in Italian) or a **Tax-Free Check** when completing a purchase. This includes hotels.

Direct refunds are offered at major airports by the three major tax free services: **Cashback, Global Refund Italia, Tax-Free for Tourists**, plus others. You can easily save hundreds of dollars doing this.

TELEPHONES
Even when making local calls the area code must be used. To dial Italy from the United States, first dial the international prefix, **011**, then the country code, **39**, then the city code (for example Rome is **041**) then the number you wish to reach.

Calling From Italy
To call the U.S. direct from Italy, dial **001**, then the area code and number.

TIME
Most of the year, Italy is **six hours ahead of Eastern Standard Time** in North America, so if it's noon in New York it's 6pm in Rome. Daylight savings time goes into effect each year in Italy usually from the end of March to the end of September.

TIPPING
In many restaurants in Italy there used to be a universal cover charge, *pane e coperto* (literally "bread and cover"), which was tacked on to your bill. Not all restaurants do this anymore, and will simply tack on a 10% tip instead. This will mean that service

is included (*servizio incluso*). If service is not included, (*servizio non incluso*) a 10% tip is customary.

ENGLISH-ITALIAN ESSENTIAL PHRASES

GENERAL PHRASES
• Excuse me, but ....
    Mi scusi, ma ....
• Thank you
    Grazie
• Please
    Per favore
• If you are in trouble, yell "Help"
    Aiuto (eye-yoo-toh)
• Where is the restaurant(name of restaurant)
    Dov'é il ristorante_____?
• Where is the hotel (name of hotel)
    Dov'é l'hotel _____?
• Where is the museum (name of museum)
    Dov'é il museo _____?

Note: (*Dov'é* is pronounced "Dove [as in the past tense of dive] - ay")

TRAVEL-PUBLIC TRANSPORT
• Where is the (name of station) metro station?
    Dov'é la stazione del Metró _____?
• Where can I buy a Metro ticket?
    Dove posso comprare un biglietto per il Metro?
• How much is the ticket?
    Quanto costa il biglietto?
• Where is the bus stop for bus number ___.
    Dov'é la fermata per il bus numero ___?
• Excuse me, but I want to get off.
    Mi scusi, ma voglio scendere.
• Where can I catch a taxi?
    Dov'é posso prendere un taxi?

HOTEL

- How much is a double for one night/two nights?
  Quanto costa una doppia per una notte/due notti?
- How much is a single for one night/two nights?
  Quanto costa una singola per una notte/due notti?
- Where is the Exit/Entrance?
  Dov'é l'uscita/l'ingresso?
- What time is breakfast?
  A che ora é la prima colazione?
- Can I get another....for the room?
  Posso prendere un altro ... per la camera?
- blanket
  coperta
- pillow
  cuscino
- bed
  letto
- key
  ciave

MISCELLANEOUS

- Where is the bathroom?
  Dov'é il bagno?
- What time is it?
  Che ore sono?
- Sorry, I don't speak Italian.
  Mi scusi, ma non parlo italiano.
- Where can I get a ticket for ...?
  Dove posso prendere un biglietto per ...?
- a soccer game
  una partita di calcio
- the theater
  il teatro
- the opera
  l'opera
- Do you speak any English?
  Parli un po d'Inglese?

INDEX

TravelNotes

Things Change!
Phone numbers, prices, addresses, quality of service – all change. If you come across any new information, let us know. No item is too small! Contact us at :

jopenroad@aol.com
or
www.openroadguides.com

Open Road Publishing

Open Road has launched **a radical new concept in travel guides**: matching the time you *really* have for your vacation with the right amount of information you need for your perfect trip! No fluff, just the best things to do and see, the best places to stay and eat. Includes one-day, weekend, one-week and two-week trip ideas. Now what could be more perfect than that?

Best Of Guides

Open Road's Best of Las Vegas, $14.95
Open Road's Best of Arizona, $14.95
Open Road's Best of Southern California, $14.95
Open Road's Best of Costa Rica, $14.95
Open Road's Best of Honduras, $14.95
Open Road's Best of Belize, $14.95
Open Road's Best of Ireland, $14.95
Open Road's Best of Italy, $16.95
Open Road's Best of Paris, $12.95

Personal Paradise Guides

... finding your perfect place to stay!
Personal Paradise Caribbean, $14.95
Personal Paradise Florida, $14.95
Personal Paradise Hawaii, $14.95

Family Travel Guides

Open Road's Italy with Kids, $16.95
Open Road's Paris with Kids, $16.95
Open Road's Caribbean with Kids, $14.95
Open Road's London with Kids, $14.95
Open Road's New York City with Kids, $14.95
Open Road's Best National Parks With Kids, $14.95
Open Road's Washington, DC with Kids, $14.95
Open Road's Hawaii with Kids, $14.95

Order now at www.openroadguides.com